ROUTLEDGE LIBRARY EDITIONS:
POLICE AND POLICING

Volume 8

THE CASE AGAINST
PARAMILITARY POLICING

THE CASE AGAINST
PARAMILITARY POLICING

TONY JEFFERSON

Routledge
Taylor & Francis Group

LONDON AND NEW YORK

First published in 1990 by Open University Press

This edition first published in 2023
by Routledge
4 Park Square, Milton Park, Abingdon, Oxon OX14 4RN

and by Routledge
605 Third Avenue, New York, NY 10158

Routledge is an imprint of the Taylor & Francis Group, an informa business

British Library Cataloguing in Publication Data
A catalogue record for this book is available from the British Library

ISBN: 978-1-032-41114-9 (Set)
ISBN: 978-1-032-44888-6 (Volume 8) (hbk)
ISBN: 978-1-032-44901-2 (Volume 8) (pbk)
ISBN: 978-1-003-37441-1 (Volume 8) (ebk)

DOI: 10.4324/9781003374411

Publisher's Note
The publisher has gone to great lengths to ensure the quality of this reprint but points out that some imperfections in the original copies may be apparent.

Disclaimer
The publisher has made every effort to trace copyright holders and would welcome correspondence from those they have been unable to trace.

The case against
paramilitary policing

Tony Jefferson

Open University Press
MILTON KEYNES · PHILADELPHIA

Open University Press
Celtic Court
22 Ballmoor
Buckingham MK18 1XW

and
1900 Frost Road, Suite 101
Bristol, PA 19007, USA

First Published 1990

British Library Cataloguing in Publication Data

Jefferson, Tony
   The case against paramilitary policing. – (Crime, justice
   and social policy)
   1. Public order services
   I. Title   II. Series
   363.3

   ISBN 0-335-09326-4
   ISBN 0-335-09325-6 (pbk)

Library of Congress Cataloging-in-Publication Data

Jefferson, Tony.
      The case against paramilitary policing / Tony Jefferson.
         p. cm. — (Crime, justice, and social policy)
      Includes bibliographical references.
      ISBN 0-335-09326-4. — ISBN 0-335-09325-6 (pbk.)
      1. Police.   2. Paramilitary forces.   I. Title.   II. Title:
   Paramilitary policing.   III. Series.
   HV7921.J43   1990
   363.2'—dc20   90-32541 CIP

Typeset by Rowland Phototypesetting Ltd
Bury St Edmunds, Suffolk
Printed in Great Britain by St Edmundsbury Press Ltd
Bury St Edmunds, Suffolk

For Mandy, Stephen and Neil

Contents

Series editor's introduction

During the weekend of 31 March to 1 April 1990 in two British cities police officers were deployed in paramilitary style and formation as a response to quite distinct but equally serious incidents. The first, on the Saturday, was a major civil disturbance on the streets of central London during and after an Anti-Poll Tax demonstration. The second, on the Sunday, was the most serious contemporary prison riot at Strangeways, Manchester. Given the high profile and dramatic media coverage, the public was presented with units of police officers trained, organized, dressed and equipped for a military-type intervention. From this coverage it was evident that a new military initiative in policing had become normalized in Britain. Sometimes called the 'third force', the equivalent of a National Guard without their automatic weapons, the paramilitary dimension has consolidated and developed during the 1980s.

In the broad sense, however, paramilitary policing is not simply a recent development. To some extent the contemporary form of policing, its roots in the 1829 Metropolitan Police Act, has always projected an image which closely resembles a military form. Although established to emphasise local, civil law enforcement as against national, military rule, the reception of the new police was mixed. As one commentator, Captain W. White, reflected in 1838: 'the latent object appears to have been that of placing at the disposal of the Home Secretary a body of well-trained, disciplined and armed men, competent to intimidate the public and to keep down the rising spirit of the population.' Internally the police retained an organizational structure which reflected military rank and while there was no clear class division, as in the army or navy, the more senior officers were drawn almost exclusively from ex-military personnel. In fact it was only in 1945, with the appointment of a civil servant as Metropolitan Commissioner, that over a century of tradition was broken. Until then the post was held by former senior military officers.

Civilian policing in appearance, training, rank system, deference to authority, powers and occupational culture has retained its familiarity with the military form. Although great play is made of the police officer as 'citizen-in-uniform' who operates, through local government, 'by consent' of the communities she or he polices, both propositions are of dubious merit given the powers vested in the offices of constable and chief constable. Further, the police use of the truncheon, the night-stick, firearms with restrictions and, in the early days, the cutlass, under the lawful discretionary powers of 'reasonable force' again has reinforced connections with military powers. This has been evident particularly in the policing of public order, political demonstrations and industrial conflict during the nineteenth and twentieth centuries. 'Riot shields' and other associated 'defensive' equipment have a long history in the police response to civil disturbance.

While not negating the historical evidence concerning the close resemblance of civil and military forms of policing and regulation, there is considerable contemporary debate over the existence of a post-war shift, particularly since the late 1960s, towards paramilitarism within the police. With one of the main British police forces, the Royal Ulster Constabulary, fully-armed and in possession of 'special powers', the carefully planned and well financed move towards more authoritarian options has consolidated during the 1980s. The revelation, in 1985, of the existence of a *Public Order Manual* developed and produced by the Community Disorder Tactical Options Inter-Force Working Group of the Association of Chief Police Officers, effectively exposed the paramilitary option. That no police officer below the rank of Assistant Chief Constable was allowed to read the *Manual*, that no parliamentary debate had taken place on its development, and that police authorities had not been consulted on strategies which would be deployed in their areas, indicated that the document and its directions were intended to stand above the parameters of political accountability. With major implications for training, equipment, organization and deployment, not to mention intervention and the use of force, the *Manual* in conception and delivery represents an initiative well outside the reassurances of chief officers concerning 'policing by consent' and 'democratic accountability'.

Whereas the Association of Chief Police Officers appeared hostile to criticisms concerning paramilitarism made in the early 1980s by John Alderson, then Chief Constable of Devon and Cornwall, within the decade Sir Peter Imbert, the Metropolitan Police Commissioner, echoed that concern. He stated, 'A subject for concern is the move towards paramilitarism in the police. I accept that such a move has occurred.' Specialist training, including the carrying and use of firearms, the use of plastic bullets and CS gas, the formation of wedges and the deployment of snatch squads, is a significant development from the 'defensive' strategies and equipment of former initiatives. While these developments have been initiated far from the public gaze or political scrutiny, the debates have been fierce over the status of such paramilitary options. There has been considerable disquiet both within and outside the police concerning the dual, and apparently contradictory, role of 'community' policing practices and paramilitary strategies. Police support units, for example, can be expected to operationalize their public order training one day only to return to patrolling a neighbourhood the next. Consequently some commentators have called for a permanent and distinct operational 'third force' resembling the US National Guard. Others have welcomed the consolidation of tactical support units which use highly trained officers within the context of operational specialization in existing forces. Further commentaries have argued that the shift towards paramilitarism is indicative of a more generalized authoritarian trend in policing linked to a marked decline in the political accountability of the police.

There has been remarkably scant attention given to these debates and virtually no research into the rise and ocnsolidation of contemporary paramilitarism. This book sets out to make a contribution on both fronts. It charts the development of paramilitary policing, linking it particularly with the policing of public order and industrial conflict in the 1980s. Central to the analysis is a thorough account of the diverse theoretical positions concerning paramilitarism and their consequences in operational policies and practices. Useful to this discussion is the introduction of comparative international material. The book continually returns to an evaluation of the impact of the paramilitary option on the policed in terms of the escalation of violence and the emergence of resistance.

Tony Jefferson presents his analysis within a broadly critical framework, supporting his discussion by research carried out with the Special Patrol Group of a large Metropolitan Force. It gives a welcome insight into the day-to-day routine of the Group's work, in which policing soccer matches had been more the order of the day than large-scale operations such as the 1981 inner-city uprisings or the 1884–5 coal dispute. Yet it does consider the role and function of paramilitary policing in the inner cities, particularly the targeting of black populations; for the real potential of the paramilitary option was realized in Toxteth, Liverpool in October 1985 when the Operational Support Division of the Merseyside Police was deployed against the wishes of the local council and the judgement of the local Superintendent, and the community was cordoned off. The arbitrary use of violence against local people, the high-speed deployment of riot-clad officers, and the restrictions on movement on the streets, virtually held the community under siege for two days. Tony Jefferson considers a range of such dramatic interventions not only in terms of their immediate consequences but also in terms of the lasting impct on police-community relations.

What is also introduced is the significance of a strident, often forceful, culture of maculinity which has become central to the camaraderie engendered by and reinforcing of paramilitary styles of policing. At a time when the police have received major criticisms concerning institutionalized sexism and the maintenance of macho values, the development of all-male units whose identity is closely connected to the worst excesses of aggressive interpersonal and collective masculinity flies in the face of the reformist rhetoric that has emerged from training programmes. *The Case Against Paramilitary Policing* presents an indictment of the shift towards authoritarianism within contemporary policing. It explores what is unique in that shift and what makes it distinct from the historical, latent paramilitarism of drill, uniforms and rank. Finally it opens up the theoretical and political debates directing future research towards the key issues, both internal and external to the institution, concerning the policing of crime, public order and industrial conflict in the 1990s.

Phil Scraton
Joe Sim
Paula Skidmore

Preface and acknowledgements

Some years ago now, Roger Grimshaw and I completed a report for the Home Office based on our research into 'the organization and control of policework', using a broadly ethnographic approach, inside a big, largely urban, police force. It was a novel and ambitious project for a number of reasons: first, because we observed senior management and policy-making as well as operational officers simply going about their various jobs; second, because we studied a number of 'specialisms' as well as the basic uniformed shift patrollers (namely, resident beatwork, the Criminal Investigation Department (CID) and the Special Patrol Group (SPG)); and, finally, because we tried to show how a whole range of apparently disparate police activities could be economically analysed and understood in terms of three underlying 'structures', namely 'law', 'work' and 'democracy'. Whether we succeeded or not, such ambition had hidden costs; in our case, an over-compressed final report, and too much material for the planned follow-up book. Since publishers generally find long academic books uneconomic to produce, and readers anyway appear to prefer the book equivalent of the three-minute pop record (under 200 pages), we did what seems almost inevitable in today's world – we bowed to market pressures. In consequence, the resulting book, *Interpreting Policework*, was based on an analysis of only part of the data, namely the policy and practice of uniformed beat policework (yet still managed to run to 300 pages).

The problem of what to do with the unused material – in my particular case, that based on my time spent with an SPG unit and its relevant senior managers, and that gleaned from going through associated policy files, records and other documentation – remained. Time passed. Other projects came and went. Still the question of this unused SPG material hung in the air. Until, that is, I was asked to write a short article on public order policing for the *British Journal of Criminology*'s special issue devoted to policing in Britain. The format chosen by the *Journal*'s special editors, Reiner and Shapland, was to invite one 'lead' and one (shorter) 'reply' article per topic. My 'lead' was P. A. J. Waddington's article 'Towards Paramilitarism?'. This prompted my 'Beyond Paramilitarism' reply. More importantly, it finally crystallized what I had to do with my unused SPG material, since it provided just the polemical framework I guess I had been unconsciously searching for all along. This book is essentially the flower of the seed first sown by that paper.

Rodney Stark's preface to his 1972 study of *Police Riots* in the United States (a book I shall be discussing in Chapter 5) talks of his taking on the task of writing the book because of the reticence of other police researchers faced 'with controversial features of policing'. For my part, I have never seen the slightest point in getting involved with police research if one is not interested in the 'controversial features'. To stay away from these in the interests of safeguarding future possibilities of research access to the police, though 'understandable' as Stark suggests, is ultimately self-defeating because it is precisely the controversial aspects that (rightly) exercise, intrigue and concern people.

Since the mid 1970s paramilitary policing has become a controversial topic of public concern. Yet, apart from Gerry Northam's recent book, *Shooting in the Dark*, based essentially on his radio and TV programmes, there has been no book-length treatment of it. This is an attempt to rectify that; but, more importantly, to advance a particular case based on an intensive reading of my own (as far as I know, unique) primary data, on general reading of an extensive body of secondary materials and, last but not least, on an active political involvement in policing issues stretching back over many years. If it manages to raise both the visibility and the level of the 'paramilitary' debate it will have served its purpose.

There are, of course, the usual debts to acknowledge: for the initial collaboration that produced the text's central ideas, to Roger Grimshaw; for (unwittingly) providing my framework, to Tank Waddington; for providing the initial opportunity to test this out briefly in the *British Journal of Criminology*, to Robert Reiner and Joanna Shapland; for written comments on the original draft, to Roger Grimshaw (again), Eugene McLaughlin and the series editors; for typing the text, to Sue Turner; for secretarial assistance, to Lilian Bloodworth; for much needed general feedback, to the audiences at the various conferences at which versions of the original paper were delivered; for funding the original research upon which the book draws in part, to the Home Office; for allowing me to observe them and discuss my observations, to the police of a large county force, especially the SPG units I 'rode' with; and finally, for general support and encouragement, especially when the going got rough, as well as for her sympathetic but critical editorial eye, to Sue Crosbie.

CHAPTER 1

Introduction

FROM 'PUSHING AND SHOVING'
TO 'SEARCH AND DESTROY'

The difference between the quasi-military and the civil policeman is that the civil policeman should have no enemies. People may be criminals, they may be violent, but they are not enemies to be destroyed. Once that kind of language gets into the police vocabulary, it begins to change attitudes.[1]

Think back to the demonstrations of the 1960s. The dominant image of policing political protest, even during the massive anti-Vietnam war demonstrations in 1968, was of lines of bobbies, with arms linked, pushing and shoving against lines of demonstrators, with whom they were in 'eyeball to eyeball' contact. This is not to deny the reality of other images – the mounted police in pursuit of fleeing demonstrators, drawn truncheons, street scuffles, aggressive arrests, and so on – nor to suggest that 'pushing and shoving' was necessarily a cosy, avuncular affair; too many bruised shins and sore heads could surely testify to the contrary. Nevertheless, this dominant image – of 'dense cordons of police to restrict movement'[2] – neatly captures the essence of the *traditional* approach to public order policing, namely, the bringing together of a number of conventionally uniformed individual officers to form a relatively static and defensive human shield. In the light of subsequent developments, it is increasingly an archaic image.

Think now of policing public order in the 1980s. The dominant image of policing, as reflected in the miners' strike of 1984–5, or in one of the many inner-city riots that punctuated that decade, has changed dramatically. The new image is not one of a line of bobbies defensively 'pushing and shoving', but of 'snatch squads': menacing teams of officers, unrecognizable in visored, 'NATO-style' crash helmets and fireproof overalls, advancing behind transparent shields being banged by drawn truncheons, making 'search' sorties into crowds

1

of fleeing demonstrators for the purpose of arrest, or a spot of retributive 'destruction'. Once again, it is not necessary to deny the continuing presence of other less aggressive, more traditional images – humorous exchanges between police and demonstrators during the frequent lulls in the proceedings, for example – to make the point. This new dominant image also neatly encapsulates the essence of the new or *paramilitary* approach, namely, the use of specially trained and specially protected groups of officers, operating as highly mobile, quasi-military units, engaged in 'search and destroy' missions against 'enemy trouble-makers' or 'ringleaders'.

Images, of course, are one thing, definitions another. And since there is no agreed definition of paramilitarism, but rather, I would suggest, a degree of confusion about the significance of various aspects, it is important firmly to establish my starting point. This will be assisted by a brief account of the actual changes in public order policing between Grosvenor Square and Wapping, and their more immediate origins. Such an account will also serve as a general reminder and as a rough illustration of the development of public concern on this topic, which has proceeded broadly in tandem with the new paramilitary developments.

The emergence of paramilitarism

Underpinning the emergence of paramilitarism were three separate debates. One was about whether Britain needed a 'Continental-style' paramilitary force midway between the police and the army (like the French riot police, the Compagnies Républicaines de Sécurité (CRS)) to deal with particular demonstrations, strikes and terrorists. The second concerned civil defence policing needs in the event of an outbreak of nuclear war. And the third involved the issue of more effective crime-fighting in a period of rising crime and a shortage of police officers. Jointly, these three debates delivered, by the early 1970s, the elements from which the British paramilitary response was to be fashioned: a commitment to developing a response from within existing police forces; the first Special Patrol Group (SPG); and the idea of the Police Support Unit (PSU) – essentially a group of officers trained to operate as a team – as the backbone of a system of inter-force mutual aid.

The argument about whether Britain needed a special 'third force' was considered and ultimately rejected by a Home Office Working Party between 1961 and 1971, on the well-worn image-conscious grounds that it would not be acceptable to the public. Instead, the Working Party recommended, by way of a compromise solution, that existing forces be retrained and re-equipped to cope better with serious civil unrest. The debate about civil defence needs, initiated by the 1971 Home Defence Review, introduced the concept of the PSU. It recommended the establishment of at least one such unit per police force division, each unit to be made up of three sections of a sergeant and ten constables supervised by an inspector, to deal with duties arising from wartime contingencies. And the debate about more effective crime-fighting produced, in

2

London (and among other things) from 1965, the first SPG – 100 officers operating as mobile support units around London, answerable to their own headquarters-based command structure, and with a mandate to assist hard-pressed divisions with particular 'high crime' problems, either through providing additional preventive patrols or, where necessary, 'saturation' policing.

The development of the story from the early 1970s on is essentially one of how the spectre of civil, industrial and political strife, and the threat of terrorism, transformed the various original debates into a single one about public order policing, and fuelled the increasingly paramilitarized police responses. The mass confrontation between police and pickets at Saltley coke depot during the miners' strike of 1972, where the vastly outnumbered police were forced to concede the pickets' demand to 'shut the gates', was the first of the 'transforming' dramatic confrontations. The high level National Security Committee set up in its wake, with its mixture of police, military and government representatives, also rejected the idea of a third force, but it did advocate the complete revamping of police training in riot control and firearms, and established a mechanism – the National Reporting Centre – for co-ordinating the provision of extra help to hard-pressed forces. Fittingly, perhaps, this National Reporting Centre was to become the controversial spine of the massive mutual aid exercise which was so important in the defeat of the 1984–5 miners' strike.[3]

At the same time, external events – the growth of international terrorism, the provisional IRA bombing campaign in Britain which began in 1972, and the protracted flying picket' industrial disputes of 1972 (the dock strike and the building workers' strike) – continued to highlight the issues of political violence and crowd control. The net result in London, after the arrival of the new commissioner, Robert Mark, in 1972, was a shift in emphasis in the work of the SPG – away from 'crime-fighting' (if indeed that had ever been its primary task)[4] and towards a greater involvement in combating political violence (assignments to Heathrow Airport, guarding embassies, etc.) and crowd control. In the provinces the effect was to stimulate the formation of SPG-type groups based on the Metropolitan model.

If the miners' strike of 1972 provided a major impetus to the growth of paramilitarism, the influence of developments in Northern Ireland should not be overlooked. The year after the Grosvenor Square demonstrations, the 'troubles' in Northern Ireland recommenced with the aggressive breaking-up of a civil rights march. The rapid escalation of events there, especially the introduction of the army onto the streets, and the formation of the Royal Ulster Constabulary's SPG in 1970, resulted in a corresponding development in the paramilitary 'solution', in terms both of paramilitary techniques of crowd control ('snatch squads', 'wedges', etc.) and of the use of paramilitary equipment and weapons (most notoriously, the use of lethal plastic bullets). Even if the 'peculiarity' of the situation in Northern Ireland enables many conveniently to bracket off what is happening there, and to fail to connect it with developments in Britain, Northern Ireland became a testing ground for a whole range of paramilitary techniques, equipment and weaponry. In that exemplifying way, it must be considered an important and constant stimulus to paramilitary thinking and developments in Britain during this period.

The Metropolitan Police SPG and public order

The year 1974 dramatically witnessed the Metropolitan SPG in its new special role of front-line public order work. The decision of the National Front (NF) to march through the West End of London in June, and end with an indoor meeting in Conway Hall, Red Lion Square, prompted an anti-fascist counter-demonstration to end with an outdoor meeting also in Red Lion Square. Naturally the police were there to keep the sides apart. As the square began to fill up with anti-fascist demonstrators, a contingent of marchers made a series of surges towards the police cordon protecting Conway Hall. These actions precipitated the decision to 'clear the square, make arrests'.[5] The clearance was conducted by two units of the SPG, supported by the mounted police.[6] The end result was one demonstrator – Kevin Gately – being tragically killed, much concern at the aggressive nature of the clearance, and a public inquiry chaired by Lord Scarman.[7]

If the SPG had come under considerable criticism for its aggressive clearance of the square, the policing operation as a whole was still very largely traditional: cordons of foot officers, everyone in ordinary uniforms, no special equipment and batons the only weapons. The same can be said of the policing of the strike at Grunwick during 1977. But, once again, the SPG were in the forefront of the 'action' – and of the subsequent criticism. The strikers' decision to call for a week-long mass picket in June, after the dispute was nearly ten months old, was met by an aggressive police response – mass arrests, forcefully executed. The role of the SPG was to clear a route through the picket line for the strike-breaking workers' bus to enter the factory. This was done extremely aggressively. Eye witnesses talked of the SPG behaving like 'animals' and of women being 'grabbed by the breasts, and punched around the neck and face'.[8] Perhaps most telling were the comments of two miners to Capital Radio. One said he had 'never seen police like this. This is not traditional policemen we have here. These . . . are thugs in uniform.' The other said that Saltley Gates 'was a children's Sunday picnic by the side of this'.[9] Unlike Red Lion Square, however, there was to be no public inquiry, for though the TUC called for one into the activities of the SPG, the call was ignored.[10]

Developments in the provinces

While London undoubtedly led the way with these incipiently paramilitary developments, the provinces rapidly followed suit during the 1970s. According to Rollo, prior to 1972 there were only six SPG-type units in all, including those in the Met. and in Northern Ireland. Eight more were formed between 1972 and 1974.[11] By 1979, the *State Research* survey of chief constables' reports showed that the figure had risen to 27,[12] and that 'the combination of an anti-crime and a paramilitary role is an almost universal feature of SPGs'.[13]

Similar expansion was taking place with PSUs. Moreover, there had been a change of emphasis – from the original idea of PSUs being for civil defence purposes to the practice of training and using them for 'in-force' public order purposes, or in response to outside requests for mutual aid. According to *State Research*, by 1979 28 forces had formed PSUs, and 14 others mentioned PSU-type training. It suggested, in consequence, that it would not be long before the Home Office idea of a national mutual aid system – each police division having at least one trained PSU – was realized.[14]

The Metropolitan Police SPG, crime control and the black community

But if the shift in emphasis from crime to public order was a feature of the changing role of the SPGs during the 1970s, crime control still remained significant, especially in the Met. It also rapidly became controversial as 'saturation policing' – the use of the roadblock and massive random stop checks and searches – became its typical method, and London's black communities, especially their youth, the latest heirs to London's run-down, 'high crime' areas, its prime targets. Relations between the police and the black community, especially black youth, were under considerable strain by the early 1970s.[15] The deployment of SPG units to 'swamp' black areas, often for three to four weeks at a time, served only to worsen matters. The scale of these operations added to their oppressiveness.

> For example, in Lewisham in 1975 the SPG were called in. In the course of their operations in the area, the SPG stopped 14,000 people and made over 400 arrests (20 per cent of the stops and 10 per cent of the arrests made by the whole SPG in 1975).[16]

Whatever the relationship between race, crime and policing – the ongoing subject of controversial academic and political debate[17] – two things about the 'stops' policy can be said with confidence: the 'strike rate' (ratio of arrests to stops) tended to be low generally (even lower for crime arrests) especially in the early years (between 1 in 10 and 1 in 16 between 1972 and 1976, for example); and it fell disproportionately on black youth.[18] Not surprisingly, then, feelings of alienation, injustice and hostility towards policing grew within black communities, especially among sections of black youth. This could and did lead to mini-confrontations, characteristically in the form of blacks 'rescuing' one of their number perceived to be unfairly arrested.

This anger finally spilled over in a more sustained way at the Notting Hill carnival in 1976, precipitated by the massive and uncompromising police presence, ostensibly to deal firmly with the problem of street thefts and robberies. The resulting confrontation was widely seen as a defeat for the police, as they beat a very public and undignified retreat from hails of stones and bricks, grabbing dustbin lids for protection. The following year saw the first appearance of the riot shield on the streets of Britain. So, ironically, the SPG's anti-crime tactics had indirectly promoted a further development in the process of para-militarization – special protective equipment.

Shield Trained Units (STUs), the Metropolitan Police's equivalent of the provincial PSUs, were formed and trained in London from the beginning of 1977. 'Each Unit comprised 20 policemen under an inspector and each of the 24 London Police Districts had a minimum of two STUs.'[19] This training was widely adopted in the provinces, with several forces sending their SPG and PSU officers to be trained by the Met.[20] Later in the year, at Lewisham, the shields were tested for the first time. Once again the NF and its opponents were involved. In this case the NF had made the provocative decision to march from New Cross to Lewisham, an area with a high proportion of black people, and the police had decided against rerouting. The result was some missile throwing at the march and its police protectors, attacks on the NF march by some incensed anti-racists and attempts to block the marchers' passage, aggressive charges by baton-wielding police with mounted officers, the SPG and snatch squads all prominent, and some angry and violent clashes. In all this, the new shields were not always confined to their intended defensive purpose.[21]

If the Notting Hill carnival of 1976 promoted the acquisition of special protective equipment, Lewisham highlighted the issue of special protective clothing. As Commissioner McNee put it to the press, 'the shortcomings of the traditional helmet were evident during the disturbances'. However, aware of what special clothing and equipment might connote to a wary public, he quickly stressed that this did 'not mean we have forsaken traditional methods of policing demonstrations'.[22] Eighteen months later at Leicester, in April 1979, a public order occasion involving a NF march and anti-fascist counter-demonstrators yet again, a similar concern was expressed by police about the inadequacies of conventional equipment. Those PSU units without the new reinforced helmets and other special protective clothing compared themselves unfavourably with those who had – a comparison doubtless made easier by the scale of the mutual aid operation with SPGs and PSUs being drawn on from twenty other forces.[23]

Southall

But it was the anti-NF demonstration just two days later at Southall that provided the most dramatic 1970s example of the emergent paramilitarism. Once again the provocative intention of the NF to hold an election meeting in the heart of an area with a large immigrant population was met by a massive counter-demonstration. The police decision to shut off the entire centre of Southall and severely constrain the movement of demonstrators by means of cordons precipitated anger, frustration and some missile throwing. The police reply consisted of mass, apparently indiscriminate and often extremely brutal arrests, the use of truncheons as offensive weapons, and the dangerous driving of SPG transit vans through the crowds. The SPG, as at Red Lion Square, 'was prominent in the worst scenes of violence',[24] with one of their number responsible for the day's worst single incident – the deliberate blow to the head which killed Blair Peach.[25]

The subsequent barrage of criticism included calls for a public inquiry. Unlike the response to the Red Lion Square incident, these were refused,[26] though the Unofficial Committee of Enquiry appointed by the NCCL produced a very thorough alternative.[27] The Director of Public Prosecutions (DPP) also refused to prosecute anyone over the death of Blair Peach, despite the internal report by Commander Cass in which he 'referred to the possibility of prosecutions not only for homicide but also for riot, affray, and conspiring to pervert the course of justice'.[28] Nevertheless, the criticism did lead to some internal reorganization of the SPG, principally in an attempt to reintegrate it into 'normal' policing and thereby reduce its elite status, a status which was widely seen to be the source of the problem and damaging to public relations. Thus the eight units were spread around the four areas of the Met. and placed under area command, an upper limit (of four years) was placed on each officer's stay in the group, and public order duties were made much less of a priority.

Urban riots

If this reorganization was intended as a brake on the development of para-militarism, it was to prove very temporary. A series of urban riots – which commenced in the St Paul's area of Bristol in April 1980, spread to Brixton in April 1981 and, finally in July, to many major urban centres, Toxteth (Liverpool) and Moss Side (Manchester) prominent among them – placed public order policing firmly back at the top of the policing agenda. The speed with which events unfolded, and their ferocity, appeared to catch the police by surprise. At Bristol, the rioters remained in control for several hours while the Avon and Somerset force awaited PSU reinforcements under the mutual aid scheme.[29] Similarly, in Brixton:

> On Saturday – the height of the disorders – the rioters had the run of Railton and Mayall Roads . . . for some three hours before the police had assembled sufficient forces to regain the initiative and quell the disorders.[30]

The addition of the petrol bomb to the more traditional 'sticks and stones' armoury of the rioters, and the force of their attacks, also highlighted 'deficiencies in police equipment'. In particular,

> protective shields and helmets . . . proved inadequate; the helmets provided insufficient protection to the head; the foam padding at the rear of the shields – themselves heavy and cumbersome – caught fire when petrol spilled over them . . . officers' uniforms were also ignited by the flames from petrol bombs. Police vehicles were totally unprotected from missile-throwing mobs.[31]

7

Both issues proved galvanising: what Saltley Gates had been for public order policing in the 1970s, the riots of 1980–81 were to be for the 1980s. The events at Bristol precipitated a 'high level review of police arrangements for the "handling of spontaneous disorder"'.[32] This, in line with the direction of previous developments, made it clear that policing public order was a national issue requiring a co-ordinated and standardized set of responses:

> all forces would develop response plans involving clearly defined command structures, the rapid assembly of adequate numbers of officers in a short time and a review of 'mutual aid' arrangements . . . *all* police officers [would] receive training in 'crowd control', including the use of riot shields, while additional training would be given to those who might be called on to deal with disorder. In addition, a further review of police equipment was set up.[33]

Henceforth, the earlier predicted national PSU system would be available for use.

After Brixton, the Home Secretary, William Whitelaw, promised stronger helmets, better protective clothing, armoured police vehicles and, most ominously of all, CS gas and plastic bullets. Only months later the Chief Constable of Merseyside, Kenneth Oxford, was to authorize the use of CS gas, for the first time in the UK outside Northern Ireland, during the Toxteth riots. It was a decision that left four citizens seriously injured.[34] In addition, David Moore died and Paul Conroy was seriously injured as a result of police vehicles being driven at crowds and bystanders. Both measures – the use of CS gas and the aggressive use of police vehicles – were examples of what Oxford euphemistically called a 'positive police policy'.[35] From our vantage point, such policing and subsequent developments demonstrate the watershed nature of the 1980–81 riots: Robert Mark's famous astute comment on the 'art of policing a free society' being to 'win by appearing to lose' was being overtaken by a new ('positive') belligerence – exemplified by Commissioner McNee's sombre warning that 'if you keep off the streets of London and behave yourself, you won't have the SPG to worry about'.[36]

In London itself, permanent area-based Instant Response Units (IRUs) replaced the temporary STUs. This meant that each police district got permanent emergency cover from such units which operated from 'carrier' transit vans on a shift basis and were staffed by local shield-trained officers on three-month tours of duty (this last change a response, no doubt, to Scarman's recommendation of 'a regular turn-over of officers to prevent too inward-looking and self-conscious an *esprit de corps* developing in the group').[37] In other words, and despite the greater turnover, 'local SPG style groups in every district was the order of the day'.[38] For public relations purposes, their name was later changed, in January 1983, to the more innocuous sounding District Support Units (DSUs).

These latest developments in paramilitarism were the results of disorders which were precipitated by the aggressive policing of crime in black communities, especially the hated 'saturation' tactics. Bristol had ignited after a heavy-handed police raid of a café in St Pauls, and Brixton, of course, was triggered by the infamous Swamp 81 – the massive 'swamping' exercise in policing street crime which involved 150 local officers in plain clothes and which 'produced 1000 stops and 150 arrests in the first ten days of April'.[39] But during the early 1980s it was industrial relations once again which were to produce the most dramatic examples of the new paramilitary developments in action.

The colonial dimension and 'controlled incapacitation'

Home-grown experiences – industrial disputes, anti-racist demonstrations and public disorders following 'saturation policing' – had produced the motive for these paramilitary developments, and Northern Ireland examples (and portents) of advanced techniques, equipment and weaponry. The period after 1981 saw a new input – colonial policing. Paramilitary policing, often seen as un-British, is certainly no stranger to the British colonies. Thus it was that the autumn 1981 meeting of the Association of Chief Police Officers (ACPO) witnessed a discussion of public order embracing the experiences of the Met., the RUC in Northern Ireland and 'a detailed outline of colonial policing tactics . . . presented by . . . the [Hong Kong] Police Director of Operations'.[40] Central to these colonial policing tactics was the planned aggression of the arrest and dispersal tactics – tactics that were to become such a controversial feature of the contentious industrial disputes of the 1980s, as we shall see. Whether or not we owe such methods directly to Hong Kong, they are certainly '"all very similar" to the methods Hong Kong taught the police in Britain', according to Roy Henry, Hong Kong's Commissioner of Police.[41]

The first public outing for these new, aggressive tactics was to take place in Warrington in 1983. Eddie Shah, then Chairman of the *Stockport Messenger* newspaper, initiated the first real test of strength between a newspaper owner determined to introduce the new print technology and a major print union determined to resist. Like George Ward and the long running mid-1970s industrial dispute at Grunwick, the strategy was equally uncompromising – the use of cheap-rate strike-breakers to operate the new technology, the exploitation of relevant legislation, and a reliance on the police to get supplies and workers through the massed pickets. Fittingly, in view of this similarity, Warrington was the scene of 'the largest mass picket since Grunwick'.[42] On the night of the largest of these, 'four thousand pickets were dispersed by police using new . . . riot control tactics implemented with unprecedented ferocity'.[43]

The evening had been characterized by violence, with the police pushing against the crowd, arbitrarily dragging people out, taking them to the back of police lines and then making them run a police gauntlet where they 'were punched and kicked and people came out bloodied [and] . . . limping'.[44] More than that, the police destroyed the National Graphical Association (NGA) communications van, thus denying the stewards the opportunity to organize the picketing themselves, and adding considerably to the anger of the demonstrators. But it was the dispersal in the early hours of the morning that was so unprecedented, as one eyewitness confirmed:

> I was at Grunwick where the SPG – and they were vicious – pushed people back, they actually knocked garden walls over, they were so forceful. But I have still never seen anything like *this*.[45]

'This' referred to successive charges by riot police against people who were clearly terrified, who were

> screaming . . . running away, falling over . . . And as people were running away and falling over, riot police were running up to them and kicking them and hitting them with their batons, even though they were already on the ground.[46]

Later a National Council for Civil Liberties (NCCL) observer 'counted over 100 people with injuries – male and female – leaving the site'.[47]

Re-enter the miners

Hard on the heels of Warrington came the fullest flowering of the paramilitary response seen to date – the year-long miners' strike of 1984–5. To the aggressive violence of Warrington, the miners' strike added two new dimensions: scale, this being the largest public order police operation ever mounted in Britain; and duration, this being the longest time-span over which such a policing exercise had ever been conducted. Road blocks became an everyday feature of life around pits or for those 'suspected' of being a miner (or supporter). Some 1.4 million officer-days of mutual aid were worked, making for extra policing costs of some £400 million. Nearly 10,000 (11,500 including Scotland) arrests were made. Almost 1,400 (1,500 including Scotland) police injuries were recorded (picket injuries, though not recorded, were doubtless higher), and there were two picket-line deaths (three including the taxi-driver killed by a rock dropped from a bridge by two strikers while he was driving a strike-breaking miner to work). Police–picket ratios were sometimes as high as 8:1, and police were willing to use 1,000 or more officers to escort even a single working miner to work. Of those arrested, 137 were charged with riot, and 509 with unlawful assembly (very serious offences, though only 130 of the latter were convicted, and then only with the assistance of guilty pleas after plea-bargaining removed the threat of immediate custody). Five hundred and fifty-one formal complaints were filed against the police (564 including Scotland), though none led to formal disciplinary action. And all this was to continue for a year.[48]

If, as Sheffield Policewatch observed, the majority of picket lines were relatively peaceful,[49] the strike will still rightly be remembered for those that were not. Of these, Orgreave, the scene of two massive confrontations, will surely become the byword, not least because it was during the riot trial relating to the second of these, on 18 June 1984, that the existence of the new Tactical Options Training Manual was made public – a year later, and then only, to all intents and purposes, by accident. It was this manual which authorized aggressive 'dispersal' and 'controlled incapacitation' ('by striking in a controlled manner with batons about the arms and legs or torso').[50]

The fact that it was during the trial of the 55 arrested at Orgreave and charged with riot or unlawful assembly that the official policy of 'aggressive dispersal' was made public is grimly ironic – given that many lawyers saw the police policy as 'unlawful' and their behaviour on that day as 'riotous'. One such was Gareth Peirce, who commented eloquently on the film record, made by the police themselves, of the day:

> In the film, you see how men arrived at Orgreave on a beautiful summer's day . . . You see them from 6 am onwards being escorted by police towards an open field . . . For two hours, you see only men standing in the sun, talking and laughing. And when the coking lorries arrive, you see a brief, good-humoured, and expected push against the police lines: it lasts for 38 seconds exactly.
>
> You also see . . . battalions of police in riot uniforms, phalanxes of mounted officers, squadrons of men with long shields, short shields and batons. You see . . . in a cornfield police horses awaiting and down a slope . . . more police with dogs.
>
> Suddenly the ranks of the long-shield officers, 13 deep, open up and horses gallop through the densely-packed crowd. This manoeuvre repeats itself. In one of those charges you see a man being trampled by a police horse and brought back through the lines as a captive, to be charged with riot. You see squadrons of officers dressed in strange medieval battle dress with helmets and visors, round shields and overalls, ensuring anonymity and invulnerability, run after the cavalry and begin truncheoning pickets who have been slow to escape.
>
> You hear on the soundtrack 'bodies not heads' shouted by one senior officer, and then see junior officers rush out and hit heads as well as bodies. You see this over a period of three hours and you see men begin to react and throw occasional missiles. After 12 noon, they begin to construct defensive barricades against further police onslaught.[51]

Although Orgreave has become the byword for the aggressive policing of the strike, it should not be forgotten that aggressive tactics were not confined to the picket lines. Mining communities generally 'felt the force'. In this respect Armthorpe – the village that was briefly sealed off and then subjected to rampaging riot police – comes most readily to mind.

The normalization of paramilitarism

After this miners' strike policing public order became so many variations on a theme: the theme being the new aggressive approach, now increasingly the policing option of first rather than last resort.[52] The scale, duration and aggression of operations might differ, but their paramilitary manner was

11

unmistakable. The most unlikely groups began to experience it – for example, the few hundred students good humouredly demonstrating on the steps of their union building at Manchester University against the visit of the Home Secretary, Leon Brittan, in April 1985 (who were violently ejected from the steps by Greater Manchester Tactical Aid Group units);[53] and the rather unfortunately named 'peace convoy', a group attempting simply to conduct its annual summer solstice worship at Stonehenge in June (who were aggressively beaten, and their property damaged, by Wiltshire police in the infamous 'beanfield' attack). The paramilitary policing response was becoming 'normalized', that is, an unsurprising feature of public order events, though not necessarily an acceptable nor everyday one. Unofficial public inquiries into such events, motivated by public concern and the failure of central government to institute official ones, were also becoming more common.[54]

Perhaps it was this growing normalization of the tough paramilitary response that contributed to the renewed urban rioting in autumn 1985. But certainly it was the issue of policing black communities and the related inner-city eruptions, especially the rioting at the Broadwater Farm Estate in Haringey in October, that were to precipitate a further reorganization of public order policing in London – and stronger threats to make lethal weaponry standard fare.

And the rioting continues

In September 1985 Handsworth erupted again. Only those unaware of the fragility of the post-1981 'resolutions' in all the major urban centres could have been really surprised by it. Since none of the underlying issues of unemployment, deprivation and discrimination, nor the more immediate concerns about intimidatory policing, had been adequately dealt with, only new 'triggers' were needed. In the case of Handsworth the trigger was provided by a perceived police crackdown on previously tolerated petty drug dealing, and an insensitively forceful arrest of an Asian motorist. Two nights of rioting – 'worse than the [1981] Brixton riot', according to Mr Dear, the area's Chief Constable[55] – and two killed by fire led to much 'law and order' talk by government ministers, police chiefs and assorted commentators. But it was the serious disturbances at Broadwater Farm a month later, during which 'one police officer was murdered, 255 police officers were injured . . . seven had gunshot wounds',[56] that produced Commissioner Newman's statement of notice to all Londoners, backed by the Home Office, that he would 'not shrink' from the decision to use CS gas and plastic bullets on the streets of London, in the event of similar attacks.[57]

The police killing and the use of guns were both unprecedented features of modern riots. The immediate trigger for this angry outburst was the death of Mrs Cynthia Jarrett, a local West Indian woman who collapsed and died of a heart attack during a police raid on her home, only days after a similar raid in Brixton, when police shot and paralysed Mrs Cherry Groce, another West Indian woman.

Further reorganization in the Metropolitan Police

The threat to bring 'Belfast-style' CS gas and plastic bullets 'back home' to the streets of London was followed by a thorough review of the Metropolitan Police's public order response capability.[58] This provided the basis for the third major reorganization of its kind in under a decade, the first being the post-Southall reassignment of the SPG, and the second the post-Brixton introduction of the IRUs (later DSUs). Essentially the change amounted to an amalgamation of the SPG and DSUs into new Territorial Support Groups (TSGs). Nearly 1,000 strong and area-based like the replaced DSUs, their remit resembled that of the old SPG – public order, anti-terrorist and divisional crime support work – as did their deployment: officers, as well as the Groups themselves, were 'permanent' as four-year tours of duty replaced the three-month tours of the DSUs. Specialist public order training beyond the basic shieldwork of the DSUs, hitherto confined to the SPG, was proposed, with selected officers to receive 'firearms training and specialist search training'.[59] Senior officer public order training was to be revamped and, for some, intensified. Communications were to be overhauled, and protective equipment was to become standard personal issue for shield-trained officers. More armoured vehicles were to be ordered, plastic bullets and CS gas were more openly touted as tactical options, and the 'clumsy' water cannon option was to be subject to further tests; though, as Northam has since pointed out, this 'option' has now been rejected by the Home Office.[60] Finally, 'authority [was to be] sought from Home Office to purchase sufficient numbers of long truncheons [a last resort 'weapon' before the use of plastic bullets] to expedite an 'early resolution' of disorder.[61] These changes – in organization, training, communications, strategy, tactics, equipment and weaponry – were all designed to ensure anti-riot measures were 'speedy, firm and effective'.[62] Launching the review, Commissioner Newman 'admitted that the new SPG-style Territorial Support Groups "take us to a point midway to a third force"'[63] – an ironic statement in the light of the original entry point in the 1960s, namely, the effective resolution of the 'third force' argument with the 'midway' compromise of the original SPG.

Meanwhile, back on the industrial front another year-long dispute was drawing to a weary close. Smaller in scale, more geographically contained and less in the public eye than the miners' strike, it was, nevertheless, subject to all the by now familiar paramilitary tactics: road blocks, the riot squads, the aggressive dispersal tactics. And it provoked the by now equally familiar unofficial inquiry.[64] One novel feature was the presence, 'for the first time on picket lines' of 'riot-trained policewomen' – in the interests of 'equal opportunities'.[65] It was, of course, the Wapping dispute, precipitated by the audacious decision of Rupert Murdoch, partly inspired by Eddie Shah's provincial success, to dismiss his powerful printworkers, switch newspaper production from Fleet Street to a plant in Wapping, and use non-print-union labour to produce and distribute his titles.

Wapping seems a reasonable place to stop our narrative, since it brings us almost to the present. More importantly, though, all the paramilitary elements we mentioned at the outset – specially trained and equipped officers, mobile and offensively orientated snatch squads subject to quasi-military command, etc. – are now well established. True, we have yet to see plastic bullets, an all too familiar feature of policing public order in Northern Ireland,[66] actually used (as opposed to being deployed) in Britain; and, no doubt, new and so far nameless paramilitary equipment and weaponry is being imagined, tested and developed right now. But, we have sufficient here to provide both a background and a basis for the subsequent argument.

DEFINING THE PROBLEM

What is it, then, that is so problematical about the foregoing? Though that might seem a simple question, the range of unsatisfactory answers on offer suggests otherwise. Consequently, in order to be in a position to mount a satisfactory argument, a spot of ground clearing is going to be necessary. This will first highlight two idealistic blind alleys to avoid, and then offer a realistic starting point.

The focus on centralization[67]

For some the key issue is centralization, that is, whether paramilitary policing should be undertaken by a separate 'third force', or national riot squad, under centralized control. The traditional argument is that centralization is something to be avoided, an argument which, as we have seen, has successfully held sway until now. It has recently been challenged, however, by an argument suggesting the reverse.

The criminologist, Terence Morris, in the context of a discussion of the problems of modern policing spread across two *New Society* articles, has recently made out the case for a national riot squad.[68] After reviewing paramilitary developments, he concludes that this 'drift towards paramilitarism' can only be halted by the paradoxical solution of making 'some policemen tougher [the national riot squad] in order to leave most policemen free to get on with a different kind of work'.[69] He defends this solution by invoking an idealistic past:

> But is [such a solution] worse than the death-by-inches of the model of consensual policing that has enjoyed popular support for 150 years and has contributed probably as much as anything else to the relative tranquillity of British society?[70]

He also invokes, for reasons we are never given, a breathtakingly unproblematic future:

> It may be easier to control the activities of a unified riot squad than those of police support groups drafted into a district from other areas. The French

14

CRS is noted for its cynical brutality. We need not follow the model in every detail.[71]

We may forgive the professor of social institutions his historical idealism, but a sociology professor ought really to be prepared to spell out how the proposed new institution of the national riot squad *not only* gets round existing problems of the control of riot-trained officers, *but also* manages to avoid new 'CRS-style' ones. One problem that centralization could assist with, to be fair, is the occupational schizophrenia endemic to the PSU concept – as officers themselves complain, one minute they are community officers, the next minute they are on riot duty.

One traditional defence of the locally based 'British way' of policing also erroneously regards the issue of centralization as crucial but as something to be avoided at all costs. In this argument, the successful avoidance of centralization is regarded as a solution to the problems of paramilitarism. An example of this is Chief Inspector Clift's post-Brixton *Police Review* article of 1981.[72] In it, he basically suggests that the then existing paramilitary approach – the system of specialist trained and equipped 'in-force' riot units – 'has stood the test of time and is so flexible that it can cover every eventuality'.[73] To take the paramilitary path, which for Clift (as for many others) is synonymous with a national riot squad, would be to risk losing the two prime virtues of British policing: the '"civil" image' and the 'reasonable approach'.[74] It is not my intention to use the exact science of hindsight against Clift, but simply to point to a similar idealism at work here. The history implied in the notions of '"civil" image' and 'reasonable approach' is, once, again, idealistically consensual. And the socio-logical thinking behind various ideas, with more excuse in Clift's case, is just wishful thinking – the idea, for example, that simply altering the military terms used to describe units somehow 'demilitarizes' them; or that offensive actions, up to and including the use of plastic bullets, can leave the revered principle of 'minimum force' intact so long as these proceed through a scientifically graded series of responses.[75] This is, of course, management 'PR-speak', unfortunately all too common in this field.

The focus on professionalism

If Morris and Clift disagree over the effect of centralization, they are agreed about the importance of professionalism, the second of our two blind alleys. Implicitly in the case of Morris, and explicitly in Clift's case, underpinning their respective preferred solutions is a notion of well-trained, highly-disciplined public order specialists, in control and under control – the 'professionals'. Like their other notions, it remains abstract and idealistic, with neither author attempting to address the question of how the obvious gap, between the present profane reality of paramilitary policing I have briefly outlined and the 'professionalism' they invoke, is to be bridged.

It is a similarly idealistic conception of professionalism that lies at the heart of

Waddington's more elaborated defence of paramilitarism, cited in the Preface to this book.[76] Essentially, he argues that policing civil disorder has always presented the police with a challenge to their legitimacy, the more so the more politically motivated or violent the disorder. Since the basis of police legitimacy is their reputation for impartiality and restraint, the art of successful public order policing lies in ensuring that police are not seen to be partisan nor unnecessarily violent.

The advent of the more violent and politically motivated disorders of the 1970s and 1980s – to which the police response has been 'the acquisition . . . of the technology of coercion and . . . [an] evident willingness to use it'[77] – appeared to pose a threat to their reputation for restraint. However, it is a mistake to associate this new aggressiveness with paramilitarism, since paramilitarism, properly understood, involves the collective disciplined approach of the military, not the sorts of disorganized, violent and ill-disciplined response we actually witnessed. So, far from being a threat to the notion of restraint, paramilitarism offers a possible way out of the current dilemma by allowing 'the police to quell civil disorder with less force than would otherwise be likely'.[78]

Despite its ingenuity, this argument suffers from the same basic flaw as that of Morris and of Clift, namely, an abstract idealism in relation to both policing's past (characterized by 'impartiality' and 'restraint') and its present (which will apparently witness a magical flowering of paramilitarism as the presently 'ill-disciplined' are suddenly transformed into the 'super-disciplined').

A concrete approach

It is my contention that only a concrete starting point has any hope of getting to grips with the problem of paramilitarism. This involves, first, embracing a simple, profane definition of paramilitary policing, namely, the application of (quasi-)military training, equipment, philosophy and organization to questions of policing (whether under centralized control or not); and second, a concretely grounded sense of the history and sociology of paramilitarism, to counteract the prevailing idealism and to provide a realistic appraisal of 'professionalism in action'.

From this (profane) perspective, Waddington's argument – that paramilitarism is the most *effective* way of maintaining *impartial* and *consensual* (or restrained) public order policing (and hence legitimacy) – needs to be systematically inverted. Far from being consensual and restrained, policing disorderly confrontations has often felt *unjustly violent*, when viewed from the 'bottom up' – the vantage point of the 'policed' (this forms the subject of Chapter 2). Far from being impartial, the discretion granted the police makes their work *intrinsically political*, never more so than in the highly controversial yet discretionary arena of public order policing, yet their independence precludes a proper democratic input (I take this argument up in Chapter 3) and an effective management input (see Chapter 4). Far from being effective, the paramilitary approach materially contributes to and thereby *amplifies* the prospect of disorder (the subject matter of Chapters 5 and 6). Thus this book essentially expands upon, demonstrates and connects these points in order to produce a historically and sociologically grounded 'case against paramilitary policing'. The final chapter summarizes the argument of the previous chapters, shows how each negative input reinforces the others, anticipates the consequences of failing to reverse present trends and lays out the framework necessary to move towards a 'just' approach to public order policing, namely, reduced legal discretion, the political direction of the remaining discretion and the institutionalization of a notion of justice, compatible with the interests of the policed, into the new framework.

NOTES

1. John Alderson, quoted in Northam, 1985, p. 5.
2. Metropolitan Police, 1986, p. 20.
3. Cf. Kettle, 1985.
4. See McCabe and Wallington, 1988, p. 44.
5. The Commander-in-Chief, quoted in Gilbert, 1975, p. 12.
6. Ibid., p. 10.
7. See Scarman, 1974.
8. Quoted in Dromey and Taylor, 1978, p. 119.
9. Ibid., p. 123.
10. Rollo, 1980, p. 183.
11. Ibid., p. 195.
12. *State Research*, no. 19, 1980, p. 152.
13. Ibid., p. 150.
14. Ibid., p. 155.
15. Cf. Select Committee on Race Relations and Immigration, 1972.
16. *State Research*, no. 13, 1979, p. 135.
17. For a summary of the issues, see Jefferson, 1988.
18. Strike rates taken from *State Research*, no. 13, 1979, pp. 134–5. See also, *Policing London*, 1983, p. 10. More generally, see Jefferson, 1988.
19. *Policing London*, no. 8, 1983, p. 10.
20. *State Research*, no. 19, 1980, p. 157.
21. Cf. *Camerawork*, 1977, p. 7.
22. Quoted in Rollo, 1980, p. 186.
23. *State Research*, no. 19, 1980, p. 158.
24. Unofficial Committee of Enquiry (UCE), 1980a, p. 182.
25. Cf. UCE, 1980b.
26. For a discussion on the reasons for granting or refusing public inquiries, see Jefferson and Grimshaw, 1984, pp. 128–32.
27. See UCE, 1980a; 1980b.
28. UCE, 1980b, p. 50.
29. See Chief Constable of Avon and Somerset, 1980.
30. Scarman, 1982, p. 115.
31. Ibid., pp. 115–16.
32. Gordon, 1985, p. 163.
33. Ibid., pp. 163–4.

34. Scraton, 1985, p. 72.
35. Ibid., p. 76.
36. For the Mark quote, see Reiner, 1985, p. 54; the McNee quote is taken from *Policing London*, no. 8, 1983, p. 9.
37. Scarman, 1982, pp. 144–5.
38. *Policing London*, no. 8, 1983, p. 10.
39. *Sunday Times*, 19 April 1981, quoted in Jefferson and Grimshaw, 1984, p. 101.
40. Northam, 1985, p. 4.
41. Ibid. The irony is that paramilitary 'colonial' policing methods were developed first not in the colonies but by the British state to deal with its first colony, Ireland. Though conventional wisdom still has it that Peel's Metropolitan Police Act of 1829 inaugurated 'modern policing', it would be hard now, in the wake of Palmer's monumental recent study, to deny that 'honour' to the Dublin Police Act of 1786 (Palmer, 1988, pp. 27–30). Moreover, given the greater rebelliousness of the Irish to British political rule, the policing system instituted in Ireland in the late eighteenth and early nineteenth centuries was altogether more centralized and coercive than the subsequent British system. Thereafter, as Palmer's (1988, pp. 542–5) conclusion makes clear, the history of the relationships between 'demilitarized' British, 'military-style' Irish, and colonial policing is complicated. And, as Brewer and his colleagues' contemporary overview of policing public order in seven different states makes clear, the situation in Northern Ireland is all but unique: 'there are few, if any, close analogies with Northern Ireland as a divided society elsewhere in the world' (Brewer *et al.*, 1988, p. 82). We should beware, therefore, of easy comparisons, even as we acknowledge the undoubted contribution of Anglo–Irish relations to a full understanding of coercive developments in the modern British state (cf. Boyle *et al.*, 1975; 1980; Hillyard, 1985; Brewer *et al.*, 1988, Chapter 3; and Hillyard and Percy-Smith, 1988, esp. Chapter 7).
42. Dickinson, 1984, p. 7.
43. Ibid., p. 10.
44. Terry Fields, MP, quoted in ibid., p. 138.
45. Colin Bourne, quoted in ibid., p. 140 (emphasis in original).
46. Ibid., p. 141.
47. Ibid., p. 143.
48. The statistical record of the strike is complicated by a number of factors: the use of alternative sources, for example the Chief Constable of Nottinghamshire's claim of 3,000 police injuries (*Sheffield Morning Telegraph*, 6 July 1985) which contrasts with the figures I have quoted (from McCabe and Wallington, 1988, p. 166); later additional charges (which increases the number of riot charges from 137 to 295; McCabe and Wallington, 1988, p. 162); and whether figures quoted are inclusive or exclusive of Scotland. My own figures have largely drawn on McCabe and Wallington's (1988, pp. 161–9) detailed statistical appendix. But see also *The Guardian* 4 and 5 March 1985; and McIlroy, 1985, p. 106.
49. Sheffield Policewatch, 1984. This finding is in line with that of an earlier study on picketing by Kahn *et al.*, 1983.
50. Taken from Manoeuvre 6, Tactical Options Training Manual.
51. Peirce, 1985, p. 7. Orgreave is analysed in more detail in Chapter 5.
52. Scraton, 1987, p. 163.
53. Cf. Manchester City Council, 1985. This incident is also analysed in more detail in Chapter 5.
54. The miners' strike and the Manchester Students' Union demonstration were both

subject to unofficial inquiries (see NCCL, 1984; Manchester City Council, 1985). Still to come were a whole spate of unofficial inquiries into the riots of 1985, including two into the Handsworth riots (see Gifford, 1986; Review Panel, 1986; Silverman, 1986); and another NCCL inquiry, this time into the policing of the printers' industrial dispute at Wapping (NCCL, 1986).

55. Quoted in *The Times*, 11 September, 1985, p. 2.
56. Metropolitan Police, 1986, p. 12.
57. Quoted in *The Guardian*, 8 October 1985, p. 1. A more detailed analysis of the disturbances at Broadwater Farm appears in Chapter 5.
58. Metropolitan Police, 1986.
59. Scotland Yard press release, 12 January 1987, quoted in *Policing London*, no. 27, 1987, p. 95.
60. Northam, 1988, p. 116.
61. Metropolitan Police, 1986, p. 21.
62. Ibid., p. 27.
63. *The Guardian*, 3 July 1986, quoted in *Policing London*, no. 23, 1986, p. 23.
64. NCCL, 1986.
65. London Strategic Policy Unit, 1987, p. 36.
66. According to a Parliamentary reply by John Stanley, 15 people had died and 383 had been injured (up to 31 May 1987), as a result of the use of plastic bullets in Northern Ireland (*Hansard*, 3 July 1987, quoted in *Policing London*, no. 29, 1987, p. 27).
67. For those who feel uneasy about my denial of the importance of centralization, let me insist that I am not sanguine about the dangers of any centralization of state powers in the absence of an adequate structure of democratic accountability. But, as I and Grimshaw have argued elsewhere (Jefferson and Grimshaw, 1984, Chapter 6), the critical question is not where (locality or centre) power is exercised, but whether adequate mechanisms exist for its democratic control. We attempted then to spell out what such democratic mechanisms might look like. But, in this particular text, I hope to show that there is an inherent problem with paramilitary policing *per se* which also needs to be recognized. Nothing I say here is intended to deny the continuing importance of the accountability debate. Hopefully, my present argument will only add to its urgency.
68. Morris, 1985; 1987.
69. Morris, 1985, p. 364.
70. Ibid.
71. Ibid.
72. Clift, 1981.
73. Ibid., p. 1482.
74. Ibid., p. 1483.
75. Ibid.
76. Waddington, 1987.
77. Ibid., pp. 39–40.
78. Ibid., p. 46.

CHAPTER 2

Minimum force:
a 'contingent' historical
'view from below'

INTRODUCTION

The tasks of this present chapter are twofold: first, to show that one of the key prongs of Waddington's argument – the tradition of restraint or 'minimum force' – cannot withstand critical historical scrutiny; and, second, to provide the rudiments of a historical approach that can, as a basis from which to begin my evaluation of the paramilitary response.

To achieve this requires that we first take a critical look at the kind of benign reading of police history that has produced the consensual backcloth of 're-straint' against which paramilitarism provides either a negative contrast[1] or a positive continuation.[2] With this approach found wanting because it is ill equipped to comprehend the continuance of disorder or the views of the demonstrators and pickets on the receiving end in confrontations, a more fruitful one is then outlined. This recognizes that consent is always *conditional* – operating only under some conditions, and not under others – and is *far from universal* among the policed. What emerges from adopting this perspective is a much more episodic and uneven history of policing public order, with violence for the policed always a potentiality. Finally, the emergence of the paramilitary response is examined from this vantage point. This scrutiny produces a far more pessimistic appraisal than Waddington's sanguine conclusion.

A TRADITION OF 'RESTRAINT'?

The idea of the restrained use of force being central to the British police tradition is a unifying feature of conservative histories of modern policing. From this perspective, the widespread cross-class hostility to the very idea of a permanent, paid police force in the late eighteenth and early nineteenth centuries ensured that the resulting police force was unarmed, without special powers, and charged to use the minimum force necessary. This restrained approach quickly won over the middle classes, and eventually the working classes once the benefits of a more orderly and less crime-prone society became evident, and the fears (of intrusion, surveillance, loss of liberty, etc.) proved relatively ground-less. With increased acceptance came a reduction in the sort of hostility and violence (from both sides) characteristic of early police–public contacts. This new 'maturity' in police–public relations inaugurated a 'golden age of policing', which in turn provided further vindication of the restrained approach. When new developments (like paramilitarism) appear to threaten this tradition of 'benign restraint' – the famous British 'police advantage' – the question becomes: how can change take place in ways which preserve this central legitimizing notion of 'minimum force'? Such a question, as we have seen, was indeed at the heart of the writings of Clift, Morris and Waddington.[3]

Restraint and industrial disputes: a recent example of the conservative approach

Roger Geary's recent book *Policing Industrial Disputes: 1893 to 1985* is a good example of a latently conservative approach informing a historical account of one sort of public order policing. For our purposes, its importance lies in illustrating how the conservative evolutionary framework – the gradual maturation and increased legitimacy of the 'police idea' – has problems explain-ing the industrial confrontations of the 1980s such as the miners' strike of 1984–5.

Basically Geary traces, and then offers his explanation for, the changing tactics adopted during industrial confrontations between 1893 and 1985. His account suggests that at least until the 1980s such tactics (on both sides) have become increasingly peaceful. This is because the early violent tactics of the late nineteenth and early twentieth centuries, characterized by stone-throwing strikers and a military prepared to shoot, give way first to violent (1910–14) and then to non-violent picketing (1915–45), both being met by the police baton-charges. In the post-war period (1946–80), these tactics are replaced with the relatively non-violent 'pushing and shoving' by both sides (in situations of mass picketing), or by the equally non-violent 'symbolic confrontations' (in situ-ations where pickets and police both sustain only a limited 'symbolic' presence). The miners' strike of 1984–5 inaugurated a reversal of 'this historical trend towards non-violence . . . once again stone-throwing pickets have been charged by baton-wielding police'.[4]

The explanation Geary offers for the de-escalation of violence is that it becomes increasingly counter-productive, the more public opinion grows in importance. For the trade union movement closely associated with a Labour Party committed to the ballot-box, avoiding violence became increasingly politically necessary if Labour's electoral fortunes were not to be adversely affected. From the other side, a well-organized labour movement made the authorities increasingly vulnerable to bad publicity from their coercive actions. In addition, the growing presence of the media and of civil rights organizations at disputes, as observers and recorders, has acted as a further restraining influence on both sides.

But, when it comes to explaining the violence of the miners' strike of 1984–5, Geary resorts to treating it as a special case, as an exception to the non-violent 'rule':

> As for the future, there is every reason to suppose that the violence of the miners' strike will not generally be repeated in subsequent disputes. It seems that several unique features – the lack of whole-hearted support from other unions, the marked absence of internal unity, the militant leadership, the sheer length of the stoppage – prevented the constraints on violence which has proved so effective in the past from being fully operative.[5]

In treating the miners' strike as a special case in the otherwise progressively more peaceful nature of industrial disputes, Geary reveals his latent conservative evolutionism. Elsewhere, he is more explicit: 'It seems then that the return to "stoning" may be a temporary phenomenon; a throwback in the evolution of successively less violent styles of industrial disorder.'[6] While he does qualify this by suggesting that 'constraints on violence have, to some extent, been offset by modern police tactics which tend to generate a vicious spiral of violence and destruction'[7] (a viewpoint on the amplifying role of paramilitary police tactics that I both agree with and develop below), as a historical framework for understanding 'restraint' it remains too optimistic a starting point for understanding the present re-emergence of coercive policing. As such, it is unable to provide an adequate basis for an appropriate response.

It is important to add, by way of a caveat, that this critique of Geary is not directed at the particular substance of his account, which is informed and informative. Rather, the critique is directed at its implicit underlying framework, which I have deliberately highlighted in order to make my particular point.

AN ALTERNATIVE EXPLANATION: GRAMSCI, CONSENT AND 'CONTINGENCY'

The impact of Gramsci on modern Marxism, and on a whole range of studies informed by a 'radical' or 'critical' approach, is probably incalculable. It is certainly immense. This has something to do with the variety of his interests. It has also to do with their enduring relevance.

Central to his concerns was the question of 'consent'. If traditional Marxism had emphasized the centrality of understanding the role of conflict between the classes for political or social analysis, Gramsci was one of the first to recognize the importance of consent for understanding how advanced capitalist democracies work. He recognized that the strength of 'civil society' in such societies rendered an 'old-style' revolutionary seizure of state power redundant. He also recognized that a well-developed civil society made coercion a strategy of last resort; what happened when the ideological struggle to produce consent failed. Both the 'ruling bloc' (the ruling class and its allies from other classes) and its opponents were constantly struggling to widen their sphere of influence by winning over allies to their vision of the world. To the extent that a ruling bloc was successful in such a struggle, its dominance could be said to be 'hegemonic'. To the extent that it was not, it was appropriate to talk of a 'crisis of authority'. Such moments of instability might have many outcomes, including, if the alliance of radical forces failed to produce a successful counter-hegemony (and as Gramsci knew to his personal cost), the horrors of fascism and other 'exceptional' modes of capitalist rule.

The idea of politics as the outcome of the balance of forces at particular moments, and of this balance being constantly in flux as each side enjoins the ideological struggle in order to 'win friends and influence people' (and disturb their opponents' similar attempts), renders a very different historical framework to that underlying the work of Geary. Rather than the conservative idea of history as progress, what we have here is the idea of history as a series of moments or 'conjunctures', each more or less stable, each more or less hegemonic (or consensual). While long-term 'organic' trends determined by the mode of production set certain limits, within these limits political outcomes are the product of (or are *contingent* upon) the successful (or unsuccessful) management of the political field. And crucial to such management is the 'battle of ideas'.[8]

Negotiation and restraint: a recent example of the 'contingent' approach

Phil Cohen's article, written in 1979, on the changing nature of the policing of Islington before and after the First World War is an excellent example of this 'contingent' approach. While I would dispute the historical veracity of his starting point, that 'the modern police force . . . was the first branch of the British State to develop an ideological as well as a purely repressive function',[9] the influence of Gramsci in that statement is unmistakable.

At the risk of diluting the article's richness, the basic argument runs essentially like this. The starting point is the idea of the new police having a 'civilizing' mission ultimately motivated by economic considerations ('designed to ensure the free circulation of commodities'[10]), which was fiercely resisted by the city slum-dwellers who bore its brunt. However – and here the importance of ideology and consent becomes crucial – this mission embodies a *contradictory* function. On the one hand, the relentless pursuit of the mission – the enforcement of 'statutory norms of public order'[11] in working-class neighbourhoods where strong countervailing norms operated – could not help but

23

overstretch limited resources and feel oppressive to the community on the receiving end. Hence the fierce community resistance. On the other hand, anything less than full enforcement threatened the very idea which gave the new police force its general legitimacy, namely, impartial law enforcement: 'the official posture of the force as neutral arbiters of justice'.[12] The result was to confront 'the force . . . with the impossible choice of enforcing law *or* order'.[13]

In terms of 'consent', the problem was one of competing ideologies: the old ideology of what was acceptable public behaviour in working-class neighbourhoods (the *popular* notion of public order espoused by the new urban proletariat); and the new 'juridical ideology of crime'[14] (the *unpopular* bourgeois legal order 'in which the bourgeoisie has enshrined its version of the rights of capital and the obligations of labour')[15] – in other words, 'proletarian order' versus 'bourgeois law'. The solution to the 'impossible choice' was, eventually, compromise: a change from the 'outright physical confrontation' characteristic of policing in pre-war Islington to 'an unwritten system of tacit negotiation'[16] in the post-war period. In practice, this meant 'turning half a blind eye to the rule book' and 'turning the other half of the blind eye to a good deal of minor infringement'.[17]

This change – from confrontation to negotiation – was not just attributable to the new ideological function of the police. A whole host of changes, especially structural changes in the labour market, assisted. Critical to the latter was the growing divide between the declining 'informal' casual labour market and the developing formal economy, with a 'labour aristocracy' at its apex and gradations of other skilled, semi- and unskilled workers beneath. While those in the casual, informal economy – led by the costermongers – remained committed to the traditional street culture with its associated popular institutions and mores, those in the regular economy, led by the 'labour aristocrats' like the 'skilled print and railway workers',[18] were establishing and participating in a whole range of new institutions – political, cultural and social – and developing a new morality to match. This new morality Cohen has termed 'public propriety'.[19] In short, a structurally-based divide was beginning to open up between those workers with a stake in the new urban order (the 'respectables') and those without (the 'roughs'). This division, and the associated development of the notion of 'public propriety', provided the material basis for the change from confrontation to negotiation, namely, 'an alliance between the spokesmen of proletarian patriarchy and propriety [the "respectables"] and the enforcers of bourgeois law and order [the police]'.[20]

However, the willingness to allow certain notions of community 'order' to prevail over juridical notions of bourgeois 'law' does not eliminate the ideological importance of the latter. In other words, the contradictory choice of law *or* order remains. The organizational solution has been to institutionalize this contradiction in the form of an internal division of labour. Within this, some officers, like local beat constables, have the task of 'maintaining negotiated order'; others, 'like the Special Patrol Group and Regional Crime Squads' are charged with restoring 'statutory order without regard for any of the factors constraining the operations of the local force'.[21] The consequence is the constant undermining of each other's work:

> The more resources allocated to increasing the efficiency of repressive policing, the more manpower has to be poured into 'community relations' to restabilize the public image of the force. The more technologically sophisticated, and hence impersonal, the systems of surveillance, the more home-beat coppers are needed on the ground.[22]

Finally, the fragility of negotiated settlements is emphasized. Because of the way in which the labour force under capitalism is constantly being recomposed and relocated, any negotiations made with existing communities will need to be constantly renegotiated with any new groups of workers (or 'non-workers') generated by these changes in the division of labour. To illustrate, Cohen particularly mentions changes in the juvenile labour market and the arrival of 'immigrant workers'. The temptation for the police with such 'new social forces' is to take the easy way by 'falling back on the more or less brutal reimposition of statutory public order when policing these groups'.[23] Thus it is that the idea of 'negotiated' consent is necessarily contingent; new contingencies constantly threaten the always 'unstable equilibria' of existing accommodations.

The advantages of this kind of approach are hopefully obvious. Unlike Geary's resort to a 'special case' explanation for the re-emergence of violence in industrial disputes, Cohen's contingent account never precludes such a possibility. Indeed, it provides a means, based on the changing material conditions of working-class life and livelihood, of predicting when such violence is more rather than less likely to occur. However, it can also explain why much public order policing is relatively peaceful, and why there is broad support for much policework, as survey after survey has shown, among many in the working classes. In short, the advantages of the approach are that neither consensus nor coercion are seen as inevitable features of police–public relations. Each is regarded as contingent. And Cohen offers an account of the relevant contingencies operating at a crucial transitional moment in the 'policing of the working class city'. Now let us see how such a historical framework can illuminate another crucial transitional moment – the emergence of paramilitary policing.

CONTEXTUALIZING PARAMILITARISM 1: CONSENSUS, 'CRISIS' AND COERCION

As we saw in Chapter 1, the transition to paramilitarism commenced in the 1960s with the mid-decade establishment of the first SPG in London. As must now be common knowledge, either through direct experience or through the variously mediated accounts now available (most recently the 1968 TV retrospective), the 1960s was generally a crucial transitional decade. A proper contextualization of the former transition obviously requires that we first comprehend the significance of the 'transitional' 1960s.

Given the sheer volume and variety of writing about the period, it is easy to become distracted by its spectacular surface and multiple myths. It is therefore important to get a proper analytical grip on the period. Here Gramsci's writings demonstrate their continuing relevance, especially his notion of hegemony. Periodization in history – demarcating particular conjunctures – is never an easy matter, and never more so than when applied schematically, as I intend, and with large brushstrokes. This is because, strictly speaking, any conjuncture is composed of 'the overlapping of different periodizations, of structurally different forces developing at different tempos and rhythms, of, in fact, different "histories"'.[24] In other words, developments in the economic field do not necessarily coincide exactly with, for example, changing political or ideological or cultural developments. Nevertheless, a loose conjunctural periodization of post-war Britain can be usefully attempted in terms of hegemony, if a certain tolerance is exercised, both towards its schematic approach and towards the 'fit' between the 'different histories' of the various developments. The pay-off for such tolerance is a revelation of an underlying importance to the 1960s which matches its significance as spectacle. This significance lies in its being the transitional moment between the consensual, hegemonic 1950s and the more coercive, less hegemonic 1970s and 1980s: the moment of the breakdown or crisis of hegemony.

'Crisis' is of course a much overused word and one which ought, therefore, to be treated with some caution. However, in relation to the 1960s, whether one is thinking of the economic, the political, the ideological or almost any arena of social life, the term seems appropriate – which is why the notion of an overall 'crisis of hegemony' does not seem far-fetched. In briefly demonstrating this below, my account draws heavily on the much longer more detailed account of this period in *Policing the Crisis*, a book whose account of the 'crisis', whatever its other shortcomings, remains substantially intact.[25]

The hegemonic 1950s

Gramsci was always clear that the bedrock of hegemony is successful mastery of the economy by the ruling alliance. Economic sacrifices to subordinate groups certainly need to be made to provide the basis for 'a certain compromise equilibrium', and mastery has to extend to fields beyond the economy – to be 'ethico-political' as well as economic – but 'hegemony . . . must *necessarily* be based on the decisive function exercised by the leading group in the decisive nucleus of economic activity'.[26] Thus, in looking at the basis of the 'period of unrivalled hegemonic domination',[27] presided over from 1951 by a Conservative government, we need first to mention the new world-wide stabilization and expansion of capitalism. In Britain this new-found stability rested on two new commitments: to the newly constructed welfare state and to full employment. These were the social costs, the economic 'sacrifices' that a reformed Conservatism knew was required of it if unemployment and welfare – 'the twin spectres of the Depression'[28] – were ever to be successfully exorcized from the collective memory of the working classes. The origins of the new expansion lay in the

26

conjunction of Keynesianism – the general strategic response to the Depression – and the new productive 'assembly-line' methods, methods whose origins lay in the revolutions in management and production first instituted in the early twentieth century by F. W. Taylor and Henry Ford in the USA, but which really only came to be extensively adopted in Britain in the post-war period. Keynesianism, through its interventionist approach to employment and demand, went some way towards managing capitalism's hitherto uncontrolled slumps; and the new methods of production greatly enhanced productivity. Together 'both made possible the high-wage, mass-production, domestic-consumer-oriented modern economy, under the governance of an expanded and interventionist "state regulator"'.[29]

The general level of political agreement about the requirements of a modern capitalist economy, for security of employment, for productivity and for a welfare net, made the question of its political management not 'what is to be done', but 'who is to do it'. In the event, the Conservatives managed to reform themselves more convincingly than Labour. If it was easier to associate Labour with the new commitments to the welfare state and to full employment, they clearly found it less easy to associate themselves with the rampant, individualistic materialism of the new consumption-led 'affluence'. For their part, the Conservatives, with no 'cloth-cap image' to shake off, nor moral scruples about opportunistic appeals to the immediate material interests of the new working classes, found themselves much more in tune with the 'politics of affluence'. And the concessions on welfare, on employment, and on the odd nationalization, offered no threat to this revival of capitalism; on the contrary, such concessions 'secured just the measure of popular legitimacy . . . required [for] . . . the expansion of a popular consumers' capitalism'.[30] If Labour had been the 'natural' party of austerity during the immediate post-war years, painstakingly presiding not over the parliamentary road to socialism as it transpired, but over the provision of a more socially conscious capitalism, the new Conservatives were to reap the reward and become, between 1951 and 1964, the 'natural' party of 'never-had-it-so-good' affluence. However, if Labour consistently failed to win the middle ground from the Conservatives, it certainly was not through lack of trying – hence the label 'Butskellism' to describe the centrist 'consensus' politics of these years.

The ideological reading of these economic and political changes that came to dominate the period, and thus to provide the 'ethico-political' justifications needed to secure the hegemony, were essentially constructed out of a consensual reading of the terms 'affluence', 'consensus' and 'embourgeoisement'. A consensual ideological reading is one which suppresses or obscures the complex, contradictory nature of social developments in favour of a simple, one(favourable)-sided emphasis. Thus the ideological reading of affluence 'referred, essentially, to the boom in working class consumer spending',[31] and successfully obscured the more complex reality: that some groups were untouched by 'affluence'; continuing poverty; a failure to redistribute wealth; as well as the very fragile, credit-based, 'live now, pay later', basis of much of the so-called affluence. The ideological reading of 'consensus' referred to the acceptance by both political parties, and the majority of the electorate, of all the measures – mixed economy, increased incomes, welfare state 'safety net' – taken after 1945 to draw people of all classes together on the basis of a common stake in the system.[32]

And, once again, such a reading suppressed a more complex reality: that some still had more of a stake in the system than others; that the 'mixed economy' was being driven by the imperatives of private capital, not those of socialism; and that beyond the consensual stranglehold of the politics of parliamentary democracy, other political voices, like the 'New Left' and later the Campaign for Nuclear Disarmament (CND), were striving to be heard.

Finally, the ideological reading of 'embourgeoisement' entailed the notion 'that working class life and culture was ceasing to be a distinct formation in the society, and everyone was assimilating rapidly towards middle-class patterns, aspirations and values'.[33] This, again, obscured a far more complex reality. Phil Cohen, in particular, has captured the contradictory nature of these changes in his idea of the post-war respectable working class in London's East End being 'caught and pulled apart'[34] by them. In other words, these changes presented not one but *two* 'options', two opposing types of social mobility: upwards into the ranks of the new suburban working-class elite or downwards into the 'lumpen'.[35] As well as presenting a rather more complex picture of the impact of the changes wrought by 'affluence', Cohen's argument also replaces the idea of the disappearance of a class (a notion which already assumes too homogeneous a notion of class) with the more historical notion of the dislocation of a class – its decomposition and recomposition.

> Perhaps the most significant aspect of . . . Cohen's analysis is the way in which he picks and redefines certain key themes in the affluence–consensus–embourgeoisement thesis: he discards their spectacular and ideological framework, relocates them within the specific historical re-lations and situation of the working class of a particular area, and arrives at a 'thesis', not about the disappearance or 'embourgeoisement' of a class, but rather about how wider social-economic changes can fragment, unhinge and dislocate its intricate mechanisms and defences.[36]

Despite the more complex reality, it was the simple ideological reading that provided the hegemonic explanation of these bewildering changes:

> Stated simply, the conventional wisdom was that 'affluence' and 'consen-sus' together were promoting the rapid 'bourgeoisification' of the working classes. This was producing new social types, new social arrangements and values. One such type was the 'affluent worker' – the 'new type of bourgeois worker', family-minded, home-centred, security-conscious, in-strumentally-oriented, geographically mobile and acquisitive – celebrated in, for example, Zweig's work (Zweig, 1961). Another was the new 'teenager' committed to style, music, leisure and consumption: to a 'classless youth culture'.[37]

Finally, there is little doubt that this 'internal' consensual reading of social change was materially assisted by the 'external' ideological climate. Here the 'cold war' united the Western democracies in the ideological defence of the 'free enterprise' system and thereby effectively contained debate within these 'icy' parameters.

But hegemonic domination, however 'unrivalled', is never absolute nor unending. In the first place, the economic base which underpinned it proved far more fragile, especially in Britain, than optimists imagined. Rising inflation, comparatively slow growth rates, and a declining competitiveness gradually revealed the structural weakness which the boom years had largely managed to conceal. Unconsensual signs – a vague sense of moral unease with the new materialism, concern about crime and immigration, youth violence and the teddy boys, sex (not yet drugs) and rock and roll, the birth of CND, the new 'satire' movement, the 'rediscovery of poverty', and so on – constantly broke through the hegemonic framework. As the 1950s gave way to the 1960s such breakthroughs became more frequent and more sustained: a sure sign that the consensual, hegemonic 1950s were beginning to enter a period of transition.

The transitional 1960s

Strictly speaking, the early part of the decade was still underpinned by hegemonic consensus, albeit a 'social-democratic' rather than a 'spontaneous' one,[38] and the last year or so, after 1968, by its opposite, namely, a conflict-ridden 'crisis of authority'. Nevertheless, for the sake of brevity, I regard the 1960s as a pivotal 'moment of transition' – between the hegemonic 1950s and the non-hegemonic 1970s and 1980s. The transition was marked, economically by a new accent on restraint and 'belt-tightening', politically by the full flowering of corporatism – the bringing together of both sides of industry and the state to thrash out a universally acceptable social and economic 'package' – and ideologically by the twin themes of 'modernization' (to enhance productivity) and 'the national interest' (above the 'selfishness' of individualistic or sectional interests). Clearly these changes were connected. The harsher economic climate required the imposition of certain painful measures. The consensual achievement of these required the willing acquiescence of all affected parties – hence the political importance of corporatism and the ideological importance of 'the national interest', the latter ideally being simply the agreed corporate plan. Those opposed to it were simply guilty of 'selfishness' – of putting their own individual or sectional interests above the 'interests of all'. 'Modernization', which was equated simply with 'greater productivity', meant 'more for all' and therefore was unproblematically 'in the national interest'.

These changes, which collectively constituted an alternative, social-democratic form of attempted hegemony, were presided over, for the most part (1964–70) by a Labour government. This is perhaps not surprising. As the 'natural' party of austerity, not affluence, it had the right credentials for the new discipline, restraint and 'belt-tightening' needed when the never-had-it-so-good apparently spontaneous hegemony of the 1950s hit troubled times. And, as the party of 'regulation for the social good', the new corporatist 'national interest' strategy was more 'naturally' in tune with its socially concerned interventionist approach to policy.

The centrepiece of the 'belt-tightening' strategy was the national prices and incomes policy. For its importance extended beyond the economic; getting political agreements on prices and incomes, and attempting to ensure these were kept ('in the national interest'), was to become the litmus test of the new 'disciplined' style of consensus management, the key to the social-democratic attempt at a hegemonic project. But as the structural weakness of the economy became increasingly visible during the period, signified by rising deficits on the balance of payments, a falling pound and mounting inflation, the successful striking of bargains satisfactory to all the relevant parties – employers, workers and the state (representing 'the people') – became more and more difficult. The real question, obscured by ideological talk of 'modernization' and 'the national interest', was who was to bear the burden of economic decline.

It was this issue above all others, in keeping with Gramsci's point about the decisive nature of the economic for hegemony, which best illustrates the period's transitional nature: its status as 'a turning point in the passage . . . from the "moment of consent" through to the "moment of force" '.[39] When the seamen went on strike in 1966, thereby delivering their verdict on the fairness of the prices and incomes policy, the Prime Minister, Harold Wilson, attacked them in a way which was to become all too familiar in the years to follow. The strike was not only selfishly against the national interest, but it was led by a 'tightly knit group of politically motivated men', by 'conspirators', by 'extremists', by 'reds'. As was argued in 1978 in Policing the Crisis, the idea of a subversive minority with ulterior political motives fomenting industrial unrest 'was to dominate the ideological signification of industrial conflict from that point forwards to the present'.[40] It is a form of signification that was also to become dominant in other areas, as the way of explaining (away) dissensual viewpoints, that is, viewpoints contrary to an assumed consensus. Thus, though Wilson's story succeeded at the time in securing an early settlement to the seamen's strike, it was, more importantly, an admission of failure – a failure to harmonize (or 'hegemonize') all interests within 'the national interest'.

Other signs that the hegemony of the 1950s was beginning to crumble stemmed from the growing disjunction between the disciplined restraint constantly being demanded in the workplace, and the new air of freedom informing people's moral and cultural lives. One consequence was the appearance of the moral entrepreneurs, as the vague sense of moral unease about many post-war changes we noted breaking through the hegemonic 1950s took the very definite shape of a concerted moral backlash. Moreover, and importantly for our purposes, the changes came to be seen as connected. The bored, 'too affluent' mods and rockers clashing on south coast beaches, the hedonism of 'swinging London', the gangland violence of the Kray twins, the Great Train Robbery, the Moors murders, the liberalization of the laws on censorship, licensing, divorce, and so on, the drug-taking dropout, 'flower power', the alternative lifestyle of the hippies, the 'mindless violence' of the skinhead, football hooliganism, the Beatles, the Rolling Stones and 'acid' rock – all came to be seen, by the moral entrepreneurs, as examples of a new 'age of permissiveness'.

The idea of 'permissiveness' linking together a number of disparate phenomena is a good example of the increasingly ideological reading that the period became subject to, as the dissensual signs grew. In the first place, the obsession with 'permissiveness' constituted a way of demarcating a boundary line or 'threshold', marking out 'symbolically the limits of societal tolerance'[41] on questions of morality. It thus performed the important ideological function of reaffirming the singularity of the moral consensus, while obscuring the bewildering multiplicity of the signs of dissensus. Secondly, the use of a single term like 'permissiveness' to connect up a number of activities is also an example of the ideological mechanism of 'convergence'. This 'occurs when two or more activities are linked in the process of signification so as to implicitly or explicitly draw parallels between them'.[42] The ideological effects of convergence are threefold: simplification of a complex reality to an alleged common denominator; amplification, because the relatively harmless activities become implicated in the more serious ones with which they are linked; and depoliticization or criminalization, when the authenticity of particular activities becomes undermined through being connected with obviously criminal or violent ones. The net result, once again, is the reaffirmation of the consensus, and, because of amplification and criminalization, the legitimation of harsher measures of control in its defence.

One final mechanism, also indicating that all was not well with the consensus, makes an appearance during this period. It occurs when, for a time, the moral backlash becomes more sharply focused on a particular group or activity, and takes the form of a frenzied overreaction, including usually the imposition of severer measures of control, often in the aftermath of a particular dramatic event. This overreaction has been called a 'moral panic', and the groups subject to such overattention, which become for a while the concrete focus of an otherwise much more generalized set of social anxieties, have been called 'folk devils'.[43] At various times during the 1960s, particular groups and activities – mods and rockers, drug-taking, students, football hooligans, and so on – have all become the focus of this stigmatizing process. But for us what matters is what the general tendency to 'panic' reveals about the state of hegemony. And this takes us back to our starting point, the 1960s as a 'period of transition'; for,

> to put it crudely, the 'moral panic' appears . . . to be one of the principal forms of ideological consciousness by means of which a 'silent majority' is won over to the support of increasingly coercive measures on the part of the state, and lends its legitimacy to a 'more than usual' exercise of control.[44]

The voluntary prices and incomes strategy – the centrepiece both of the social-democratic economic strategy and of its hegemonic project – finally came to grief in the closing years of the 1960s. The worsening of the economic crisis made the question of who was to bear the burden of the decline more urgent, and the answers, from both sides of industry, more militant. Capital's 'answer' was double-edged: the productivity deal (effectively designed to make labour pay for its own wage increases by working harder or by agreeing to its partial replacement by new machines) and rationalization (typically in the form of a state-supported takeover or merger leading to a shake-out of labour and/or greater mechanization). Labour's 'answer' was similarly duplex: the 'unofficial' strike (led by stewards from the shop floor and not by full-time union officials) and 'wage drift' (usually the object of a strike, namely increasing the gap between local earnings and nationally agreed rates). The government presided over the accompanying debate. Three key documents appeared – the Royal Commission Report on Trade Unions and Employers' Associations (the Donovan Report), and two party-political replies, namely, the Labour government's *In Place of Strife* and the Conservatives' *Fair Deal at Work*. Each proposed a different solution, but each had its sights set on the same (ideologically defined) problem – how to get (sectional) union militancy to conform to a higher (national) interest (without resorting to compulsion).

The less hegemonic 1970s and 1980s

The failure of Wilsonian 'voluntary restraint' to provide a framework to stem the 'flood of wage demands', or to deal with 'rapid price inflation, rising unemployment and a period of zero growth',[45] led to a lost election in 1970 and to the evolution of a new more openly confrontational strategy. The Conservatives' new strategy, under the leadership of Edward Heath, had three prongs: a decisive turn towards Europe and the Common Market (and hence away, to some extent, from the 'special relationship' with the USA); the unleashing of market forces at home to flush out the uncompetitive 'lame ducks' (and the consequent dismantling of the corporatist framework); and a new legally-backed framework for industrial relations (to replace the failed voluntaryism). One unintended effect of the new *laissez-faire* was a bonanza for property speculators – capitalism's 'unacceptable face'. Another (no doubt also unintended) effect, a result of introducing legislation to regulate trade union activity in various ways (enshrined in the new Industrial Relations Act), was the stiffening of working-class resistance. For example, more days were lost through strikes in 1972 (now, unlike the 1960s, characteristically 'official' rather than 'unofficial') than in any year since 1919. Even the jailing of five dockers for contempt – during a dock strike in defence of jobs threatened by container rationalization – failed to have the desired impact. And, although the successful 'Saltley Gates' miners' strike of 1972 prompted fresh legislation against 'flying pickets' (which was to lead to further jailings, of the 'Shrewsbury picket' building workers, in the following year), the alternative Heathian attempt to solve the British Crisis had by then effectively failed.

The deepening of the recession on a global scale, illustrated most dramatically by the massive rise in OPEC oil prices, forced Heath reluctantly to return to corporate bargaining – though the first phase, a six-month total freeze on wages, hardly looked much of a 'bargain'. A final showdown with the miners led, in

1974, to the electoral defeat of the Conservatives and the re-election of a Labour government – the 'natural' custodians of corporatism. But the return of a social-democratic form of crisis management – the 'social contract' years of the Callaghan government – coincided with a still militant working class, and (not unrelated, of course) the full flowering of a novel and devastating form of capitalist recession, namely, 'slumpflation' (a slump in production combined with rising inflation). The result, effectively, was simply a 'softer' way of managing the decline – a resolution which, in the event, confused many and eventually paved the way for another radical attempt at turning the economy around, in the form of Thatcherism.

The installation of a radical Conservative government under Margaret Thatcher from 1979 witnessed a return to the concerns of Edward Heath, but executed in an even harsher economic climate and with a new ruthlessness. The release of market forces, and the attacks, by recourse to the law, on all centres of resistance, such as the unions and local government, did, for a while anyway, cut inflation. But it did so at a very high cost – a massive reduction in manufacturing output, a huge rise in unemployment and severe cuts in public expenditure (the 'social wage'). These changes have effectively institutionalized a dual economy, or what has come to be called by many on the Left, especially those connected with *Marxism Today*'s 'New Times' project, the ⅔:⅓ society. One-third – the unemployed living on state benefits, the low-waged participating either in the unprotected nether world of the 'informal' economy, or in the unskilled, still labour-intensive, traditional end of the labour market – live at or below the poverty line. Two-thirds – those making up the professional or 'recomposed' sectors of the economy – live on high or relatively rising incomes. Whatever the ultimate stability of such an economic solution, it can hardly be said to be built on consensus – unless it is one which simply ignores the voices of the dispossessed one-third.

To sketch in the economic changes characteristic of the 1970s is, as we have seen, impossible without touching on the political struggles around such changes, principally over the use of coercive legislation to impose what could no longer be voluntarily agreed. This more ready recourse to law is a more general feature of the politics of the period – and is, simultaneously, symptomatic both of the growing dissensus and instrumental in deepening it. By way of illustration, let us look at just four examples from the proliferating signs of dissensus: youth, women, race, and Northern Ireland.

Nineteen sixty-eight is probably best remembered as the year of global student rebellion – the revolt of the 'brightest and best'. Coming fast on the heels of the hippy rebellion, it proved that youthful rebellion no longer simply embraced the frustrated alienation of certain working-class youngsters. Moreover, the depth and scope of the critique emanating from those most aware of the political and cultural dimensions of these simultaneous 'refusals' amounted to a completely new vision of the 'good life'. The conventional wisdoms of the dominant culture about the importance of materialistic affluence, 'career', status, repressive sexual taboos, the nuclear family, and so on, were systematically inverted. Alternative media (such as the underground press in the form of *Oz*, *IT* and others) and institutions (like the arts lab and the commune) sprang up to meet the very different emergent needs and mores. Dominant 'straight' culture was faced with a fully-fledged, 'deviant' set of alternatives: a freewheeling, concrete series of embodiments of dissensus, which collectively constituted an anti-authoritarian, libertarian counter-culture.

The origins of this 'revolt against affluence' are too complex to attempt to unravel here, though undoubtedly they had something to do with certain contradictory developments within a capitalism whose expansion now *required* a modification in the traditional, dominant ideology: away from a thrifty and repressively puritanical, work-based outlook, and towards a more liberated approach to the pleasures of spending, sexuality and consumption. In some respects the counter-cultural critique merely pushed this required internal modification to its limit position, thereby exposing its contradictory nature. The most important consequence of this, for our purposes, was its importance in sharpening the tools of legal repression, a point to which I return below.

If the counter-culture was spawned partly within the new ideological needs of an adapting capitalism, the new women's movement constituted a 'revolution in the revolution'. Though it had much in common with the counter-culture – most especially, of course, a profound awareness that 'the personal is political' – it was critical of the blindness to gender. And so, like the counter-culture's completion of the logic of the new capitalism's licensed 'permissiveness' (Marcuse's 'repressive desublimation') which ended up exposing its contradictoriness, the women's movement also completed the counter-cultural 'logic' of liberation (by 'genderizing' the agenda) which also ended up exposing the contradictory nature of a 'liberation' which remained solidly male-defined and male-dominated.

Though the counter-culture produced some lasting cultural innovations and remains still an influential reference point for many, and though it also provided the seedbed feeding other political movements like the revolutionary left-wing sects in the early 1970s, its only indigenous political formation was an ill-fated attempt at urban terrorism – the Angry Brigade. The women's movement, on the other hand, totally transformed the ideological landscape, even if the translation of anti-sexist rhetoric into effective, practical reality still has a long way to go, and the issue of male violence towards women remains as severe a problem as ever. But the feminist voice remains essentially a dissensual one, a constant reminder of the lack of consensus on the gender question.

It is sometimes hard at this point in time to recall that the present situation in Northern Ireland has specific origins – the attack in 1969 on the new civil rights movement demonstrating against the systematic discrimination in everyday life practised against the Catholic minority. Unravelling the spiral of violence triggered by the original attack is, thankfully, unnecessary for my very restricted purpose of providing further illustration of the breakdown of consensus. For this purpose, I wish only to mention two features of central importance to my argument – the role of legal repression and the question of violence, both of which I deal with more fully below.

However one regards these things, there can be no denying the crucial role played by the panoply of coercive measures variously designed to deal with the situation – the use of the army, internment, special powers, 'Diplock' courts, CS gas, armoured vehicles and plastic bullets, strip searches, the routine harassment of street stop or house search, armed police and surveillance helicopters, the refusal to grant prisoners political status, the subordination of legality to higher 'interests of state' in dealing with suspects, the sanctioning of 'shoot-to-kill' policies, and so on. Such repression, which has now become an intrinsic part of the problem, not only illustrates the absence of consensus but, in strengthening the resistance, has exacerbated further the level of dissent, as Hillyard has also argued.[46]

As for violence, there is no doubt that the struggle has become a very bitter and violent affair in reality. However, it is equally clear that the signification of violence has had profound ideological importance throughout. The reduction of the politics of urban guerrilla warfare to 'criminal' and 'senseless' violence – the dominant form of media and of popular signification – has been the means through which legitimation, and hence popular support, has been sought (and largely achieved) for the various repressive measures introduced.

Finally, then, race. As with Northern Ireland, the 'transitional' 1960s first sees race emerge nationally as a dissensual issue. The open endorsement of racialism by the Conservative candidate, Peter Griffiths, in the 1964 Smethwick election first broke the official silence of the liberal consensus. Thereafter Enoch Powell, by successfully casting people's everyday fears and anxieties in racial terms and imagery in a series of provocative speeches in the late 1960s – most notoriously in his infamous 'Rivers of Blood' speech – became the voice of popular racism and, almost singlehandedly, shattered the liberal consensus. The new dissensual parameters set by Powell affected every part of the political spectrum on race from then on. The centre became bogged down in the numbers game – seeing 'immigrants' as problems whose numbers must be restricted (a perception informing the succession of ever more racist Immigration Acts, which consistently contradicted the accompanying anti-discrimination legislation). Repatriation became the rallying cry of the right-wing extremists summoned up by Powellism, and confrontation the tactic: the official confrontation of the National Front marches through 'black' areas; and an increase in the 'unofficial' confrontation of the cowardly racial attacks – both, regrettably, ugly and shameful features of 1970s-style racism. For black people, some already watching the emergence of 'black power' in the USA out of the urban riots and the struggle for civil rights, Powellism provided the internal stimulus for the growth of new, radical and oppositional black political groups, and for the emergence into the public arena of an informal 'politics of resistance' – the reggae-influenced 'rastas' and 'rude boys' – which were to become so characteristic a response of black youth. And, as we saw in Chapter 1, the confrontations between the NF and its anti-racist opponents, and the culturally defiant lifestyles of black youth, became particular objects of the more repressive, paramilitarized policing response of the 1970s, one result of which was the urban, anti-police riots of the 1980s. After Northern Ireland, race, in the aftermath of the riots, is the next most dramatic symbol of the breakdown in hegemony.

Within each of the four examples chosen, the increase in repression has been one important symptom of the collapse of consensus. But the sheer extent of this shift to coercion during the 1970s – what has been referred to as the 'birth of the "law-and-order" society'[47] – can only be properly captured when all (together with examples from areas not highlighted here) are considered together. For example, following the election of a Tory government in 1970 committed to a more vigorous approach to law and order, the year 1971 saw the passage of new 'tough' legislation to deal with dissidence wherever it raised its head: an Emergency Powers Act to deal with the situation in Northern Ireland; a Misuse of Drugs Act to counter one aspect of the counter-culture; a Criminal Damage Act directed at squatters, pickets and demonstrators; an Immigration Act restricting further the rights of 'non-whites'; and an Industrial Relations Bill, which was to become in the following year the ill-fated centrepiece of Heath's new strategy. The enforcement of the law during the same period, using a combination of both the new legislation and some very ancient common law offences, most notoriously in the use of conspiracy charges, was similarly comprehensive. Drug busts, obscenity trials, internment, the jailing of protesting students and picketing workers, raids on black clubs, the discriminatory use of the old 'sus' laws (since repealed) against black youngsters, the clampdown on squatting, and exemplary sentencing were all symptomatic features of the new attempt to 'bring about by *fiat* what could no longer be won by consent – the disciplined society'.[48]

This extraordinary 'mobilisation of legal instruments against labour, political dissent and alternative life-styles'[49] in the early 1970s produced first resistance, then Heath's U-turn, and finally his defeat at the polls. But a new bench-mark had been established for the 1970s – a 'tendency to "criminalise" every threat to a disciplined social order, and to "legalise" (i.e. raise to the legal threshold) every means of containment'.[50] As we saw in the previous chapter, these are the years when the paramilitarized response to strikes, protest and inner-city crime gradually became institutionalized. These are also the years when this more coercive response itself becomes the focus of organized dissent – most emphatically in the growing concerns about policing, as the establishment of a Royal Commission on Criminal Procedure in 1978 bears official witness (and to which we return, briefly, below). Thatcher's response in 1979, after Callaghan's vain efforts to build some sort of 'social contract' consensus out of this proliferating dissensus, was to push the attempted Heathian revolution to a successful conclusion – by extending police powers and by strengthening the law against powerful centres of resistance. The result, as the year-long miners' strike and the inner-city riots bear particular witness, to say nothing of the continuation of the bitter struggle in Northern Ireland, has been the creation of a more divided Britain, albeit one presided over by a radical right-wing government whose 'politics are "hegemonic" in their conception and project'.[51]

Obviously in a democracy any movement towards greater coercive power needs to be justified. Thus, unsurprisingly, the increasing recourse to law during the 1970s is accompanied by further developments in the mechanisms of ideological signification, and by their readier use. The particular 'subversive, conspiratorial minorities' held responsible for industrial unrest or political protest in the 1960s quickly became parts of a general undifferentiated 'threat' – 'the enemy within' – an enemy which was extended far beyond the 'tightly knit group of politically motivated conspirators' to encompass, in Enoch Powell's telling phrase of 1970, the 'conspiracy of liberal causes'. This conversion of conspiracies into a single extensive conspiracy is also the ultimate 'convergence' – one in which protest and permissiveness, conflict and crime, strikes and students, race and terrorism, *and* liberal 'fellow-travellers', were seen to present a single challenge to the erstwhile 'silent majority' (in the guise of 'the nation'). The role of the mass media, both in constructing and relaying such significations, should not, of course, be overlooked.

The preoccupation with a legal solution to the crumbling consensus at the start of the decade is not only an example of increasing coercion; ideologically it is also an example of an increasing threat to 'societal tolerance limits': an escalation from the 'threshold' of permissiveness (breaches of which threaten only social authority, or the moral order) to the more serious 'threshold' of legality (where breaches threaten the legal order, or those morally disapproved activities deemed serious enough to warrant proscription by law). A further escalation quickly followed in 1972 – to the threshold of violence, where, because of the state's monopoly on legitimate violence, transgressions threaten not just the legal order but that which laws are designed to protect, namely, the very idea of social order itself. It is hence the final or ultimate threshold. Nineteen seventy-two – 'a year which began and ended in violence', according to *The Times* review of the year[52] – was riveted by it: 'it is *the* axis around which the public signification of the crisis turns in 1972'.[53]

This is not to deny the fact that 1972 was a year when politically motivated violence reached new peaks – in Northern Ireland (where 'Bloody Sunday' triggered a systematic retaliatory Provisional IRA bombing campaign); in international terrorism (most dramatically in the carnage of Lod airport, where 24 were killed, and of the Munich Olympics, which left 14 dead); in war (as the USA subjected Vietnam to the heaviest bombing assault of any modern war); and in industrial relations (where the confrontations between police and striking miners became the symbol for the *massive* resistance to the new Industrial Relations Act). However, what matters for our present purpose is the rapid way such violence became denuded first of any political meaning, a result of crossing the threshold of legality which renders all activity subject to the simple label 'criminal', and then denied any meaning whatsoever, a corollary of crossing the 'violence' threshold in a situation where only the violence of the state can be meaningful. Thus the bitter and intensely political republican struggle in Northern Ireland became successfully reduced to its terminal signification: the mindless and pointless violence of criminally motivated thugs. It was a form of signification that became increasingly common, the more political dissent grew, the most dramatic recent examples being the depiction of the riots and the miners' strike of 1984–5. In none of these cases, of course, has this ideological depiction gone unchallenged, a further indication that the consensus it assumes – the (consensual) 'nation' threatened by 'the enemy within' – increasingly exists only as a figment of the ideological imagination.

Finally, the proliferating signs of dissent first speeded up the production of moral panics and then precipitated a change in their shape. The former process culminated in 'a *general panic* about social order',[54] which then became an important ideological backcloth to Heath's 'law and order' campaign of 1970. The latter process witnessed an increasing tendency for the normal 'bottom-up' sequence of moral panics (dramatic event, public disquiet, moral entrepreneurship, firmer control) to become inverted, with firmer control, itself the product of a more highly sensitized moral and political climate, becoming instrumental in producing the 'scapegoat' dramatic event (which in turn gets used to justify yet tougher action). The 1960s panic reaction to the 'mods' and 'rockers' is representative of the normal sequence; the early 1970s panic about 'mugging' typical of the latter.

The overall achievement of this set of changes was the installation of an ideological repertoire capable of 'reading' all dissent in consensual terms – part of a violent conspiracy against 'our' way of life requiring legal constraint and firmer control. The irony was that 'our' way of life – the threatened consensus – seemed, in reality, less and less inclusive as time wore on.

CONTEXTUALIZING PARAMILITARISM 2:
THE CONSTABULARY IN CRISIS

The completion of this rudimentary account of change in post-war Britain – in terms of the hegemonic 1950s entering a crisis in the 1960s which was followed by the breakdown of hegemony in the 1970s and 1980s – is an essential starting point for this chapter's stated object, which is the provision of a firm (that is to say, not 'idealistic') historical basis from which to commence an evaluation of paramilitary policing. Before finally concluding it, however, we need to narrow the focus somewhat and look briefly at the more immediate context – the changes and developments taking place specifically within policing. In doing so, the single most relevant point is that the transition from the consensual 1950s to the conflictual 1980s is clearly echoed in policing; as Reiner evocatively put it, the period 1959–81 saw the police change 'from plods to pigs':

> From a position of almost complete invisibility as a political issue, policing has become a babble of scandalous revelation, controversy and competing agendas for reform. The police institution is beset by innovation and undergoing changes which seem the most momentous since the 1829 establishment of the Metropolitan Police. The tacit contract between police and public, so delicately drawn between the 1850s and 1950s, had begun to fray glaringly by 1981. The still open question is whether current efforts will suffice to repair it.[55]

Behind the 'babble' and the 'controversy' the issue, as in 1829, boiled down to one of legitimacy, which, by the 1950s, had come to mean 'accountability'.

Indeed, it was a series of *causes célèbres* in the 1950s which led to the 1960 Royal Commission with a brief to look precisely at the question of police accountability. The Commission's proposals led to the 1964 Police Act, though this only strengthened the hands of chief constables and the Home Office, and did nothing to make policing more democratically accountable. Thus, the controversial changes that took place during the 1960s and 1970s – the new emphases on specialization, technology, managerial professionalism and eventually, as we have seen, paramilitarism – all happened without public consultation, even though they were partly motivated, ironically enough, by a desire to improve relations with the public. The introduction of unit beat policing – an attempt to 'specialize' the patrol function using area constables in contact with local communities, panda cars for emergency services, and a collator to analyse incoming information – is a case in point. Attempting, simultaneously, to use resources more efficiently, increase public contacts and improve force morale, placing bobbies in cars scored a spectacular double own goal – it successfully *reduced* overall public contacts *and* police interest in the job. The call-dominated 'fire-brigade' approach of the pandas rendered public contacts transitory and inconclusive, and the proliferation of specialist units and squads increasingly left the unit only the 'rubbish' work to deal with.

At the same time, concern with the abuse of police powers in dealing with suspects – a subordinate factor in the establishment of the 1960 Royal Commission – became more central. And, after the particularly notorious Confait case prompted the official Fisher inquiry – which found that the three teenage boys (one of whom was mentally retarded) convicted of murdering Maxwell Confait had falsely confessed after serious violations of their rights – another Royal Commission, this time on criminal procedure, was established. Though ostensibly concerned with clarifying the existing position and balancing citizens' rights against police powers, the end result, the Police and Criminal Evidence Act (PACE) 1984, has only strengthened the hands of the police and done little of substance to enhance police accountability.

A whole series of matters have also become, during the same period, causes for concern: the appearance of a police 'law and order' lobby; the gradual arming of our 'unarmed' police; police violence, most dramatically in cases of death in custody; declining effectiveness in the 'fight against crime'; the use of Special Branch and the question of criminal intelligence, especially computerized information gathering; and, of course, the use of the SPG, both in public order situations and to 'saturate' so-called 'high crime' areas. Two matters in particular have proved both problematic and highly resistant to reform: police corruption, which in the Metropolitan Police has survived the best efforts of Robert Mark's A10 squad and David McNee's 'Operation Countryman'; and, probably the most tangible of the accountability mechanisms available to the individual, the complaints machinery. Despite changes introduced by three successive Police Acts – 1964, 1976 and, most recently, PACE 1984 – the procedure still lacks public confidence, a situation produced in part by the persistently low substantiation rates.

The net result of all these changes, in the absence of reform efforts to affect the question of accountability, has been an accentuation of conflictual relations with the socially dispossessed, the economically marginal and unemployed of whom, currently, young (especially black) males form a disproportionate part, a politicization of the police debate not seen since the 1820s, and a proliferation of non-statutory and unofficial attempts – independent inquiries, police committees, monitoring groups and the like – to highlight, publicize and protest against the accountability crisis in which policing is currently stuck.[56]

UNDERSTANDING PARAMILITARISM CONTINGENTLY FROM BELOW

It is, then, this double crisis – the broader general one 'requiring' it and the more immediate one concerning police accountability 'allowing' it – which jointly provide the historical context for the examination in Chapter 1 of the emergence and development of paramilitarism, and the starting point for seeing what all this looks like 'from below', that is, from the viewpoint of the policed.

Obviously the two crises are integrally related, the issue of police accountability being both symptom and outcome (since crisis conditions 'require' tougher policing) of a breakdown in hegemony (which is not the same as saying that the one can be 'reduced' to the other). Now, if the above accounts were to be used as a sort of template for the more particular 'paramilitary' account presented in Chapter 1, a good (if rough) fit would clearly be evident, with the 1960s witnessing signs of 'crisis', concern about police accountability, and the advent of paramilitarism, and the 1970s producing a breakdown of hegemony, persistent unease about accountability, and a highly developed paramilitary capacity. Of course, to push this idea of a 'fit' too far would be to ignore, for example, those early, influential, more 'internally' generated third-force debates – about crime and civil defence, for example – which slightly pre-dated the 'crisis' years. But equally, to overlook the relative snugness of fit would be to miss the way in which more internally generated debates themselves tend to be influenced and fashioned by broader, more 'externally' generated ones. In this case the important *developments* in paramilitary policing during the 1970s seem to have been fuelled more by the 'external' debate over problems of public order (itself symptomatic of the breakdown of hegemony), even if the initial *emergence* of the paramilitarized approach owed something to a more restricted and internal debate with more disparate origins. To put it at its simplest, it seems reasonable on the historical evidence of both this and the previous chapter to suggest that the 'moment' of paramilitarism broadly coincides with the 'moment' of a crisis in police accountability and a more general hegemonic crisis and breakdown.

Casting our minds back to Phil Cohen's historical account of policing in Islington can now assist our understanding of this 'coincidence'. Reducing the above account to its barest bones, the essential features of the current breakdown of hegemony have been: an economic crisis in which the accompanying recomposition and relocation of the labour force has entailed a massive (and for some seemingly permanent) shake-out of labour, and the creation of what might crudely be called 'the new lumpen'; a political crisis characterized by a tough 'law and order' response to increasing numbers of belligerent dissidents of all persuasions; and an ideological crisis in which a repertoire of negative evaluations is constantly applied to all forms of dissent, which in turn is constantly challenged by dissenting replies. The defining feature of the crisis in police accountability has been a growth in police power and influence, combined with a decreasing ability of citizens to contest or check it. The essential feature of the paramilitary response has been a rough and uncompromising 'no nonsense' approach to the swift reimposition of (an essentially police-defined sense of) 'order'.

Applying Cohen's terminology, the paramilitary response represents the option of last resort – the 'falling back on the more or less brutal reimposition of statutory public order'[57] in dealing with those groups (in this case 'the new lumpen', in which sections of male, especially black, youth, and militant dissidents of all kinds – pickets, demonstrators, etc. – figure prominently) with whom the (preferred) negotiated approach – the 'unwritten system of tacit negotiation'[58] – has never been properly established or has broken down. This breakdown may be fairly temporary, in the case of say a particular industrial dispute, or, in the case of some highly alienated groups – Afro-Caribbean youth, for example – apparently irrevocable.

The irony of this, as Cohen points out, is that the straightforward repressive legal approach constantly threatens to undermine the order it is designed to uphold (witness the way the repressive Swamp 81 contributed to the first Brixton riots), a dilemma Cohen refers to as the police's 'impossible choice of enforcing law *or* order'.[59] The result is that 'the more resources allocated to increasing the efficiency of repressive policing, the more manpower has to be poured into "community relations" to restabilize the public image of the force'.[60] And that is precisely what has happened. The growth of paramilitarism has been accompanied by a parallel growth in community relations policing (that is, all forms of policing variously concerned with the question of 'negoti-ated' rather than strictly 'legal' order), though this also has an 'internal' logic, that is, to compensate for the unwanted side-effects of the specialization that devalued the all-purpose beat patroller to such an extent that the only altern-ative was to make traditional, generalist policing itself a specialism! Moreover, and in line with this logic, such initiatives *are* largely aimed at those groups furthest removed from the existing 'tacit negotiations', such as the black communities (to whom community relations departments owe their very existence),[61] and youngsters in Northern Ireland (for whom a routine search may be offset by a dance in one of the many police-run 'blue-lamp' discos).

This contingent historical approach, using Gramsci's concept of hegemony, seems well able to explain, then, both the emergence of paramilitarism and its subsequent development, and in a way which does not see violence as excep-tional (as does Geary). Rather, the shift from the hegemonic, consensual 1950s to the less hegemonic, coercive 1970s produces (in line with the new coercive 'requirements'), as one outcome, a 'tougher' form of policing. Of course, the precise shape of the response (specially trained and equipped officers, operating in groups, and so on) builds on existing organizational features (specialized squads, for example) and according to the available technology currently in use. But the benign image bequeathed by Waddington – paramilitarism as a simple continuation of the tradition of 'minimum force' – hardly matches the far less benign social context of the 1970s.

But it is necessary also to say something about the particularity of the present – the 'moment' of Thatcherism. For if paramilitarism belongs broadly to the moment of hegemonic breakdown, certain features of the Thatcherite years make the idea of paramilitarism even more chillingly dangerous. First, the multiple crises (economic, political and ideological) producing the divisions and confrontations that serve to justify further paramilitary developments have continued to worsen. Second, these developments are increasingly technologically sophisticated, which makes them not only more dangerous, most obviously in the case of the new weaponry, but also prey to 'technological drift' – the internal technological dynamic whereby the technologically feasible constantly threatens to pre-empt the politically desirable. Third, the Thatcher government is *committed* to the tough political response, unlike, say, the social-democratic government of the Callaghan years – which also presided over paramilitary developments, but less willingly. Within this political climate paramilitarism is not only a 'necessary evil' but is also seen as a positive weapon to enforce key changes (witness the absolutely central role of the police in breaking the miners' strike in 1984–5).[62]

Finally, and most depressingly, there is the crisis of alternatives. This has both general and specific features. One of the most surprising features of the Thatcherite years has been the degree of support the government has managed to maintain while implementing a highly divisive strategy. Though there is a debate about the relative strength of Thatcher's ideological hold which is beyond the scope of this book,[63] I subscribe to Hall's idea that these have been years of essentially 'authoritarian populism'. That is to say, though Thatcherism has not achieved hegemony (a notion Hall regards as 'preposterous') its whole thrust is hegemonic – the attempt to achieve leadership across the social formation as a whole, rather than mere narrow economic dominance.[64] In the area of policing specifically, despite an ongoing challenge on the question of police accountability, this has tended to concern itself with the reform of constitutional arrangements.[65] The equally needed debate about the 'content' of a reformed police – its organizational shape and operational conduct – has tended to be left very much to the 'professionals', or to outsiders operating from a similar, managerialist starting point (who therefore fail to address the need to think about the content and (constitutional) form of police *together*).[66] These particular features – the intensity of the conflicts to be policed, the technological capacity of police, the willingness of the government to sanction 'tough' methods, the relative support for these and the absence of ideas about alternatives – jointly make the present moment (the late 1980s) one when the paramilitary option seems far removed indeed from Waddington's consensual tradition of the restrained use of force.

This becomes even more the case when paramilitary developments are viewed from the 'bottom up' rather than the 'top down'. Waddington's idea that paramilitarism stands within the consensual tradition holds *only* if the idea of consensus refers simply to *majority* (or top-down) viewpoints. But the majority of people are *not* the objects of policing. Those traditionally on the receiving end of policing have always been a minority. Those currently on the receiving end of paramilitary policing are also minorities – dissidents of various sorts. So, any argument that relies on the idea of the *general* high level of support for the police – for which there is much opinion-poll evidence[67] – essentially misses the point, namely, the importance of a 'bottom-up' viewpoint. And indeed a closer inspection of opinion-poll surveys provides substantiation for this argument that support for the police is dependent (at least partly) on whether the viewpoint is 'top-down' or 'bottom-up'. As Brogden's review concludes: 'lower class and minority groups in the inner city, the recipients of primary police experiences, give only a tenuous approval to policing'.[68] And the later Policy Studies Institute study produced evidence of a similar sort in documenting the (well-known) antipathy to police of young West Indians.[69]

So, when these paramilitary developments are set within their historical moment *and* viewed from the vantage point of those on the receiving end – the policed minorities – the notion that these have anything meaningfully to do with 'consent' must disappear. This, then, must be the historically realistic starting point for the subsequent appraisal. Though I go on in subsequent chapters to discuss the problems with paramilitarism, it is important constantly to bear in mind this problematic historical starting point, for it sets important limits on what other reforms might achieve in the absence of more general changes. But this is part of the subject matter of the final chapter.

NOTES

1. Morris, 1985; Clift, 1981.
2. Waddington, 1987.
3. See Chapter 1.
4. Geary, 1985, p. 133.
5. Ibid., p. 147.
6. Ibid.
7. Ibid.
8. For an elaboration of Gramsci's key ideas, see Gramsci, 1971.
9. Cohen, 1979, p. 120.
10. Ibid.
11. Ibid.
12. Ibid., p. 130.
13. Ibid.
14. Ibid., p. 128.
15. Ibid.
16. Ibid., p. 123.
17. Ibid., p. 130.
18. Ibid., p. 124.

19. Ibid.
20. Ibid., p. 132.
21. Ibid., p. 134.
22. Ibid., p. 133.
23. Ibid., p. 132. For a similar understanding based on the theoretical insights of both Gramsci and Foucault, see Grimshaw and Jefferson, 1987, pp. 269–82.
24. Hall *et al.*, 1978, p. 219.
25. Ibid., Chapters 8 and 9.
26. Gramsci, quoted in Hall *et al.*, 1978, p. 227 (emphasis added).
27. Ibid., p. 227.
28. Ibid., p. 228.
29. Ibid., p. 229.
30. Ibid., p. 229.
31. Clarke *et al.*, 1976, p. 21.
32. Ibid.
33. Ibid.
34. Cohen, P., 1972, p. 21.
35. Clarke *et al.*, 1976, p. 31.
36. Ibid.
37. Ibid., p. 21.
38. Hall *et al.*, 1978, p. 235.
39. Ibid., p. 239.
40. Ibid., p. 238.
41. Ibid., p. 225.
42. Ibid., p. 223.
43. Cohen, S., 1972. See also Hall *et al.*, 1978, pp. 16–17.
44. Hall *et al.*, 1978, p. 221.
45. Ibid., p. 272.
46. Hillyard, 1985.
47. Hall *et al.*, 1978, p. 273.
48. Ibid., p. 284.
49. Ibid.
50. Ibid., p. 288.
51. Hall, 1988, p. 154.
52. Quoted in Hall *et al.*, 1978, p. 293.
53. Ibid., p. 300.
54. Ibid., p. 222.
55. Reiner, 1985, pp. 61–2.
56. For fuller accounts of the emergence of this crisis in policing, see ibid., pp. 61–82; Jefferson and Grimshaw, 1984, pp. 1–10. For a broad overview of the achievement of recent 'post-Scarman' developments, see Brogden *et al.*, 1988, pp. 173–96.
57. Cohen, 1979, p. 132.
58. Ibid., p. 123.
59. Cohen, 1979, p. 133. Strictly speaking, this is not really a *choice* between law and order since the nature of public order law *allows* police substantial discretion, a point I expand upon in Chapter 3.
60. Ibid., p. 21.
61. See Judge, 1974, p. 201.
62. See McCabe and Wallington, 1988, p. 130.
63. See Hall, 1988, pp. 123–60; Jessop *et al.*, 1984, pp. 32–60.

64. Hall, 1988, p. 154.
65. See Greater London Council, 1983; Jefferson and Grimshaw, 1984; Scraton, 1985; Spencer, 1985; Downes and Ward 1986; Lustgarten, 1986.
66. On the importance of the relationship between 'internal' reforms and 'external' constitutional arrangements, see Grimshaw and Jefferson, 1987, pp. 282–97.
67. Brogden, 1982, pp. 199–202.
68. Ibid., p. 205.
69. Policy Studies Institute, 1983, Vol. 1, p. 326.

CHAPTER 3

Impartiality, discretion and the real world of policing disorder

INTRODUCTION

We saw in Chapter 2 how a more concrete, 'contingent' view of police history was much better equipped to explain the recent paramilitary developments when compared with more idealistic versions, that is, those who see paramilitarism simply as a continuation of the consensual, restrained tradition of British policing. In a similar fashion, this chapter will take a more grounded look at the sociology of public order policing. This will entail, first, exposing the idealism of 'impartial law enforcement', the foundation of liberal-democratic approaches to the question of paramilitarism; second, considering the actual determinants of law-enforcement decision-making; third, showing how these determinants operate specifically in relation to public order policing; and finally, demonstrating the way in which certain features of the present, including new legislation such as the Public Order Act (POA) 1986, are increasing police discretion and hence rendering policing more, not less, partial. As before, the conclusion of this appraisal will prove far more pessimistic than that of idealists like Waddington.

THE MYTH OF IMPARTIAL LAW ENFORCEMENT

The idea of impartial law enforcement stems from the office of constable (the police office common to all officers whatever their rank) and the obligation this imposes to uphold the law generally, that is to say, against all offenders without fear or favour. This unique obligation is mirrored by a unique form of accountability – not to a statutory body, but to the law itself. Together these notions make up the hallowed doctrine of police independence – the idea that the

46

police do not operate at the behest of others, but are servants only of the law. Breaking with this idea of police as independent legal officers would make policing a political matter and result in selective (or partial) law enforcement.

This, in essence, is the conservative justification for placing 'impartiality' at the heart of the policing task. It constitutes a fine ideal, but it is based on a very unrealistic sociology; and this is so whether we take the chief constable, with his specific task of upholding the law generally, or other officers, with their more limited task of dealing with those particular infractions that come to their notice. Either way, impartial law enforcement constitutes an 'impossible mandate':[1] for the chief constable because he is obliged to do something – uphold the law generally – which limited knowledge (about offences) and lack of time and resources render impossible in any strict sense; for the constables under his command because the necessary prerequisite for impartial law enforcement – clear law activated by a particular complaint – is often simply not applicable to the area of law being enforced. In reality, then, the chief constable must make choices and select priorities (which types of offence will get more attention and which less; what resources will be poured into rooting out offences, such as drug-taking, that rarely come to light through public complaint, and so on); must 'adopt, in short, a policy of partial law enforcement (in flat contradiction of the underlying principle)'.[2] And the constable on the street is faced with a similar dilemma in those situations 'where the law is not a clear guide for action and/or where there is no necessity for a complainant'.[3] In such situations the constable *must* supply the missing clarity or the hypothetical complaint before acting: must, in other words, make an inevitably subjective (and hence partial) judgement about the right course of action.[4]

This gap between the ideal (impartial) obligations imposed by the office of constable, and the actual (partial) decisions made every day by existing police officers took a long time to be acknowledged. When it was, the notion of police discretion was born. The conservative assumption that the exercise of this discretion was relatively benign enabled the belief in impartial law enforcement to survive more or less intact. But the growth of a radical sociology of policework, which emphasized the class-based *outcomes* of discretionary decision-making, exposed a hidden politics of policing. What was also needed was an understanding of the *processes* through which such outcomes were routinely achieved.

THE ACTUAL DETERMINANTS OF DISCRETION: THE STRUCTURES OF LAW, DEMOCRACY AND WORK

In thinking about the processes underlying the routine use of discretion, a first port of call has to be liberal sociology, with its explanations of the use of discretion, either in terms of how socialization in a police subculture (or 'cop culture')[5] provides the practical common-sense 'rules' and working knowledge ('a working personality')[6] necessary for handling discretion, or in terms of how the environmental contexts of policework – what Reiss and Bordua called the police's 'environing system'[7] (the legal system, crime and the system of civic accountability) – could produce 'varieties of police behaviour'[8]. But both these sorts of explanation were relatively one-sided and failed adequately to address *together* what each had managed singly (namely, a focus on the subculture *or* the environmental contexts). Moreover, neither properly took on the radical critique which had tried (if sometimes too reductively) to examine the broader social function of law-enforcement activity. So, the question of the actual determinants of discretion, or the processes through which outcomes broadly reflecting existing power structures are achieved, and – crucially – the relationship between all these determinants, still remained to be uncovered.[9] If the presence of discretion tells us that the law alone is not the sole determinant of police behaviour (a tendency among conservatives), we should not make the opposite mistake (a tendency in the subcultural approach) and conclude that the law is never a constraining influence. The point is to ascertain the *degree* of discretion or permissiveness in any given situation. Since this is *inversely* related to the constraining power of law – the more discretion the less constraining the law and vice versa – this will reveal the *degree* to which the law is operating to constrain police behaviour in particular instances. As we shall see, in the case of public order law, which is riddled with discretion, the law hardly constrains police-defined activity at all.

The starting point for this approach is to render the abstract notion of 'the law' more concrete: first, by treating it as an overall system or structure with many 'sites' (Parliament, the courts, and so on) where 'law' gets defined and interpreted; and second, by breaking it down into its component powers and demands. This latter aspect essentially involves a thorough knowledge of 'procedural' powers and 'substantive' demands. And, just as the legal powers of the police differ from situation to situation (with corresponding differences in the degree of discretion entailed), so do the legal demands of the criminal law, as the following quotation, taken from a much fuller consideration of this subject, argues:

> We need not rehearse here a full examination before suggesting that offences will *differ* in several ways. They will differ as to their *legal complexity*, which will be a function of the number of legally significant factors they encompass. They will differ as to the degree of *citizen involvement*, as witnesses or injured parties, necessary to meet minimal legal requirements. They will differ as to their *legal clarity* . . . These differences mean that the effect of the law on police behaviour will be a function of the particular offences with which they routinely deal, with the more 'complex', 'citizen-involving' and 'clear' offences being more legally constraining, and the least legally constraining being those offences requiring only the discretionary subjective judgement of a single officer.[10]

The more concrete notion of law as an overall system with many points of definition, interpretation (and challenge) entails the idea that formal powers can remain inert unless used; so a further level of constraint over police discretion is the concrete use citizens and legal authorities (like the courts, the Home Office and police authorities) make of their powers to constrain activities (essentially by mobilizing alternative definitions or interpretations), because 'where powers are extensively, persistently and consistently used, they are likely to be more effective as a constraint on police behaviour than where the reverse obtains'.[11]

In sum, in thinking about how constraining (if at all) is the legal structure,

> we need a thorough knowledge of the legal powers of police, the legal demands made by the criminal law, the legal powers of citizens and legal authorities and the uses made of them – before we can begin to think about how law affects police behaviour in particular situations.[12]

The particular situation we are interested in is, of course, the policing of public order. But, before we can consider the operation of discretion in this context, we must first outline the other 'extra-legal' constraints, and then how all the various constraints – legal and otherwise – are interrelated.

We can all think of situations where 'extra-legal' factors come into play to affect police decision-making: the probationer issuing a parking ticket because of a desire to please superiors; the traffic officer more likely to book the irate than the polite motorist; the readiness to intervene in the gang fight but not the domestic dispute. The question is how best to conceptualize these. In a simple descriptive sense the obvious constraints, apart from the law, will be the organization itself (through its policies, standing orders, use of rewards and punishments, and so on), 'the public', or immediate colleagues. It is not, therefore, surprising that the first two of these, the organization and the public, together with 'the law', broadly correspond, as we saw earlier, to the 'environmental' contexts of policework; the last (immediate colleagues), again as we saw earlier, to the source of the informal 'cop culture'. However, problems remain with the conceptualization offered by both the 'environmentalists' and the 'subculturalists'. Take, first, the question of 'the public'. This has tended to be seen in rather gross dichotomous terms (middle class/working class; white/black; old/young; law-abiding/criminal; supportive/hostile), with the first of each of these terms exercising a greater constraining influence on police behaviour. (Ironically, though feminists will not be surprised, the influence on police behaviour of one major social division – man/woman – has not been similarly analysed.) This sort of analysis is fine, if the only interest is in terms of outcomes in a macro sense, which clearly, as these examples bear out, favour the relatively powerful, however that is defined. But, these distinctions alone do not permit precise enough answers if the interest is in the concrete processes through which such outcomes arise, something a study of this sort, concerned with addressing a *particular* area of policework such as public order, must be. Given this interest, the central question must be, 'under what conditions are various "publics" . . . able to have an affect (*sic*) on policework practice?'[13] For this we need a more differentiated approach to police–public contacts. We need to be alert, first, to the various potential *roles* through which members of the public come into contact with the police (as potential witness, injured party, suspect, community representative, elected politician, professional expert, and so on, which largely encompasses the power dimension so central to the macro studies mentioned above; second, to the comparative *status* of those in contact ('respectable' or otherwise, known face or stranger, representative or ordinary citizen, and so on); third, to the *nature of the contacts* (reciprocal versus one-sided, sporadic versus (recurrent); and finally, to the *type of issue* motivating the contact (contentious or consensual).

With these distinctions in mind, it should not be difficult to see how 'contacting roles spelling "trouble" or "inconvenience" [are] less likely to influence behaviour, since they are resisted, than those offering more desirable prospects', nor how 'least influence . . . [is] exerted by non-respectable individual strangers who have nothing to exchange and with whom contact is sporadic and contentious'.[14] For various fairly obvious reasons, these will collectively tend to constitute 'the powerless'. How this reconceptualization assists in thinking about policing public order we return to below. For the moment, one final reconceptualization is in order, that is, to regard 'the public' as a democratic structure (just as we earlier reconceptualized 'the law' as a concrete legal structure) because the variety of public contacts with the police are, in *practical terms*, the principal, concrete mechanisms through which some sort of democratic influence can be brought to bear on policework, especially given the present very undemocratic system of accountability.[15]

The other two 'obvious' constraints – 'the organization' and 'other colleagues' (or the 'cop culture') – have usually been considered separately. This has been largely a function of research access; quite simply, it has traditionally been easier to examine an organization's rank and file than its senior management. The result has been a very full portrait of cop culture – its zealous but cynical action orientation, its prejudiced, pragmatic and suspicious conservatism, and its macho solidarity,[16] coupled with a very incomplete picture of management culture. This has led to assumptions about the latter, usually that it shares the formal goals of the organization. Consequently, the sociological consensus in this area talks about a gap between the technologically orientated, legalistic 'managerial professionalism' of senior officers and the action-orientated, corner-cutting 'practical professionalism' of the lower ranks.[17] The problem then becomes how to bring the latter into line with the former. But

since the organizational structure has not been submitted to the same rigorous observational examination that the occupational culture has, the empirical possibility remains that the two might not be universally in conflict.[18]

In which case it is much better to regard the whole as one

work structure . . . with two dimensions: an 'organizational' one – referring to the vertical dimension of rules, policies, approved procedures, command and control – and an occupational one, referring to the horizontal dimension of the norms and practices of colleague groups.[19]

Having done that, the question of the relationship between management and the rank and file can be concretely addressed by looking at whether specific management practices, such as supervision, policy and the like, operate as constraining influences on specific policing tasks; at whether, in other words, there are *any* areas of policework that *some* kinds of management practices can touch or not.

With these constraints on policework, the actual determinants of discretion, reconceptualized in the form of three structures – legal, democratic and work – we are now in a position to consider how they operate together in particular concrete instances: how, in other words, the processes of policework routinely reproduce the policing of the powerless – the hidden political agenda that the notion of 'impartial law enforcement' obscures. In thinking about the relationship between these three structural determinants of police discretion it is essential to bear in mind the importance of being able to grasp, simultaneously, the *unity* (the concern of the radicals) and the *diversity* (the concern of the sociological liberals) of policework practices. It is the former which enables the broader question of the social function of policework in reproducing the established contours of power to be addressed; the latter which enables it to be done in a non-reductive fashion. With this dual structure in mind, I submit 'that the relationship between the structures is structured [or 'determined'] by law . . . without that in any way implying that law will be the dominant structure in particular instances'.[20] In other words, the legal structure always determines 'which of the structures [law, work or democracy] is the dominant one'.[21] It is important not to confuse this idea of law determining which of the structures is dominant with the straightforward and simplistic notion of law being the most significant determinant of police discretion.[22] Perhaps only an example will help here, which brings us to our particular object of concern – public order policing – to which I now turn.

THE ACTUAL DETERMINANTS OF PUBLIC ORDER POLICING: A DOMINANT WORK STRUCTURE

In discussing how the three structures identified above jointly affect the use of discretion in the particular instance of public order policing, I am only concerned with the use of discretion 'on the ground'. I am not, therefore, concerned with why chief constables have used their discretion 'at the top' to choose (increasingly, as we have seen) the paramilitary option, though the previous two chapters have addressed the political and historical 'logic' underpinning that choice. It is, however, worth saying that the doctrine of police independence generally produces an antipathy to 'sectional' (political) interests (effectively, any group within the public with an identifiable interest) especially on matters (like public order policing) which are likely to prove contentious. The result is to fall back on and utilize a discourse or logic addressed only to legal and occupational audiences[23] (rather than 'the public', with its 'partisan' axes to grind), what some would see as a 'professional' discourse, one within which the (idealistically presented) paramilitary option appears superficially appealing. If my case against paramilitarism is premised partly on supplying the hidden historical and political discourse (see Chapters 1 and 2) that the strictly legal-occupational one ignores, it is also concerned to dispute the legal-occupational discourse *on its own terms* (see Chapters 5 and 6). This chapter and the next provide the link by supplying the sociological spadework necessary for the latter enterprise.

In thinking about what determines the use of discretion in public order policing contexts, we need to start, as always, with the legal structure, that is, the legal powers and demands of the relevant law, and the use various authorities and citizens have made of their countervailing powers. The scope of the relevant law is wide, ranging from the common law offence of breach of the peace, through the numerous statutory offences, including obstruction (of the highway and of a police officer), and those of riot, violent disorder, affray, threatening behaviour and disorderly conduct (all now covered by the POA 1986), to the various local 'by-laws for good rule and Government and for the suppression of nuisances'.[24] We cannot possibly review all of these here, nor others which may also be utilized in the public order context. But, a key feature of most of them is the high degree of *discretion* involved. To illustrate this, I intend to look briefly at the now repealed Section 5 of the POA 1936, not only because it was in force during the period of the development of paramilitarism, but, more importantly, because it used to be the staple public order offence; 'the most frequently used of all public order offences'.[25] More than 10,000 offences were charged during the miners' strike of 1984–5, of which over 4,000 were 'Section 5s'.[26] My own time spent with a SPG unit also confirms its centrality (see Chapter 4).

Section 5 of the POA 1936 said:

Any person who in any public place or at any public meeting

a) uses threatening, abusive or insulting words or behaviour or
b) distributes or displays any writing, sign or visible representation which is threatening, abusive or insulting, with intent to provoke a breach of the peace or whereby a breach of the peace is likely to be occasioned, shall be guilty of an offence.[27]

The key terms are clearly 'threatening, abusive or insulting' and 'breach of the peace'. But what do they mean? Thornton says of the former that these 'are to be given their ordinary meaning',[28] which for Lord Reid is 'easily recognisable by the ordinary man'.[29] However, knowing that 'telling a constable to "fuck off"',[30] that shouting 'scab' from behind heavily policed picket lines,[31] and that indulging in 'an overt display of homosexual conduct . . . at a bus stop' in the middle of the night[32] have all been adjudged 'behaviour likely' makes me, for one, less sanguine. The same point can be made about 'breach of the peace'. Thornton tells us that 'the most authoritative definition' specifically states 'that the word "disturbance" when used in isolation'[33] is an insufficient description;

yet also that in 'G v *Chief Superintendent of Police, Stroud, The Times*, 29 November 1986, it was held that a mere disturbance could amount to a likelihood of a breach of the peace'.[34] And few can be unfamiliar with the fact that Kent miners were successfully prevented from travelling to Nottinghamshire (some 200 miles away) on the grounds that a breach of the peace was 'imminent', nor that the peace convoy was similarly prevented from reaching its destination in the summer of 1986.[35]

What this amounts to is a highly discretionary or 'permissive' legal context: key words and phrases have very broad (and thus ambiguous) meanings; no particular words or behaviour are proscribed; no actual breach of the peace is necessary; and no actual complainants or witnesses are needed. In short, almost *any* activity taking place in a public arena involving an element (however ritualistic) of unseemliness or hostility lies potentially within its scope, should a constable and court deem it so. One could go further and say that the law, as expressed in Section 5, actually *required* a police officer to make subjective judgements about which words or behaviour, in which contexts, constituted the offence. It is hardly surprising, then, that it has been described by 'one academic lawyer . . . "as a form of dragnet provision against those whose behaviour is considered by the police and the courts to be worthy of punishment"'.[36] To put that back into a macro context, it is a reminder that in upholding 'law and order', order is paramount.

One way of reducing legal discretion is through the use by legal authorities like the courts, or by citizens, for example, of their countervailing powers. We have already seen, in the brief survey of cases above, that the Court of Appeal has not generally used its powers in a restrictive fashion. But, of course, most cases never get that far. Since the offence could only be tried summarily (that is, by magistrates), the routine interpretation of 'behaviour likely' has been in the hands of magistrates. And they are generally recognized as being more deferential to police evidence than a barrister, judge or jury in the Crown Court. As for citizens and their countervailing powers, this effectively means the complaints system. One chilling statistic, already referred to, tells the whole story here: of the 551 complaints originally made against the police during the 1984–5 miners' strike (in England and Wales) *none* led to formal disciplinary action.[37]

If the legal structure is highly discretionary, and therefore very weak as a constraining influence on police behaviour, what of the democratic structure? This entails examining the police–public contacts generated in typical public order situations. Take, first, the question of *role*. Whether as demonstrator, protester, picket, football fan, or simply 'member of a crowd', to the officer on public order duty, and especially to the trained 'paramilitary', the only envisaged role for contact is as potential trouble-maker or would-be offender. As for the *status* of those in large crowds or demonstrations, they are at best anonymous citizens, at worst dissident minorities or 'disreputables' of some kind (or their 'dupes') – the more so in highly conflictual periods (like the present; see Chapter 2) when ideological denigration of dissidence and deviance, especially in certain sections of the media, is rife. Further, the *nature of the contacts* is largely confined to sporadic 'warnings' or arrests of strangers with whom no basis for reciprocal relations exists. And the *sort of issue* (that is, warning or arrest) motivating the contact is intrinsically contentious – a factor heightened by the absence of any need for complainants or non-police witnesses. Consequently, arrests in this area are often highly contested affairs with protestations of innocence common.

Contacts with anonymous or 'disreputable' offenders, which are sporadic, non-reciprocal and contentious – the 'troublesome powerless' – are the least likely, as argued in the last section, to be a strong constraining influence on police behaviour. Thus, the democratic structure, like the legal structure, is 'weak'. It is this dual 'weakness' of the other two structures which enables the work structure to be the dominant one in the particular case of public order policing. As such it is what *actually* determines the use of discretion on the ground in this area.

But since, as we saw earlier, the work structure consists of two dimensions, there is a final question to be answered – what is the relationship between the vertical dimension (the 'organizational' rules, policies, and so on) and the horizontal one (the 'occupational' norms and practices)? Are the two in conflict, as the subculturalists would have it? And if so, which is the one actually determining the use of discretion? Or is there some other way of explaining the dominance of one or other dimension?

Remember, I am only concerned here with the use of discretion 'on the ground'. But it is worth reiterating that the chief constable's discretion 'at the top' in this area has been used (increasingly) in favour of the paramilitary option. This means that, whatever the argument here about the relationship between the two dimensions of the work structure, we should not overlook the fact that the organizational dimension – which lies very much within the chief constable's discretionary powers – is clearly dominant (at the top) in terms of establishing special patrol groups, purchasing riot equipment, deciding about the deployment of resources and overall policing strategies, and so on.[38] But, once again, my concern is with the (disastrous) *effects* of the choice of the paramilitary option, not what *caused* the option to be chosen.

To return to the question of the relationship between the two dimensions, the simplest way of answering this is to look at the relationship between supervision (obviously a key feature of the organizational dimension) and behaviour (the obvious manifestation of the horizontal dimension) in the policing of public order. Take supervision. On public order occasions there is a lot of it. And this increases directly with the size of the operation. In the first place, there will be a complement of supervisors from the local subdivision looking after their own officers, and possibly the divisional commander as well. If the SPG is needed it will arrive with its own supervisors; sergeants constantly with their units; inspectors responsible for several units; and a chief inspector or superintendent in overall charge of it. And, if the event is big enough, there could well be some headquarters 'brass' out as well, perhaps even the chief constable himself. Leaving aside the latter, who will usually have delegated operational command on the day, means, minimally, that there is a dual supervisory structure – the routine internal command structure of the SPG, and the operational command structure, to which all officers will be subject on the day – which makes for double supervisory oversight. Moreover, since both sets of supervisors will be sensitive to 'their' officers letting them down in front of colleagues, the supervisory hold will be tightened further.

In addition, the supervision on such occasions is very *direct*. The general problem of supervising police officers is often put down to the 'low visibility' of much of their work.[39] But, public order work is *highly* visible to the supervisory gaze – as it is to members of the general public who happen to be present, and, through the presence of the media, sometimes to the whole world. And this is particularly true of the potential 'trouble spots' which, for obvious reasons, attract more supervisory and media attention, as well as a greater SPG presence.

What about behaviour? The important point is the twofold nature of its relationship to supervision. On the one hand, the high level of direct supervision can be an absolutely effective constraint on behaviour: if a unit is given positive instructions – to remain on standby (in the van or in the canteen) or to link arms and 'hold the line' – it will almost certainly do so. In these situations the organizational dimension is clearly dominant. On the other hand, supervision often appears to break down completely when an order is given to 'clear the streets', arrest the 'trouble-makers' or otherwise move onto the offensive. It is *these* moments, often ironically in the most 'exposed' locations and involving the most highly-trained officers (the SPG), that produce the violent arrests and other examples of 'unprofessional' conduct with which we are all now familiar.

How can we explain this apparent paradox – that the most supervised form of policing can produce the most apparently unconstrained type of police behaviour? The answer is that when police move on the offensive, the independence of the office of constable takes over. In such situations offences take precedence and the rank structure is effectively neutralized. In other words, supervisory powers become subordinated to constabulary ones.[40] And, so long as individual arrests are judged lawful by the courts (which does not mean that each arrest must lead to a conviction), the Police Complaints Authority finds nothing to warrant formal disciplinary proceedings, and official inquiries are deemed unnecessary, there is little incentive to consider operations as a whole beyond the obvious question of whether there were sufficient resources to maintain order. And there is certainly no incentive to intervene and supply an alternative judgement about the appropriate use of discretion.[41] In this particular way, as an unintended by-product of police independence and not the result of a clash between 'street cops and management cops'[42] (a distinction much more real in rhetoric than in substance, in my view), the occupational dimension of the work structure becomes the effective determinant of operational discretion in the street policing of public order. We will return to this occupational dimension of paramilitary policing, particularly the working norms and practices of the SPG and their amplifying effects, in Chapter 6. For the moment, and to end this section, an example illustrating the three structures 'in action' might help make some of the above comments more concrete.

A 'Section 5' arrest from my field notes

The venue is a first division football match, a local derby. Trouble is expected and there is a strong police presence from early on. We arrive at the ground nearly one-and-a-half hours before kick-off. The acting sergeant of the SPG unit I am with is told by the inspector, who is with the chief inspector in charge of the Group, to park the van and have the unit patrol around the ground in pairs. I stay with the acting sergeant (PS) and his partner (PC).

The focus of police attention seemed to be on large groups of fans singing loudly. As this was a local derby, rival fans were arriving from all over and intermingling, thus exacerbating the usual police problem of separating rival fans. Two youths passed by singing 'Up the ——', a reference to a local team other than the two playing that day. This amused PC.

Around 2 p.m. one group of fans approached another group of rival fans, all of whom looked to be aged between fifteen and eighteen. One group started singing 'You're coming down [a reference to potential relegation] with us'; to which their rivals replied 'You're going down'. Given the numbers of police on duty, the singing seemed to be deliberately symbolic rather than provocative since both groups threaded peacefully through each other without making contact. However, PS and PC went into the group and grabbed two young men. I had not heard what they specifically had been saying or singing. They were then taken over to the unit's van and told they were under arrest. PS accused them both of swearing, which was vehemently denied. They protested that they had only been singing and having fun. PS told them to 'shut it' and then went off to find the unit van driver. Meanwhile PC, with one hand on each youngster, delivered a very speedy and intimidating sounding caution, closing with 'Have you anything to say?' I doubted whether its meaning or implications were understood by either. They said they had only been singing and having fun. PC said such singing was a provocation – behaviour likely to cause a breach of the peace (or fight). One of the lads nodded assent. After further conversation, PS returned with the driver. He wanted PC to deal with both arrests on his own. PC thought PS should accompany them to the station. I thought this was because the young men were disputing the swearing. PS acceded. Inside the van the youngsters again denied the swearing; one said: 'I don't swear, you can ask my mother.' PS again told them to 'shut it'. By now PC was beginning to mellow and joke a little with them, though PS still came over aggressively. The defendants were then bundled into the station, protesting that they did not need manhandling, though no notice was taken of them. Before PS left PC to deal with the charge sergeant, both went off for a moment. I presumed this was in order to agree their account. Then PS gave over his arrest to the SPG detective constable and returned, with me, to the ground.

Back at the ground supporters singing 'provocatively' again attracted attention. I witnessed the SPG chief inspector shout a warning to a group of young fans. But, once safely past, they recommenced their singing regardless. A SPG sergeant then took out a young man from this same group to 'warn' him, and then let him on his way. I also saw a mounted officer lean over from his saddle, grab someone by the ear and 'advise' him; a divisional officer on traffic patrol manhandle a child and tell him to go; and an SPG constable 'abuse' another young man in the 'usual' way, by placing his face as close as possible to the young man's and then 'bawling him out'. At this point I began to wonder why PS and PC had chosen to arrest rather than 'advise'. At 2.50 p.m., an SPG inspector told us which 'end' we were in, and we entered the ground and took up position.

Postscript

Though both denied the charges at the subsequent trial, they were both found guilty. One was fined £150 with £50 costs. The juvenile was committed to the juvenile court for sentencing, and a request was made for a social inquiry report on him.

Comment

The highly discretionary nature of public order powers, and the subsequent weakness of the legal structures as a constraining influence, were clearly much in evidence. PS and PC, for example, made two 'Section 5' arrests for abusive behaviour in a situation where similar behaviour was being dealt with informally by fellow officers, and in which facts relevant to the likelihood of a breach of the peace, such as the good-humoured, ritualistic nature of the singing and the strong police presence, were simply ignored. Later, the magistrates took a similarly blinkered view. The weakness of the democratic structure as a constraining influence was also apparent: both in the almost exclusive focus of police attention upon groups of unknown, potentially 'troublesome' but relatively powerless young males singing and shouting 'provocatively', and in the similar restriction of actual contacts to arresting (contentiously in the case discussed here since both young men disputed that they had done anything wrong) or warning individuals from these same 'disreputable' groups. As for the work structure, the dominance of the occupational dimension (the norms and practices of the rank and file) was the obviously striking feature. For even the strong presence of supervisors (the key organizational dimension in this context) did not preclude individual officers freely using their independent powers as police officers to 'advise' or 'arrest' as they saw fit. Indeed, many of the supervisors, as we saw, were similarly engaged. And though individual officers came to different decisions about whether to advise or arrest, there was evidently substantial agreement as to what sort of behaviour – singing and shouting – warranted 'discretionary' intervention. This obviously suggests a reasonably consensual set of norms and practices informing the use of their discretionary powers.

In line with my account of the interrelationships between the structures, then, the wide discretion granted by the legal structure together with the weakness of the democratic structure gave the work structure – the police themselves – the dominant say. Within that, the independence of the office of constable effectively made the working norms and practices of the occupational culture the *actual* determinant of police discretion in this instance, just as my model would have predicted.

POLICING PUBLIC ORDER NOW: INCREASED DISCRETION, DECREASED CONSTRAINTS

This situation, which enables the norms and practices of operational officers in the field effectively to dominate discretionary decision-making in the case of public order policing, is getting worse – because both the legal and the democratic structures have been further weakened (both, of course, being part of the historical worsening recounted in Chapter 2, though not then expressed in these terms). A good example of the weakening of the legal structure is the new POA 1986. This extends police powers partly by increasing police discretion. In so doing, it thereby weakens the legal structure as a form of constraint on police behaviour. Section 4 of the POA 1986, for example, which replaces the highly discretionary Section 5 of the POA 1936 we examined above, grants police greater discretion; but it is the completely new Section 5 offence of 'disorderly conduct' which represents the most significant extension of discretion. As Thornton says: it is 'more widely drawn' than the repealed Section 5 and 'embraces behaviour which formerly would generally not have been punishable as a crime. In particular it covers behaviour which falls short of violence or the threat or fear of violence.'[43] Examples Thornton cites as being the 'minor acts of hooliganism' aimed at include 'banging on doors, peering in at windows and knocking over dustbins . . . someone turning out the lights in a crowded dance hall . . . rowdy behaviour in the streets late at night'.[44] If the old Section 5 was a 'dragnet provision'[45] covering most forms of untoward behaviour, I have to conclude, despite Thornton's learned discussion of disorderliness in which merely ill-mannered behaviour is not deemed illegal,[46] that the 'bad taste' conduct of male youths in future will be, nevertheless, more easily penalized. McCabe and Wallington would appear to agree:

> The wider new offence, covering threatening, abusive or insulting words or behaviour which the perpetrator can reasonably foresee will lead to harassment, alarm or distress, gives a much enhanced discretionary power to the police on the street. The original, at least ostensible, reason for including the new offence was to deal with young gangs of hooligans, but its potential for reinforcing the 'do as I say' style of policing, whether of political demonstrations or picketing, is clear.[47]

A similar argument could be made about the comprehensive codification of police powers contained in the Police and Criminal Evidence Act (PACE) 1984. It too extends police powers, in this case 'of search, seizure, arrest and detention', in ways which increase police discretion, though ostensibly these have been 'balanced' by more effective supervisory procedures and compulsory community consultation.[48]

In thinking about the weakening of the democratic structure,[49] we have only to cast our minds back to the end of Chapter 2, to the breakdown of hegemony. Symptomatic of this breakdown was the growth of political and ideological conflict. The effect of this was an expansion of the range of dissident and deviant groups, coupled with a new readiness to bring negative ideological significations into play. The overall result has been to increase the level of hostility generally in police–public contacts, especially in public order contexts, the 'symbolic location'[50] *par excellence* for confrontations between society (represented by the police) and 'its enemies'. This has effectively reduced further the influence of the democratic structure as a practical constraint.

SUMMARY AND CONCLUSION

This chapter has contrasted the ideal of impartial law enforcement with the real discretionary world of police decision-making, illustrated the argument with examples from the field of public order, and shown how currently the constraints on a widening police discretion have decreased. Having established the selective (and hence political) nature of law-enforcement decision-making, it was necessary to examine the real determinants of such activity. This involved a critique of various existing attempts to understand such determinants, and a reconceptualization centred upon combining the strengths of radical sociologists' concern with *outcomes* with liberal sociologists' greater attention to the *processes* through which such outcomes are routinely produced. Essentially, this reconceptualization attempted to make the already identified constraints – both legal and 'extra-legal' (the organization, the public, immediate colleagues) – considerably more concrete, in order to be able to understand better the *variable* nature of discretion – how different situations produce different *degrees* of discretion. The resulting approach redefined the constraints in terms of three structures – law, democracy and work – with the latter comprising two dimensions, the organizational and the occupational. When applied to public order policing, we saw how the legal and the democratic structures are weak relative to the work structure, and how the occupational dimension was strong relative to the organizational dimension in those (critical) operational situations when officers are acting in accordance with their 'independent' constabulary powers. A single arrest was used to illustrate this, and then the present weakening of both the legal and democratic structures was outlined.

While a dominant work structure, which in the context of police independence means a dominant occupational dimension, is problematic at the best of times, in the context of weakening legal and democratic structures (themselves both symptom and product of deepening political and ideological conflict), it can only be regarded with extreme concern. But when the organizational dimension of the work structure uses its discretion in this area to introduce paramilitary policing, the result can only be described as disastrous, because the very problem it is ostensibly designed to tackle is *exacerbated* by the chosen solution. The way

59

this happens is the subject of Chapter 5. But first we need to take a closer look at the relationship between the two dimensions of the work structure.

NOTES

1. See Manning, 1971.
2. Jefferson, 1986, p. 278.
3. Ibid., p. 279.
4. The ideas in this section are more comprehensively covered in Jefferson and Grimshaw, 1984, Chapter 5.
5. See Reiner, 1985, Chapter 3, for a full summary of the relevant literature.
6. See Skolnick, 1975, Chapter 3.
7. Reiss and Bordua, 1967, p. 25.
8. See Wilson, 1968.
9. For a fuller development of this critique, see Grimshaw and Jefferson, 1987, pp. 5–11.
10. Ibid., p. 17 (emphasis in original).
11. Ibid., p. 18.
12. Ibid.
13. Ibid., p. 21.
14. Ibid., p. 22.
15. Ibid., pp. 20–21.
16. See Reiner, 1985, Chapter 3.
17. See James, 1979, p. 70.
18. Grimshaw and Jefferson, 1987, p. 19.
19. Ibid.
20. Ibid., p. 25.
21. Ibid., p. 23.
22. For a fuller consideration of this question, see ibid., pp. 22–5.
23. See Jefferson and Grimshaw, 1984, p. 70.
24. Thornton, 1987, p. 91.
25. Ibid., p. 32.
26. McCabe and Wallington, 1988, p. 163.
27. See Thornton, 1987, p. 210.
28. Ibid., p. 34.
29. In *Brutus* v. *Cozens* [1973] AC 854, 862, quoted in Thornton, 1987, p. 34.
30. *Simcock* v *Rhodes* [1977] Crim LR 751, quoted in Thornton, 1987, p. 36.
31. Thornton, 1987, p. 32.
32. *Masterson* v *Holden* [1986] 1 WLR 1017, quoted in Thornton, 1987, p. 36.
33. In *R* v *Howell* [1982] QB 416, 427, quoted in Thornton, 1987, pp. 73–4.
34. Thornton, 1987, p. 74.
35. Ibid., p. 97. For cases see *Moss* v *McLachlan*, *The Times*, 29 November 1984; *Foy* v *Chief Constable of Kent*, 20 March 1984, unreported; and *The Guardian*, 21 March 1984.
36. A. Dickey [1971] Crim LR 265, quoted in Thornton, 1987, p. 32.
37. See McCabe and Wallington, 1988, pp. 166–7.
38. For a fuller discussion of this aspect of police discretion, see Jefferson and Grimshaw, 1984, Chapter 3.
39. See Brogden *et al.*, 1988, pp. 35–7.

40. For a fuller illustrated discussion of this issue, see Jefferson and Grimshaw, 1984, pp. 104–26.
41. Ibid., pp. 126–32.
42. See Reuss-Ianni and Ianni, 1983.
43. Thornton, 1987, p. 40.
44. Ibid.
45. Ibid., p. 32.
46. Ibid., pp. 41–2.
47. McCabe and Wallington, 1988, p. 117.
48. Jefferson, 1987b, p. 19. Though less directly relevant for present purposes, the passage of the new Prevention of Terrorism (Temporary Provisions) Act 1984 and the decision to make it semi-permanent until 1990 also contributed to a weakening of the legal structure by extending police discretion – to search, arrest, detain and exclude – and by officially 'normalizing' the erstwhile 'extraordinary' use of coercion (cf. Hillyard and Percy-Smith, 1988, pp. 256–9). The passage of the Act was also a reminder, once more, of the role of Northern Ireland in the British state's calculus of repression.
49. Which is not, of course, to imply that the democratic structure in relation to policing has ever been 'strong'.
50. A term used by Sir Kenneth Newman, former Commissioner of the Metropolitan Police, about 'black' areas of the inner city, in his Sir George Bean Memorial Lecture, 'Policing London post Scarman', 30 October 1983.

CHAPTER 4

Policy, supervision and the dominance of the occupational dimension

One of the most difficult things to understand about how policework 'works' is the relationship between management and the rank and file. This is because most commentators fail to appreciate the concrete implications of the paradox of making officers 'independently' liable for their own actions and, simultaneously, disciplined agents expected to follow orders within an organized bureaucracy with militaristic leanings. Consequently, when things 'go wrong', blame is generally attached to poor management, a recalcitrant rank and file, or to a breakdown in communication between them. Rarely, however, does the relationship between the top and bottom of the police organization, *in all its uniqueness*, come under scrutiny.

It is that uniqueness that I made central in discussing the two dimensions – the organizational and the occupational – of the work structure at the end of Chapter 3. To understand this relationship fully requires, first, a recognition that the strength (or weakness) of the work structure depends upon the relative strength (or weakness) of the other two structures, namely, the legal and the democratic. As we saw in Chapter 3, public order situations are ones in which the legal and democratic structures are weak and, in consequence, the work structure is strong. Second, a grasp is then needed of precisely why it is that sometimes the organizational dimension is 'in command' and, at other times, the occupational dimension. This far, I have argued, again as we saw in Chapter 3, that it is in those *operational* contexts where constables are expected (and required) to rely on their broad, discretionary legal powers, as in public order situations, that the occupational dimension comes to the fore.

It is time now to secure that argument by expanding it and offering a variety of illustrations from my fieldwork notes.[1] Crucial to this endeavour will be a consideration of what has hitherto received little attention – policy, and its relationship with supervision. Above all, the task will be to show that the idealistic conception of policy, which regards it as 'a set of instructions, guidelines or principles which ought to be followed',[2] cannot come to grips with the complex reality of this relationship.

THE INSTRUMENTS OF MANAGERIAL CONTROL

The instruments which enable managers of any sort to manage range from the very direct, such as *advice* or *commands*, to the more indirect, such as *training*. Somewhere in between come instruments such as *deployment*, fitting the right people into the right jobs; *rewards*, like promotion; and finally, *discipline*, what happens 'in the last resort' when all else fails. But the central instruments are undoubtedly seen to be *policy* and *supervision* – the former because its achievement is ostensibly also the end towards which the whole managerial enterprise is directed; the latter because it is also regarded as the principal means of implementing the whole repertoire of managerial instruments. The pre-eminence of both is well recognized by police managers. The Chief Constable of the force where the fieldwork was conducted, for example, described policy as the tool for ensuring that the decisions of subordinates conform 'pretty well' to the way he 'would act':

> The really essential thing for a chief constable to do, in my kind of force anyway, where you *can't possibly* take all the decisions . . . is to develop policies, so that those who have to take the decisions can take them in such a way that they know they're conforming pretty well with the kind of way in which I would act.

And, ensuring this happened – the job of 'front-line supervision' – remained one of management's 'biggest problems', as the Deputy Chief Constable outlined:

> I think one of the biggest problems that faces this force, and indeed it may well be a problem facing the service generally, is that . . . we are a very young force, we have a large number of very inexperienced policemen (*sic*) out on the ground . . . because a lot of senior officers have left, younger elements have been promoted, so the level of experience at sergeant and inspector level is not as great as it might have been, and I think . . . one of the big problems is what I call 'front-line supervision'. Because you are asking young and inexperienced policemen to go out and do a very difficult job, they are under more pressures than they were when I was doing the job . . . the complaints procedure's heavier, the television . . . the glare of the publicity on them, the increased number of black and brown people in a force like this, they produce a bit of tension . . . unemployment, all these sorts of things, it's a bit like a cauldron out there and we put these young, inexperienced people out there, and naturally they make mistakes and I think that . . . it will put itself right because in two or three years from now the force will be that much older, the people who have been made sergeant,

inspector will have grown in experience and that will be the way in which it will be put right.

While the above comments attest to the importance of both policy and supervision, neither is based upon the kind of concrete notion of policy that is needed both to address the difficulties of ensuring that practice 'conforms with' policy, and to explain why greater experience alone will not solve the recurrent problem of front-line supervision – particularly in public order contexts.

THE POLICY PROCESS: A CONCRETE NOTION

Lying behind the Chief Constable's remarks quoted above is a conventional conception of policy, one based on the idealistic assumption 'that for each force practice there is a definite set of principles which form an authoritative guide to action'.[3] Thus, for public order policing, for example, when Roger Grimshaw and I were doing the research upon which this chapter is based, we expected to find, somewhere, a definite statement of the principles to which the Chief Constable wanted his officers to 'conform', in practice. But the reality was rather different, and, 'in general, we found that the various institutional sites (conferences, meetings and "policy" files) where policy was discussed did not routinely involve the making, or revision, of such statements'.[4] What we did find was that 'policy' was a term applied to all kinds of 'discussions and statements which only in limited and specific cases approached a degree of definiteness and authoritativeness that we could reconcile with the conventional conception'.[5] Consequently, in order to make sense of our 'policy' data, and to clarify its distinctiveness as a managerial instrument, we defined policy as 'an authoritative statement signifying a settled practice on any matter relevant to the duties of the Chief Constable'.[6] This then enabled us to distinguish between policy and other sorts of statement made by senior officers: those which are not 'authoritative' because 'they are invisible beyond the immediate circle to which they are directed (such as supervisory advice)';[7] those which 'do not signify a practice (such as an announcement of the need for better relations with the public *tout court*)';[8] and those 'which signify practices which are not meant to be settled or continuous (such as a direct command)'.[9] One final distinction will prove helpful; that between policy-*making*, the moment when new policy is inaugurated (which we found to be a comparatively rare event), and

> the wider [and much more common] process of policy *consideration* – a process which can draw upon a whole gamut of resources and result in reminders and information about, or review and clarification of, existing policy, as well as the making of policy.[10]

With these definitions and distinctions in mind we can now begin to look at the relationship between policy and practice in the area of public order policing and begin to see just why it is that the occupational dimension is 'in command'. The important points that emerge from all this, as we shall see, are that policy-making in this area is much less frequent an activity than the process of policy consideration; and that policy in operational areas is either 'permissive' or non-existent.

Policy and public order offences

The charge is a basic police practice; like many operational practices, it is one for which we found no policy. Attempts had been made to introduce policy in this area, but without success. Since such attempts had been made in areas which bear mostly on public order law, and since this was probably the only example we came across of policy debate about concrete operational matters concerning legal duties in the area of public order, I intend to use it to illustrate the basic point about operational matters of this kind – the lack of policy at the point where legal duties come into play.

One attempt to establish policy in the area of charging was that made by the Joint Branch Board (JBB). Writing to the Chief Constable, they recommended that a force policy be introduced that when officers were resisted or wilfully obstructed when arresting, charges should be brought under Section 51(3) of the Police Act 1964 in addition to any other relevant charges. This, they argued, was necessary for the protection of officers in the event of subsequent complaints. The Chief Constable's response was to canvass the views of his chief superintendents on the proposal, through the medium of an HQ circular. Their views were collated and discussed at a chief superintendents' conference. Their collective view was that the Federation recommendation should be refused; that individual cases should continue to be judged on their merits; that such a proposed policy would degrade the charges; that proper disclosure to the station sergeant and a pocketbook entry would prove sufficient protection; and that an officer should act within the law. The notion of 'blanket' charging, as a matter of policy, was thus decisively rejected in favour of the continued use of existing legal powers and the discretion these afford. On the basis of this discussion the Chief Constable decided to write to the JBB informing them that their recommendation would not be acceded to, and citing some of the reasons expressed by the chief superintendents. After the matter was raised again, it was discussed at a management team meeting of the Chief Constable, his Deputy and the Assistant Chief Constables, where it was agreed to raise the matter at the next subdivisional superintendents' conference. Here the necessity of judging each case on its merits was explained and the policy of 'no blanket charging' reaffirmed.

If the above illustrates an attempt to introduce a standard policy on charging in a particular area being rejected outright through a process of policy consideration, the next two examples illustrate the difficulties of implementing a policy decision in this area, even when a degree of standardization was recommended policy.

The origin of the first example was a letter from the Clerk to the Justices complaining that the use of different charges with very different maximum penalties for all but identical offences was causing embarrassment to local magistrates. Specifically, the reference was to the use of local by-laws and Section 5 of the POA 1936, apparently indiscriminately, in relation to similar public order offences, and to the limited penalties available under the by-laws. The Chief Constable replied immediately explaining that only in the previous decade had the divisional court indicated that Section 5 of the POA 1936 could be used for offences other than those in connection with public meetings and processions. However, he continued, he was drawing the attention of all operational chief superintendents to the need to use the POA. This letter was followed by a memorandum to the chief superintendents, enclosing the original letter and his reply, and a reiteration that the POA was to be used 'where the evidence is appropriate'.

Two years later, the Chief Constable received an all but identical letter from the same source as the original one. Apparently discrepancies in charging for similar offences were a continuing problem. The response this time was to initiate an enquiry, through a Chief Superintendent, with details of persons arrested and charges at the previous local football match – the apparent root of the trouble. This enquiry revealed that one particular division had been responsible for the majority of by-law charges. The matter was discussed between the Chief Superintendent and the relevant divisional commander who had already decided that the problem had arisen as a result of an error in judgement by the staff responsible for receiving charges, and, consequently, had already issued a directive to his subdivisional superintendents advising them that, wherever practicable, Section 5 of the POA was to be used. The Chief Superintendent and the head of the SPG then saw the Clerk to the Justices and informed him of the results of the enquiry. This, apparently, satisfied the Clerk. The details of these actions were then conveyed through a memorandum to the relevant Assistant Chief Constable, along with recommendation that a letter be sent to the Clerk to the Justices confirming the information given to him, and a suggestion that an HQ circular be sent to all chief superintendents regarding the preference for POA Section 5 charges, where practicable. The Assistant Chief Constable decided to follow the advice, wrote to the Clerk along the lines suggested, and then issued a memorandum to divisional chief superintendents, along with the letter from the Clerk to the Justices, asking them to ensure that Section 5 be used 'where the evidence justifies this course of action'.

Two similar incidents; two similar policy directives. Both, in their permissive wording, amounted to no more than a reiteration of legal duty and thus effectively placed the discretion where the law places it – in the hands of constables. Hence the practical failure of the first policy directive to eliminate discrepancies in charging – and the consequent need for a second directive. In so far as the second directive simply reproduced the first, its practical effect, as we saw in the case of the first directive, cannot be the total elimination of discrepancies.

Whatever the source of the impetus for the standardization of policy on charging, and whatever the wishes of those responsible for policy in this area, whether they approved or disapproved of the impetus for standardization, the clear fact is that legal duties are necessarily paramount in this area. Thus even where the preferred policy was in the direction of greater standardization, as in the latter examples, the permissive wording of policy revealed the importance of the law in such matters. Legal duty in operational contexts is an overriding factor. Policy in these areas was and is, therefore, necessarily non-existent, or, effectively, irrelevant.

A look at a public order policy file

Another way of illustrating this basic point about the lack of policy in operational matters is to have a brief look at the contents of a sample public order policy file. Policy files are the 'repositories of policy consideration'[11] which contain 'every type of force record . . . relevant to the topic . . . items of correspondence, records of conferences and meetings, documents, orders, circulars and memoranda'.[12] They are extremely variable both in length and detail, with some 'containing a long historical narrative of changing force policy and policy consideration',[13] while others are much briefer and, even, in some cases, empty. We found a similar variation can be within the files, with some items warranting quite lengthy attention, and others being given much shorter shrift. But, whatever the length of the files, or the items therein, the important points for our purposes are the comparative absence, first, of 'operational' items (and this in a body of files, 62 in all, chosen for their likely relevance to operational matters), and second, of policy in those operational matters which were considered.[14] It is this lack of policy that concerns us in the following look at a file, which was, in fact, one of the lengthier and more 'operationally' dominated ones examined.

The file covered the period from 1936 to 1979 and contained 21 different items. Of these, about three-quarters were 'operational' items, that is, were concerned with the law, police operations or deployment. All except one of the rest were concerned with training, equipment or procedures which collectively we classified as 'administrative' items.[15] Examples of operational items included: the notes of assistance issued by the Home Office to chief constables about certain sections of the POA 1936 (the law); a report by a superintendent to the Deputy Chief Constable (DCC) detailing his observations on the use of the force PSUs during the 1972 dock strike (operations); and a 1971 memorandum from an Assistant Chief Constable (ACC) to the DCC about the need for a Force Working Party to consider arrangements for calling out officers from other divisions at short notice for demonstrations (deployment). Examples of administrative items included: the 1969 letter from the General Secretary of the Association of Chief Police Officers (ACPO) to all chief constables informing them about a police training film on 'crowd control techniques' and requesting orders for it (training); the request from the Police Superintendents' Association, in the aftermath of the Notting Hill carnival disturbances of 1976, for information from all chief constables about the 'availability, suitability and accessibility' of protective clothing and equipment (equipment);[16] and the 1975 production under the DCC's guidance of a specimen letter, based on a similar one used in the Metropolitan Police District (MPD), to be served on march organizers (procedures).

About half the items were initiated internally. Of the rest, the majority stemmed from the police themselves, usually ACPO or the Central Conference of Chief Constables (CCCC), and, in a couple of instances, the Home Office and the local police committee. Examples of all these included the 1972 internal Working Party Report on the planning and operational aspects of public order, the 1979 'Notes of Guidance on Public Order for Senior Officers' issued by ACPO, the 1974 extract from the minutes of the CCCC on the handling of public order at pop festivals and other large gatherings, and the already mentioned Home Office notes on the POA 1936 and the police committee discussion of 'vigilante' groups. The file is, thus, very much police-dominated. Only three items stem from outside these professional groups: the 1970 booklet on public order by a Committee of the Society of Conservative Lawyers; a 'crank' letter in 1971 from an individual about the peaceful controlling of crowds; and a newspaper report dated June 1978 of a local councillor calling for new public order laws.[17]

For the most part, items were not subject to a wide-ranging process of enquiry, nor were they discussed much below the Chief Constable's management team. This has a lot to do with the fact that they were initially defined as being for information or guidance rather than subjects requiring a decision which needed implementation. Consequently, they did not generally lead to changes in ongoing practice, much less to policy. Only in five instances could one talk of changes emanating from the consideration of items. Two of these involved administrative items, namely, the aforementioned production of a specimen letter to be issued to march organizers, and the 1976 decision to follow the MPD in having a liaison officer to deal with local first aid services in public order situations where trouble was expected. The other three, which involved operational items, led only to the 1978 decision to deploy an officer in the incident room of major civil disorders to ensure that correct details of police injuries were circulated to the media, and, in the other two cases, to a series of suggestions based on 'lessons learned' from two particular public order incidents – such as, in the case of the Prime Minister's visit of 1968, the need for a press liaison officer, for a 'jailer' to convey and check in prisoners, and for the prison van to be static – some of which were 'agreed', though whether the changes occurred remained unclear.[18] Thus, in the file of most obvious relevance to the operational aspects of public order policing we found only a police-dominated pot-pourri of items touching on public order, most of which were concerned with information and guidance, and little enquiry, discussion or change in practice or procedure. Policy (never mind policy-making) was noticeable only by its absence.

Lest there be any misunderstanding here, let us go through the two items which at least touch on the issues that most concern us in order to demonstrate this absence of policy: first, the report on the use of force PSUs in connection with the 1972 dock strike; and second, the internal Working Party of the same year on the planning and operational aspects of public order. The former was a lengthy and extremely detailed item commenting upon everything from 'welfare', 'catering' and 'accommodation' to 'operational control', 'use of manpower' (sic) and 'views of the dockers'.[19] It embraced numerous suggestions, such as the advantages of carrying a spare uniform (as some had been damaged in one of the confrontations) to the need for the operational commander to wear a coloured armband (to assist identification). It commended various aspects of the operation: the support unit ratio of inspector, three sergeants and 30 PCs, the communications, the *esprit de corps*, and the briefing – which was 'excellent'.[20] Part of this 'excellent' briefing consisted of warnings about the dangers of police becoming isolated and of the unnecessary use of violence. It also stressed the need to curtail provocative action. Criticisms, too, were offered: of some support units not reporting to operational control; and of overpolicing, following a particular 'fracas', which risked the loss of public sympathy.[21] The 'views of the dockers' included further criticisms: of coppers, sporting short sleeves and leather gloves, or handcuffs on their belts and truncheon thongs showing, who were earmarked as 'aggressive', as opposed to 'real coppers' who wore helmets; and of the police for being inside the confines of the port, an act which was seen as siding with the port authorities and their employees.[22]

All in all, a range of important issues which have been central to my concerns – overpolicing, 'aggressive' appearance, the unnecessary use of violence and provocative actions – were all raised here, albeit briefly, either by the police themselves or by the dockers. They were not invisible as issues. Yet they did not emanate in policy. Rather, the DCC informed the Chief Constable that there were 'some interesting points which we would do well to bear in mind in our plans', to which the Chief Constable added a single word reply: 'interesting'.[23] The final comment, and a suitable end point to our narrative, was left to the relevant ACC. In a note to another ACC, he said that they 'should consider including a mobile shower unit in our estimates', or borrow one from the army if occasion requires.[24]

Our second example, the Working Party report, was even lengthier and more detailed; the Working Party was chaired by a chief superintendent, and included three superintendents, a detective superintendent, two inspectors and a sergeant Federation representative. It was originally established to make recommendations 'on the grading and manning of demonstrations', though it found it necessary subsequently to widen its focus to embrace also 'the wider aspects of public order in relation to police planning and organization'. And it did indeed range widely, considering and making recommendations in connection with 'intelligence', the 'grading' of demonstrations (in terms of their 'danger to public order'), the 'availability of manpower' (sic), the 'command structure', the 'duties of other officers', 'planning and reporting', 'briefing', 'debriefing', 'deployment of manpower', 'communications', 'catering and rest centres', 'arrests', 'transport' and 'training'. In all this, as with the last item, the issues that particularly concern us were variously touched upon; the mounted police were recognized as being 'particularly useful' but also provocative, particularly to students; in situations of extended working, changing personnel every two to three days was regarded as advantageous since it prevented both 'staleness' and officers 'developing grievances against provocative demonstrators'; 'under no circumstances should police dogs be used to control crowds'; 'overpolicing' should be avoided since it leads to criticism; there should be a 'clearly determined policy' for arrests which 'might vary according to the type of demonstration'; officers should be carefully briefed as to 'the required action in varying situations'; the 'rigid enforcement' of 'minor matters' was likely 'to aggravate' the situation; and public order was 'often best maintained by tolerance'. But, when it came to the summary of recommendations these issues disappeared. Instead, there was a welter of firm proposals concerning organizational and procedural matters to do with intelligence, grading demonstrations, the unit structure, shiftworking, command structures, planning and reporting, briefing, equipment, catering, transport and training – but nothing on any of the above matters.[25] These remain, apparently, either beyond the scope of policy, or, as we have already seen in the case of the attempt to introduce a 'clearly determined arrest policy', permissive.

Take, finally, a further example from the above, namely, the idea that 'under no circumstances should police dogs be used to control crowds'. This, in fact, merely reiterated existing force policy as contained in Force Standing Orders, the ultimate 'bible' of force policy. But, once again, as the following interchange between myself and the Chief Constable demonstrates, the policy of keeping dogs in static 'deterrent' positions and away from crowds is, ultimately, in the final analysis, discretionary rather than 'peremptory':

cc: I believe it's important that people should have some kind of instruction book, if you like, which they can go to, which sets out for them the main policies and procedures and systems of the force, the standards which are expected of people and so on. But at the same time, I would hope that people don't think that those have to be slavishly followed, and that failure to comply with them to the letter is going to mean automatic discipline; to that extent they ought to be much more guidelines than peremptory orders.

tj: Can I . . . explore . . . that with a specific example? The Standing Order in the area of the use of dogs in public order, which I know you have strong views about, is that they are to be on static point duty . . . and . . . well away from crowds as a deterrent. Now . . . in practice they tend to accompany crowds . . . rather like the mounted.

cc: . . . What I hope that that Standing Order gets across, if it does nothing else, is that dogs should not be used as weapons and that it's foolish trying to arrest someone with one hand, and hold a dog back with the other, that's all I'm trying to get across. And if people understand that, then, whether they walk with them alongside a crowd, or, whether they do or whether they don't, doesn't worry me overmuch, it is the common-sense use of an animal.

A particular kind of 'common sense', of course, is what guides the occupational dimension of the work structure – as we shall see in more detail later.

Policy, on the other hand, ought to be about attempting to put the 'best sense' that the organization can produce 'in command'. But, since it clearly does not, it is hardly surprising that supervision, to which we now turn, is unable to provide an effective alternative to 'occupational common sense'.

SUPERVISION

Supervision can be either direct, as occurs when a sergeant accompanies his or her officers on patrol in order to oversee their activities, or indirect, as happens when senior officers monitor the paperwork traces of prior police activity – arrest figures, complaint statistics, completed crime files, pocket book entries, and so on. My intention in what follows is to show that, despite closer supervision and greater opportunities for it, the concrete reality of the SPG's 'bread and butter' work – public order operations in which discretionary legal duties are uppermost – renders both kinds of supervision effectively redundant.

Direct supervision

The importance of close direct supervision of SPG work, because of the difficulties of controlling the activities of not one but a group of officers, was recognized from the outset, as the following quotation from an ACC reveals:

> When we set up the present Special Patrol Group . . . my advice was that you want close supervision, and so we agreed on one and eight and it was agreed a sergeant to eight . . . I think that was right for those times because a lot of their work was . . . flooding an area on observations . . . and dealing with crime . . . the sergeant would have a fairly wide spread . . . [of] men deployed you see, and I think about eight was about right. And similarly, if they are dealing with any public order situation . . . I was always conscious of the fact that if you get a group of people, you can call them a group but if there's something happens and they all go their own way, they get strength from each other and they soon become a mob, and it was for that reason again I wanted very close control so that they were more disciplined, acted as individuals, thought as individuals but acted as a group, and this was the all important thing.

This view was by no means confined to the ACC. The Chief Constable, speaking of a later time (hence the reference to ten not eight men), makes substantially the same point:

> They've got to keep together in order that they can be properly supervised, because we have one sergeant to ten men, and if those ten men keep together as a group under the sergeant, if he's doing his job properly they will not get themselves into trouble, either as victims or as aggressors, 'cause he's there to see that it doesn't happen.

But, in addition to the sergeant, who was always with his unit on public order occasions, the inspector responsible for several units would also often be on hand, as would the chief inspector in charge of the whole Group. Asked when he would decide to go out with the units, the Chief Inspector said:

> I try and be with 'em all the time, purely and simply because I have always believed it's no good talking about it. One can theorize about dignity of man and all the rest of it. From sitting in a seat we're not being confronted with the violence, so I make a point of going to all of them, and in the early days, every situation that was on, regardless of whether it meant me working 12 hours a day or 16 hours a day, I was there . . . There's a question of leading by example more than anything else. Once they see that I'm about, I know that things are going to run smoothly.

Moreover, public order occasions will usually have a complement of subdivisional supervisory officers, including sometimes the divisional commander, which adds a further supervisory layer. The presence of subdivisional supervisors is not, incidentally, simply additive. Because SPG supervisors will want 'their' officers to perform creditably in front of 'outside' supervisors, and subdivisional supervisors are concerned that 'outside' departments do not mess up on 'their' turf, this introduces a level of sensitivity into the situation which effectively further enhances the already high degree of supervision. Beyond that, there is the fact that the deployment of the SPG is always to the spots where 'trouble' is expected – and to which primary operational attention, supervisory and otherwise, is necessarily directed. Finally, such spots tend to be those where 'incidents' will arise, and these inevitably attract supervisory notice. SPG public order work is thus highly supervised.

Unlike ordinary policing, it is also highly *visible* work, not only to the various supervisors around, but also to the public, and sometimes the media. Once again, this is particularly true of the 'trouble spots', and when 'incidents' arise. SPG public order work is thus extraordinarily exposed to the gaze of supervisors, the public and the media.

Now, as I argued in Chapter 3, in situations where the instruction is to 'hold formation', this close supervision can be absolute and highly effective. But when specific incidents occur which require officers to break formation and go into action, and offences are spotted or suspected, the rank structure is in practice effectively neutralized. At this point, supervisory powers become secondary to constabulary powers, and, given the discretionary nature of public order powers, the occupational dimension, not the organizational dimension, 'takes command'. Though an ACC did not put it this way, his remarks at least recognize the important distinction:

> In the structured . . . public order situation I think the . . . supervision is pretty tight and can be kept tight . . . Now unless [the] . . . sergeant is in full control of his unit then they are out of my control, they are out of the structured control of that public order event. So in those circumstances I make it very clear that the sergeant has got to exercise strict control, and it

is there that I think that the problems might arise, where they go out to deal with any number of incidents . . . In 1968 . . . we had a very big exercise . . . we had the political spectrum from the extremists of extreme left to [those of the] extreme right and in some situations we had Colin Jordan and his band there and we had the lefties there with just three policemen standing in between them and there was close supervision. We could see everything that was going on because they were all in —— Square and we kept tight control of it and when it all broke up they moved away and it was when everybody was breaking up and the supervision of the people moving away that . . . we . . . lost one area. There was trouble in one area, but it wasn't as tightly controlled, there wasn't a superintendent in charge in that area at that time. They splintered out into such small groups that . . . there wasn't the tight control. I'm sure that the officers acted properly because they'd got a bit of a punch-up situation that . . . it wasn't as tight then. I think I'm just trying to make the point that when it breaks out this is where the structure might break down.

Another way of illustrating what the ACC calls situations 'where the structure might break down', and what I call those (structured) situations where the occupational dimension (necessarily) takes command, is to look at a number of arrests that I (along with various supervisors) observed at first hand. No supervisors queried any of these arrests, nor the subsequent police accounts. Indeed, supervisors were sometimes involved in the arrests. Yet my observations clearly differed. Here, then, we can hardly talk of a 'breakdown' in the structure. Rather, we are forced to recognize the 'normality' of the occupational dimension being 'in command' in such situations, and the organization's subordinate status.

The following four incidents are drawn from my field notes made during my time spent with two SPG units. They are drawn from a much larger body of similar notes encompassing a vast number of police–public interactions resulting variously in arrests, ejections, 'warnings' and the like. They have been chosen not simply because in these particular cases I was able to compare my own notes directly with the official police accounts, but also because they demonstrate, each in a slightly different way, the particularly 'tough' interpretation of their highly subjective powers routinely made by SPG officers working in public order contexts peopled by a relatively powerless public. They are thus a graphic way of illustrating the concrete meaning of the occupational dimension being 'in command'.

The incidents all took place on fine days at heavily policed football matches where there was strong 'away' team support, a police expectation of 'trouble', and many ejections and arrests. All four resulted in POA Section 5 arrests for using abusive language 'liable to lead to a breach of the peace', three before the match, one after. My notes appear just as I made them at the time; the police accounts are substantially verbatim transcripts. In both cases, only names and other forms of identification have been altered or removed.

The first example occurred before the match and is an illustration of abusive language being construed as 'behaviour liable' in a situation in which only police were present. The police account is as follows:

> Walking with 200 [same side] supporters chanting 'We're all pissed up and we're going to Wembley'. Approached, told to be quiet. Shouted, 'I'm a press officer and know the fucking law'. Again told to be quiet. Warned about language. Quietened down. Walked ten yards, turned, shouted: 'I'll fix the fucking bastards'. Arrested 'for using abusive language likely to cause a breach of the peace'. Caution, reply: 'Can I see the match. I want to phone my fucking paper'.

Here are my field notes:

> Attempt to close gap between fans. Hurrying them. Using horses. Horse-man holds fan by ear/hair. [SPG] van driver apparently arrests same fan after shoving him. Two fans: one protesting at treatment of fans and/or at being hurried. Mate trying to calm. Horseman shooing him. Most of [one SPG] unit and division concentrated on him. Horseman on pavement (provocatively). Rumours of 'press card'. Separated from mate. Taken up alley by SPG man. Horseman blocked entrance. Inspectors walk up road. PCs take no notice. Journalist reappears with press card aloft. Allowed to proceed. All seems reasonably amicable. Horseman mouthing off about him ('more like a member of football hooligan's union'). Speculation as to which (radical) paper he worked for. Attempts to buy pie with others. Hurried up by divisional man. Objected (told later he said 'fuck off'). Arrested by [SPG officer] (picked up by scarf) thrown in van, driven off, squatting on floor though seats vacant. Later [arresting officer] said he'd arrested for 'mouthing off' – telling divisional man to 'fuck off' after three warnings.

The second example is an arrest before a local first division 'derby' match and exemplified the use of Section 5 for refusing to comply with police pushing and shoving by running off. We begin with the police account:

> At front of 50 [home team] supporters. Ran down a road towards larger group of [opposing team] fans awaiting buses. Seen by officers shaking his fists and beckoning to fans. Calling companions on. No other PCs between groups. [Offender] arrested. Companions ran away. Caution reply: 'I didn't think I'd get arrested: we was only baiting them.'

My field notes are as follows:

> Group of [away team] fans being escorted onto buses. Group of [home team] fans, unescorted, nearby – singing, waving, provoking, etc. [SPG sergeant] spotted. He and [another SPG officer] broke into a run, booted them off (those that hadn't shot off fast enough), pushed and cuffed. One didn't 'shoo'. Arrested by [the other SPG officer]. Being cautioned as I arrived. (Wore glasses, white trousers, braces, skinhead.) Seemed quiet.

Shoved in van. Not fast enough, apparently, since hit round the head (offering no resistance).

The third example took place after the same match as the second example and illustrates police 'embellishment' of the facts. Here is the police account:

Seen after match walking towards [railway] station. Heard shouting 'have a fucking go you cunts' at group of youths just in front. [SPG officer] said: 'be quiet, where are you going?' [Offender] replied: 'to the fucking station you cunt now fuck off and leave me.' He pushed [SPG officer] aside and went to continue. From [offender's] actions breach of peace feared if he reached other group. His words heard by women shoppers and children. Arrested.

And here, by way of comparison, are my field notes:

[Away team] fans being escorted. [SPG sergeant and SPG officer] seemed to pick one out as having done something provocative. SPG sergeant smiled. Raced up steps. Seemed to be too late. Watched fans pass. Meanwhile, mention that [SPG officer] had arrested. [SPG sergeant] went over to see prisoner being loaded into van. Prisoner squatting in van, though seat available. Allowed to sit. Asked various questions including last time locked up. Asked 'what for?' Asked whether at football (yes). [SPG sergeant] in front: 'I don't know what it's all coming to, I really don't'.

The final example took place before an FA Cup semi-final between two 'big name' teams, and shows the use of Section 5 in an exemplary way. This is the police view:

Seen walking along [road] with [one set of] supporters. On opposite side of road large crowd of [opposition] fans. [Offender] seen by officer calling over to them with his hand and was shouting: 'come and have a fucking go you cunts' whilst beckoning with his arms. If he had continued, fight feared.

My field notes record:

[SPG officer] driving arrestees. Shouting between rival fans across road. [Team] fan shouted. [SPG driver] said 'that's mine'. [Another SPG officer] popped out and arrested on [driver's] behalf. [Driver] continued. Later found his [the fan's] foot to be in plaster (not known at time).

These contrasting accounts, and others like them, collectively constitute two very different ways of 'seeing' incidents. I referred earlier to the SPG's interpretation of Section 5 as 'tough'. In Chapter 6 I shall address how they come to see incidents in this particular way, how they acquire this particular 'working norm'. For the moment, it remains only for me to summarize the essential differences between these police accounts and my own (see Table 1), to remind readers that these police accounts are the concrete manifestations of the dominance of the occupational dimension in such situations, and to reiterate the

Table 1: SPG arrests at football matches

SPG accounts emphasize	My observations emphasize
Noisiness, drink	*concrete* context (few or no people around to object; fun/'symbolic' nature of chanting, etc.)
Police warning(s) reasonably delivered	Police role in precipitating aggression (where applicable)
Aggressiveness of fans	Police use of violence/'street justice'
Abusiveness of fans	Police abusiveness
Caution given	Meaningless delivery of caution/no caution given
Clear identification of persons, actions, words	Difficulty of identifying persons, actions, words
Clear motives	Ambiguity of motives
Unambiguous nature of general situation	Arbitrariness of arrest in terms of person and alleged offence
Breach of peace imminent	Breach of peace *impossible* in many situations

essential conditions for this – weak legal and democratic structures, and an organizational dimension of the work structure which cannot, as we have just seen, either through policy or supervision, effectively control it.

Indirect supervision

By monitoring the various records of police activity, management can attempt to extend its supervisory gaze indirectly, beyond that which can be directly observed *in situ*. And, as we saw was the case with direct supervision, SPG activity is highly exposed to such indirect supervisory scrutiny. Yet, once again, this high exposure fails to dislodge the dominance of the occupational dimension. What follows will illustrate this paradox and thus the essential complementarity between the two forms of supervision.

In an organization committed to the preservation of order, and the prevention and detection of crime, it is hardly surprising that records relating to offences, especially arrest records, loom large. Though not the 'be all and end all' of policework, few would strongly disagree with the SPG inspector who said 'as far as I'm concerned, a man is judged on his prisoners, to some extent'. The qualification 'to some extent', in his case, was a reference to the fact that some offences are easier to detect than others. Some, such as public order arrests – 'the sort of thing that any policeman should be able to do' – show only that a 'man' is 'functioning'; others – 'self-created work . . . where an officer brings a prisoner in and . . . can relate . . . a course of actions that he has followed by observation, which led him to a certain suspicion . . . which culminated in the arrest' – that he is 'functioning well'. Given the nature of SPG work –

predominantly public order supplemented by plain clothes crime patrol work – SPG officers have little else but offence-related activity to demonstrate that they are 'functioning' at all, never mind 'functioning well'. And this was reflected in the nature of the paperwork records used to monitor them.

The paperwork circulating through the SPG system I looked at related solely to offences of one kind of another. And the records of this activity constituted the *only* permanent records kept, namely, four master record books: one kept by the inspector in which *everything* he dealt with was entered, together with the results of action taken, including the court results of prisoners that had passed through the units' hands; a 'prisoners by surname' book, kept by the two detective constables assigned to the units, in which all prisoners handled by the units were recorded; and two 'unit prisoner' books, one kept by each unit, in which were recorded all prisoners taken, as well as details of the offence, date, charge, arresting officer(s), witnessing officer(s), court decision and sentence, and monthly totals of arrest figures classified by offence.

The consequence of this singular offence orientation, and of the resulting record-keeping, is that it was possible for supervisors to compile quickly arrest records by officer, by pair, by unit, by offence; and to compare 'involvement' ratings, by looking at how often officers make an appearance either as arresters or witnesses. In other words, it was easy to draw up comparative 'work profiles' of individuals, pairs and units; to measure, objectively, activity or 'functioning' (something I in fact did, quite easily), even if judgements about 'functioning well' required a much closer look at the sorts of arrest made by officers and inevitably involved a more subjective element.

The complete absence of other records (incident and radio logs, for example) and the lack of feedback from a wide variety of community contacts, such as resident beat officers can expect – both absences, of course, a consequence of the kind of work routinely undertaken – inevitably gave such records of work achievement a heightened salience. Moreover, as a standby force lacking specific tasks, the Group had constantly to justify its existence to the organization – a fact attested to by the unique requirement to submit a quarterly report (to which I return below), which left the Group as a whole unusually exposed to scrutiny by force management too.

Thus the direct supervisory oversight possible in public order situations where supervisory staff were routinely present, was complemented by the singularity and importance of these indirect offence-related records of work; in either case, the SPG was peculiarly exposed to supervisory scrutiny.

In addition, SPG supervisors had a great deal of freedom to check paperwork submissions and consult records. With no probationers to consider, and lacking the routine demands on subdivisional supervisors' time – dealing with serious incidents, licensing inquiries, 'missing from homes', fatal accidents, and so on – supervisory officers on the Group had more time available for supervision. On top of which, standby duties and the lack of necessity for patrol super-vision increased further the time available for supervision, as compared with subdivisional unit supervisors, a fact which was not unrecognized by supervisors:

TJ: So, from what you're saying . . . it's less immediate now and you do have more chance to sit back and perhaps train the PCs.

SPG INSPECTOR: Yes, yes . . . that is true generally . . . you get the sort of thing that we've had recently where other things start to cut across. Because you are here as an inspector somebody can use you for a particular job . . . and then you get the . . . intense end to the football season followed by the various public order situations . . . you know the general election and all that went with that, but normally, I mean now, for instance, you see, I've just had, this week has been an absolutely clear week when I am totally available to the two units of the SPG.

As might be expected, this comparative freedom was used by particular supervisors in accordance with their predilections. Some used the time to get out more, others to subject submitted paperwork to intensive oversight or to set up more informal advisory sessions about the kind of work expected and how to achieve it. But what was noticeable was the failure of such supervisory activity to connect with specific incidents – crucial if the organizational dimension is to 'take command' over the occupational *where it matters*. It is here, as the ACC (operations) recognized earlier, that problems arise; that, as he put it, the structure 'breaks down'. The 'unit of supervision' was not, however, built around the analysis of incidents, their antecedents, why particular courses of action were taken, alternative options, and so on. Take paperwork, for example. Overseeing paperwork was not used to reconstruct incidents for the purpose of subsequent analysis with the officers or unit concerned. Rather, it was concerned with promoting a standard of presentation which was designed to ensure that evidence was presented in the clearest, most consistent and uncontradictory fashion for the court – to ensure that written statements did not contradict the officer's statement; that caution replies in officers' statements corresponded where more than one officer was involved, and so on. Not that such oversight is unimportant. But it is simply not enough.

Here, then, we can see the essential complementarity between the two forms of supervision. In both cases, despite the high visibility of the work, and manifold opportunities to exercise supervisory powers, specific incidents remain a neglected 'blind spot', and hence, effectively unsupervised. We can make the same point another way by looking at the relationship between force management and the Group as a whole, for the same problem arises. Despite the visibility of the Group's activities through the medium of the quarterly report, critical reflection upon specific incidents was missing.

Quarterly reports, submitted by the chief inspector in charge of the Group, covered the activities of the Group during the preceding quarter. A breakdown of arrests – into crime and public order – was given, other events taking up time, the role of the detective officers, new developments, requests for assistance, the quality of personnel, any special events that had happened, relations with divisions, the unique opportunities SPG work provided for officers, establishment, and various miscellaneous items. The reports would then be submitted to the chief superintendent responsible, then to the relevant ACC and finally the

Chief Constable, all of whom would append their comments. The notion of activity loomed large – 'extremely busy in terms of requests and arrests'; 'demands heavy'; 'fully committed', and so on. So also did arrest behaviour, particularly good-quality arrests – 'notable arrests after observations with the division in the city centre'; 'some successes in detection of recorded crime by plain clothes observations in high theft areas'; commendations for two PCs for an off-duty arrest and for nine PCs for prompt action in connection with [a political group] attempting arson; 'good observations'; 'alert action'. The reports bristle with 'keenness' and 'enthusiasm' – 'duties accepted without complaint', detective officers 'continue to give excellent service', their 'keenness, enthusiasm and efficiency' is 'a credit to the group', their 'devotion to duty a model of what true police officers can achieve'; 'fortunate to have so many experienced and willing PCs promoted to police sergeant'; officers conducted themselves in a 'thoroughly professional manner' (a reference to the policing of a National Front meeting); searching coaches (prior to another political meeting) was done in a 'convivial, friendly, good-natured' way, which 'contributed to keeping a potentially dangerous situation at an acceptable level'. Relations with divisions were uniformly good – the Group was now 'well accepted' throughout the force; written thanks were recorded from a divisional chief superintendent for help with a murder inquiry. The 'variety' of the work made it 'an excellent training ground for PCs and prospective future supervisors'. Training emphasized 'calmness, restraint and firmness'. Only one comment recognized another reality, when the chief inspector expressed a hope that the nicknames 'rent-a-mob' and 'dial-a-disturbance' had gone for ever. In the light of such activity, enthusiasm and the general air of success, the receiving officers' comments could hardly be otherwise – 'once again an excellent report' showing the 'positive industry of the group'; 'no doubting the value and enthusiasm of the Group'.

Perhaps it is in the nature of such reports to put the best foot forward and emphasize the positive. Who does attempt to justify their existence in negatives? All the same, if one looked a little closer at all those arrests and activity, there was at least room for a certain questioning of their value. I did just that when I looked at two units' total arrests for a 12-month period. What this revealed painted a slightly different picture. Certainly I agreed with the quarterly reports about the centrality of public order arrests. These were 'the bulk' of the arrests – at least 61 per cent of them. However, I also discovered that these produced a high number of 'not guilty' pleas – 68 per cent of (the known) pleas. (Even if *all* the unknown pleas were guilty pleas, the figure for 'not guilty' pleas was still a relatively high 21 per cent.) In the light of what was said earlier about the SPG's 'tough' interpretation of Section 5, this should not surprise *us*; but it ought perhaps to cause *supervisors* at least to take notice. Moreover, a breakdown of these public order arrests revealed the high number of arrests for being 'drunk and disorderly' and 'drunk and incapable' – 22 per cent of the *total arrests*. Once again, it seems at least noteworthy that one-fifth of all arresting activity concerned such relatively trivial offences.

Crime arrests were relatively insignificant as a proportion. Depending upon how 'crime' is defined, it could have been as low as 17 per cent if 'theft and burglary' is the yardstick. In the proactive crime areas, 47 per cent of illegal gambling and drug offences led to 'no further action', an indication, perhaps, of the 'arm-chancing' nature of such arrests. Also, the most 'active' individuals, judged by overall arrest rates, were prominent in proactive arrests – a finding which also lends support to the notion of arm-chancing. One of these, for example, was involved in all five gross indecency arrests. A third of all assaults were 'assault PC', mostly in public order situations, a figure which should at least cause some reflection about the nature of the police approach in such situations.

Looked at in this light, in a way which attempts, through the raw figures, to shed at least some light on the possible circumstances of arrests (specific incidents), 'arrests', 'activity' and 'enthusiasm' take on a rather different meaning. But, as with indirect supervision generally, the reports are blind to the circumstances surrounding arrests. Consequently, they are not able to address, let alone dislodge, the dominance of the occupational dimension.

SUMMARY AND CONCLUSION

In showing concretely how the occupational dimension is 'in command' over the organizational dimension in public order situations, that is, in situations where the work structure relative to both the legal and the democratic structures is strong, I have focused upon the two key instruments of managerial control – policy and supervision. I did this by first distinguishing between the various instruments of managerial control and then by offering a series of definitions – of policy, policy-making and policy consideration. Next I examined a range of actual examples – policy on charging, a particular policy file, the use of dogs in crowd control – which jointly illustrated the relative infrequency of policy-making, and the absence or 'permissiveness' of policy in operational contexts. This effective absence of operational policy in turn explained the paradox of SPG supervision: why, despite the work being highly supervised, both directly and indirectly, and highly visible, occupational 'common sense' nevertheless dominates. This was illustrated by looking at two different sorts of fieldwork evidence, one relevant to direct, the other to indirect, supervision, demonstrating the failure of management to 'take command': first, some public order arrests; and, finally the organization's failure to use the extensive paperwork records to monitor the handling of specific incidents, despite ample time to do so.

This routine inability of management, or the organizational dimension, decisively to affect operational matters stems, it should be recalled, not from a lack of will or poor communications, but from the unique relationship between police managers and officers under their command, where all are also 'independent' officers of the Crown. It is *this* which 'allows' the occupational dimension, not occasionally but *regularly*, to be dominant at the critical 'operational' moments in the policing of public disorder. Though the fieldwork examples in this chapter are drawn in the main from the policing of football matches, the similar problem posed by this routine occupational dominance, and the dire results this can lead to in the policing of more exceptional public order events, form the subject matter of the next chapter.

NOTES

1. A much fuller consideration of these issues can be found in Grimshaw and Jefferson, 1987, Part IV.
2. Ibid., p. 198.
3. Ibid., p. 203.
4. Ibid., p. 204.
5. Ibid.
6. Ibid.
7. Ibid., p. 207.
8. Ibid.
9. Ibid.
10. Ibid.
11. Ibid., p. 245.
12. Ibid., p. 246.
13. Ibid.
14. For full details about the methodology adopted in choosing and analysing the files, see ibid., pp. 245–8.
15. 'Administrative' also covers establishment, supply, finance and conditions, inspection, organization and systems, recruitment, and promotion. The final 'other' category covers 'extra-police' and unclassified items; in this case, the single item which was neither 'operational' nor 'administrative' was a police committee discussion about some publicity given to proposals that private organizations of citizens be set up to assist the police, an idea which they resolved to oppose. For the full classification schema upon which this analysis draws, see ibid., p. 211.
16. File notes.
17. For a more comprehensive and detailed look at the appearance of external bodies across a range of policy files, see Grimshaw and Jefferson, 1987, pp. 248–52.
18. A more analytically rigorous account of the method adopted for analysing policy data is to be found in ibid., pp. 207–8.
19. File notes.
20. Ibid.
21. Ibid.
22. Ibid.
23. Ibid.
24. Ibid.
25. Ibid.

CHAPTER 5

Effectiveness or amplification? The work structure in action

INTRODUCTION

If the first two prongs of the idealistic argument about the superiority of paramilitarism stress its 'restraint' and 'impartiality', the third and final prong stresses its 'enhanced effectiveness' when compared with 'the traditional approach'. And just as Chapter 2 trained a spotlight on the 'real world of restraint' and Chapters 3 and 4 on the 'real world of impartiality', the spotlight in this chapter will focus on the 'real world of effectiveness'. This concrete focus, as we shall see, far from producing agreement with the idealistic claim about the effectiveness of paramilitarism, leads to the opposite conclusion that paramilitary policing has an inherent tendency to exacerbate or amplify problems of violence and disorder (which is not to suggest that amplification is an inevitable feature of such policing, merely that there is a constant tendency towards it).

My route to this conclusion encompasses four stages. First, I highlight the idealism behind the notion of 'effectiveness'. Second, I establish a typical 'sequential account of the paramilitary policing of public order'[1] based on a concrete view of the routine dynamics involved and their amplificatory tendencies. Third, I illustrate how this amplificatory sequence was operative in three different, contemporary public disorders: one social, at Broadwater Farm on 6 October 1985; one political, Leon Brittan's visit to Manchester University on 1 March 1985; and one industrial, at Orgreave on 18 June 1984. Finally, I demonstrate, using evidence from the United States and Australia, that this phenomenon is not peculiar to the United Kingdom.

EFFECTIVENESS AND PROFESSIONALISM:
THE IDEAL VERSUS THE REAL

The argument about the greater effectiveness of paramilitarism rests on a positive endorsement of its defining features, that is, military organization, supervision and discipline, specialist training, protective clothing and equipment, and the availability of suitable weaponry – the very features I find profoundly problematical. The enthusiasm is a function of the idealism. For, in considering actual policing operations, the term 'paramilitary' is restricted to describing only those (ideal) occasions which exhibit apparently trouble-free policing. Thus, Waddington, for example, can claim, on the one hand, that the 'raids by the Metropolitan Police on the Afro-Caribbean Club in Brixton and "Bentley's" public house in the East End during the summer of 1986' were 'carried out with paramilitary planning and precision',[2] but, on the other hand, that 'the aggressive policing of demonstrations at Oxford and Manchester Universities . . . and the violent confrontation between police and the "Peace Convoy" . . . did not display the use of distinctively paramilitary tactics, still less paramilitary discipline'.[3] Using this tautologous logic, paramilitary policing cannot be other than 'effective'; for, when it fails to live up to the ideals of planning, precision and discipline Waddington demands of it, he simply denies it the label 'paramilitary'. Such purity may make for a certain theoretical neatness; but it hardly does justice to the very messy and impure reality it purports to explain.

This idealism has its origins in an idealistic conception of professionalism – the notion of the disinterested search for optimal solutions to problems posed by their work allegedly characteristic of certain occupational groups. From this perspective occupational groups achieve 'professional' status – meaning, effectively, a high degree of occupational autonomy – to the extent that they apply their specialist expertise in the service of ever more efficient problem-solving. In so far as police have acquired 'professional' status they can be similarly entrusted; and, to the extent that they successfully live up to such trust, their professional status is enhanced commensurately. It is a cosy, beguiling notion, very much in line with the police's own image of themselves as impartial law enforcers operating (disinterestedly) 'above politics'. But it is certainly out of line with most recent work in either the sociology of professionalism or the sociology of policework.[4]

Its lack of concreteness is a function basically of its failure to consider how the actual conditions of policework do affect police behaviour (rather than how ideally they ought to): how, in the case of public order policing (as we saw in Chapters 3 and 4), discretionary law and a 'weak' democratic structure place occupational norms and values (or subcultural 'common sense') at the decision-making helm; and how, in consequence, we get *routinely* the sort of 'unprofessional' arrests I detailed in Chapter 4, rather than the (professional) ideal of 'impartial law enforcement'. A similarly profane look at paramilitarism, one attentive to the actual (not the ideal) conditions of such policing, cannot help but reach the ironic conclusion that this most 'professional' of solutions to the problem of disorder has an inherent tendency to make matters worse. How this comes about forms the subject matter of the next section.

THE ACTUAL WORLD OF PARAMILITARISM: A TYPICAL SEQUENCE

The following typical sequence has been distilled from a consideration of the paramilitary policing of a number of actual events. Though not a description of any one particular occasion, its general features apply to them all, as the various examples considered in the next section attempt to demonstrate. Broadly, there seem to be four stages in the paramilitary policing of a public order event – 'preparation', 'controlling space', 'controlling the crowd' and 'clearance'. I intend to look briefly at the characteristics of each in turn.

Preparation

The essence of a paramilitary capacity, as we saw in Chapter 1, is a group of officers (centrally directed or otherwise) with specialist training and equipment readily available to deal with disorder; in other words, a group of public order specialists. As such, they must always be potentially available, on standby and in sufficient numbers for when trouble is expected. Their special training, like their special equipment, ensures that they are well prepared for all eventualities. And though they may hope for the best, they must be ready psychologically for the worst.

'Standby', as the name suggests, is waiting time. It may be undertaken in various ways. But, when the object is to play down the number of officers on duty so as not to relay the idea that trouble is expected, this can mean being cooped up in vans or buses or police canteens. Like all periods spent waiting for possibly unpleasant events, it can be stressful and, if prolonged, frustrating – especially for 'action-orientated' police officers. It is also an occasion for swapping tales about 'the enemy' in order to pass the time, boost morale, or provide justifications for past (or future) actions. Even before the event is properly under way, then, the physical and psychological preparation for the 'worst case' scenario contains the germ of a self-fulfilling prophecy, especially if unprotected demonstrators can see the protected vans, the large numbers and the riot control equipment. To them, 'preparation' can look suspiciously like 'provocation'.

Controlling space

As the event gets under way, ensuring control of space – that which the crowd may use and that which it may not – is the next objective. This entails the police demarcating areas reserved for themselves and separating these from the spaces allowed to the 'general public'. However this is done, since it inevitably involves moving people from (police-defined) proscribed areas, it is almost certain to be resented by some members of the crowd, especially if the manner of clearance is with paramilitary shield and truncheon rather than more traditional forms of persuasion. Consequently, a response (verbal or physical) from some of the crowd is highly likely. Once this happens, police will have their initial expectations of trouble confirmed, the paramilitary response will be justified, and, to ensure the situation does not worsen, perhaps a little 'nipping in the bud' activity may be in order. This will serve to confirm the crowd's expectations about police violence, and resentment may become more widespread, especially if the pre-emptive deterrence has been of the paramilitary kind. Once the rumours start to circulate among the crowd, amplification becomes even more likely.

Controlling the crowd

Once space has been successfully marked out and controlled, the crowd must then also be controlled, forcibly if necessary. Crowd anger will almost certainly follow such containment, a situation which will serve only to confirm further police expectations and justify police use of violence. In this situation, with tempers becoming frayed and frustrations mounting, the paramilitary nature of the response – horses, dogs, riot shields, and so on – only serves to make matters worse, by seeming to invite the stone-thrower. This will probably lead to the release of the snatch squads, at which point the potential for amplification increases dramatically. This is so both because the manifest injustice of heavily protected officers with truncheons drawn chasing defenceless members of the public fuels crowd anger, and because, for reasons I outlined in Chapters 3 and 4, almost *any* police actions, however apparently outrageous to public onlookers, will be sanctioned where it matters, namely, legally, organizationally and occupationally.

> That is the *profane* meaning of Waddington's 'disciplined' response: a snatch squad unloosed on the crowd has the multiple protections of almost infinitely permissive public order law, a conception of supportive team work and an occupational culture which requires that the most aggressive and bull-headed individuals be supported in the field and defended in the aftermath, and an ideology of the demonstrator as violent sub-human undeserving of either respect or sympathy.[5]

Once this stage has been reached people are being hurt and becoming even more angry. From then on violence can increase or be contained by a massive and highly oppressive police presence.

Clearance

After the demonstration, the only concern of police is to get things over quickly. But crowds who are both hurt and angry will probably wish to salvage something. This may take the form of dumb (or not so dumb) insolence or reluctance to leave. Aggressive dispersal in this context exacerbates the situation, especially, once again, if conducted paramilitary-style. Confrontations occur with increasing bitterness. As both sides hear about injuries sustained and indignities suffered by friends and colleagues, the bitterness of confrontations increases. Police remain multiply 'protected' in the ways mentioned in the previous stage. Sooner or later the police 'succeed'. The confrontation is over, but next time both sides will come better protected and prepared. For the police this means yet more riot-control equipment, for example. And the amplification spiral goes up another notch. If all this sounds somewhat abstract, let us test it using some actual examples.

ILLUSTRATING THE SEQUENCE

In the following three accounts, I shall start with a brief sketch of the event in question and then offer a more detailed account of each, highlighting both the stages and the exacerbating role of paramilitarism.

Broadwater Farm, 6 October 1985

In the early evening of Saturday 5 October a black woman, Mrs Cynthia Jarrett, died after a push by a police officer caused her to fall during a police search of her house. The following evening, after 24 hours of meetings and impromptu demonstrations of protest, black youths attempting to leave the Broadwater Farm estate clashed with police, who then quickly sealed it off. Several hours of violence followed, mostly the throwing of missiles, including many petrol bombs, at the static lines of police officers waiting behind their riot shields. At one stage guns were used and several officers and two cameramen sustained gunshot wounds. Brief sorties by snatch squads occasionally attempted to force the crowds to retreat and make arrests, but largely without success. Inside the estate, many cars and several shops and buildings were burned, and some looting took place. Around 10.15 p.m. one of a group of police officers protecting fire officers allowed to enter to deal with burning shops was stabbed to death. Not long afterwards the fighting stopped, though police remained at the various entrances to the estate for many hours and forcefully dispersed any remaining crowds. Around 4.30 a.m., large numbers of police aggressively entered and occupied a by now quiet estate. Altogether the night's disorder produced one police death and around 240 injured, most of them police.[6]

86

Preparation

There is a lot of evidence that the police were well prepared for a major disorder on the Broadwater Farm estate well before the death of Mrs Jarrett on 5 October. Such preparedness was partly a response to the persistent rumours of imminent riots after the September disturbances in Handsworth and then, after the shooting of Mrs Cherry Groce, in Brixton. It was also partly a result of worsening police–community relations on the estate, following a summer of inaction against newly arrived drug traffickers, and an inept and alienating one-day stop and search operation on 1 October conducted, apparently, with little specific purpose and no consultation.

Against this background of mounting tension and rumour the provocative circumstances of the death of Cynthia Jarrett, and the community anger it unleashed, added further reason for 'expecting the worst' – as the build-up of police resources prior to the first clashes confirms. The search which resulted in Mrs Jarrett's death was conducted with 'a district support unit and an area car . . . provided to stand by in case there should be any trouble'.[7] But after the death of Mrs Jarrett and its predictable impact on the black community, 'the reserve manpower for the area was increased for Sunday to 200 officers in each of two eight hour shifts, made up of some coach serials and some district support units in transits'.[8]

Interestingly, in the light of my argument and of subsequent events, these reserve units were not called upon to deal with the afternoon demonstration of 'over a hundred people' outside Tottenham police station.[9] Instead:

> The police response was restrained and sensible. They blocked off the High Road in both directions to give room for the demonstration. They policed the demonstration with a thin line of officers in ordinary uniform with special units well out of sight. They stood while the crowd shouted angrily and made intimidating gestures, without reacting or making arrests.[10]

And, according to Nick Wright of the police research unit, it worked: 'They didn't arrest anybody, they didn't get angry, they just stood their ground and argued the point and it gradually went down.'[11] Unfortunately this traditional response led by Chief Superintendent Couch – 'perhaps the most sophisticated politician amongst the police locally', again according to Nick Wright[12] – was to prove short-lived. Meanwhile, among the paramilitary reserves on standby 'the atmosphere must have been charged with anticipation of trouble'.[13] Specific events – including two attacks on police officers by black youths and a report of large numbers of youths, some masked, 'running through the estate banging on doors'[14] – no doubt heightened this sense; as no doubt did the subsequent order, around 6.30 p.m., 'that only protected district support unit vehicles should answer calls to the Broadwater Farm Estate'.[15]

The first clashes occurred when youths coming away from a very emotional and angry meeting of the Youth Association, having resolved to renew the demonstration outside Tottenham police station, met up with a transit van full of riot-clad officers. Predictably, this example of police preparedness for all eventualities was perceived as an intrusive provocation by the youths, who proceeded to bang on the van with their hands, forced it to reverse and then gave chase. During this, two more vans appeared in support and were also forced to reverse back. By the time the youths reached the edge of the estate, police in riot gear were out of the vans blocking the exit, and aggressively and abusively forcing people back onto the estate, hitting out with truncheons. The youths' angry reaction to the provocative paramilitary police presence had effectively ended the preparatory stage. The disorders had begun. The new police imperative became that of 'controlling space'.

Controlling space

The immediate response of the police to the youths' angry banging on the side of the transit van was to reverse and seal off the estate exit. It is also clear that the youths' actions also provided the justification for sealing off the estate generally – within minutes riot police were observed arriving at two of the three other exit roads and blocking them off, even though they were disturbance-free at that time. In other words, the initial clashes provided the necessary legitimation for police control of space to be imposed.

As the initial provocation of the transit van entry onto the estate shaded into the broader provocation of besieging the estate, angry resentment, in line with the paramilitary logic now thoroughly inscribed on the situation, grew and spread, becoming violent. Youths at the first exit turned over cars and set them alight, threw missiles, and knocked down and dismantled a wall for use as ammunition to throw at police lines. And similar responses were subsequently observed at all the other exits with a strong paramilitary presence. Exceptionally, the Gloucester Road exit 'remained quiet for the greater part of the evening [with] . . . never the same pattern of missiles being thrown at lines of police officers',[16] though burning vans were observed there around the time the police siege commenced. I shall return below to the question of the relationship between this response and the rather different style of policing witnessed here.

Apparently, the initial actions of the youths had confirmed the police's worst fears about 'trouble' and so, once again in accordance with paramilitary logic, pre-emptive police action to prevent the situation worsening – advancing onto the estate down at least one of the exit roads[17] – followed. This, in turn, apparently served only to confirm the crowd's expectations of police violence, since the 'pre-emptive' police entry onto the estate was resisted and violently beaten back. And so the amplifying spiral unwound further. At this point, with exits successfully blocked off and the space thus under control, the question of crowd containment and control became central.

Controlling the crowd

The extreme anger of the crowd – a product of the multiple provocations of the preceding 24 hours: the death of a black woman; the apparently vacillating police response; the paramilitary presence on their estate; and then the siege –

finally boiled over during this stage, resulting in several hours of violent hostility directed towards the waiting lines of police. The primary police tactic appeared to be containment – probably waiting for crowd anger to subside a little – behind lines of perspex shields. These became, predictably, an invitation to the missile-thrower, or, as *Police Review* put it, 'Aunt Sallys of the petrol bombers'.[18] But containment was not the only tactic. In line with (paramilitary) expectations, the snatch squads were periodically unleashed, even if only 'half-heartedly' and with little success, given the confined and unfavourable nature of the terrain.[19] However half-hearted, though, such sorties could still aggravate the situation, as the attempt by members of the West Indian Leadership Council to stop a van moving into the crowd for this reason clearly showed.[20] A further source of aggravation, undoubtedly, was the 'aggression, and abuse directed at black people' (one example of the ideology of the violent, sub-human demonstrator manifesting itself) evident in situations (such as the Willan Road exit) 'where the police had more of the upper hand'[21] – the more so since apparently unchecked by police leadership. And black anger was no doubt matched by mounting police anger – as the 'constant volleys of dangerous missiles' rained down on them 'for many hours'.[22]

Yet not everywhere was quite like this. At the Gloucester Road exit, the 'exception' mentioned earlier, the 'situation was far more calm and controlled'.[23] In other words, there was no disorder. Why? Because the man in charge was Chief Superintendent Couch, who had successfully contained the afternoon demonstration, and his chosen style of policing, once again, was largely traditional:

> In contrast to the other entrances many people were able to get in and out through Gloucester Road without being stopped or harassed. Many of the officers there were not in riot gear.[24]

In other words, the response was not paramilitary.

It was, of course, during this stage that the most violent event of the evening – the killing of PC Blakelock – occurred, while he was operating as part of a group protecting fire officers. In some respects this seemed to signal the beginning of the end of the fighting; for shortly after news of his death was communicated to the youths on the estate, the violence subsided. With the crowd at that point effectively 'under control', only 'clearance' remained. No doubt news of police injuries and the tragic death of PC Blakelock was circulating rapidly prior to this phase.

Clearance

Once the fighting subsided, 'the ranks of police remained for several hours at the entrances to the estate'.[25] Meanwhile, off the estate, 'severe attacks on the police line in Mount Pleasant Road from Wimbourne Road' took place 'for over an hour', though only 'a minority [were] doing the brunt of the attacking', 'the majority [being simply] . . . involved in verbal abuse'.[26] Here, the still angry crowd, reluctant to leave, met a similarly angry police force intent on dispersal, with predictable results – 'fairly violent' clearance.[27]

With the streets cleared and the estate quiet, that would normally have been the end of the affair. But, perhaps because of the severity of the disorder, or because of the killing of PC Blakelock, or because a point needed to be made about 'who's really in charge around here', a decision was made to enter and occupy the estate, in the dead of night: 'at 4.30 a.m. a massive number of police in riot gear entered the estate'.[28] At this stage, with no crowds to disperse, the heat of anger seems to have been replaced by the coldness of retribution. Eyewitnesses, who observed the fate of isolated youths unfortunate enough to be caught by police, described several such vengeful actions. For example: 'They kicked and punched and threw him on the floor and stamped on him, kneed him. Then they hung his head over the balcony.'[29]

The bitterness of the evening's violence is clearly expressed in such vengeful actions, as are the multiple police protections – legal, organizational and occupational – which 'allow' the venting of such anger with little fear of reprisal, even in front of supervisors or 'the public'. (The witnesses to these actions included several community leaders and at least one high-ranking community liaison officer, Superintendent Stacey, all of whom obviously had no constraining influence on police actions at that time.)[30] Meanwhile, back at headquarters, the lesson to be learned from the disaster was the need for *more* and *tougher* paramilitarism, as expressed in Commissioner Newman's angry warning to Londoners the next day that he would 'not shrink' from the decision to use CS gas and plastic bullets (held on standby on this occasion) in the event of future similar disorders.[31] The logic of paramilitarism thus finds its tragic denouement: tough paramilitary policing produces bitter hostility between the police and the community, and the threat of an even tougher and more paramilitarized response 'next time'.

Manchester, 1 March 1985

Once it was known that the then Home Secretary, Leon Brittan, had been invited to speak at their union, a group of Manchester University students met and decided to demonstrate by picketing the union. On the evening of 1 March, several hundred demonstrators assembled on the steps of the union and the pavements around it. Shortly before the Home Secretary was due to arrive, a column of police officers appeared and, without warning, moved into the densely packed crowd on the steps and aggressively cleared a large area. The crowd was then contained behind police lines on either side of the steps and the surrounding pavement area during the whole time of the Home Secretary's arrival, speech, and subsequent departure. Angry shouting and swearing, scuffles, and numerous fairly forceful arrests took place in this period, with plain-clothes officers in the crowd sometimes coming to the assistance of uniformed colleagues. After the Home Secretary's departure, the steps and surrounding area were unceremoniously cleared, with several students being pushed or dragged down the steps, one of whom was knocked unconscious as a result. The whole operation, which lasted some two-and-a-half hours from start to finish, left some 40 demonstrators injured and produced a similar number of arrests.[32]

Preparation

A number of pieces of evidence all point towards the police being well prepared for any possible trouble that night. First, the security for the visit the year before of another government minister, Michael Heseltine, had been inadequate to prevent paint being thrown over him. A repeat performance would obviously have been extremely embarrassing. Second, the Home Secretary's explanatory letter to the Manchester MP, Alf Morris, shows that he never had any intention of acceding to student requests that he make a conciliatory back door entry to avoid any trouble (which he found 'in principle quite unacceptable'),[33] and that police planning incorporated this potentially confrontational decision:

> It was also agreed that in the event of trouble, officers from the Tactical Aid Group [TAG] would provide me with an escort into the building, assisted by the Divisional Police Support Unit.[34]

And third, the police briefing plan itself, available thanks to the percipience of a freelance photographer accidentally noticing it on a blackboard through an open police station window and deciding to photograph it, makes it clear that six TAG units (probably the whole group, in other words) were to be on hand, as were vans for 'prisoners'.[35] We know also, from an eyewitness, that a dog van was also in the vicinity.[36]

Between 6.30 and 7.10 p.m., some 400–500 people gradually gathered on the steps and pavements nearby. Political banners were displayed and there was much chanting. The police and the media came in for some abuse. But the few police officers in attendance apparently accepted such behaviour as part of the normal rituals of political demonstrations, and ignored it. In short, at that time, 'as one eyewitness put it, the demonstration was "noisy but passive"; it was also good-humoured'.[37] Probably contributing to this basically good-natured atmosphere was the lack of an obvious paramilitary presence, since, at that time TAG units, and any other PSUs on standby, were unobtrusively parked in surrounding side-streets. But the impending arrival of the Home Secretary meant that a space was needed for his determined front-door entry; and, at this moment in time, the demonstrators clearly controlled the required space, namely, the front steps.

Controlling space

Around 7.10 p.m. the demonstrators began to notice a group of policemen led by a single officer, marching in pairs . . . to the Union building. Once the column of what appears to have been between 20 and 40 officers reached the steps, it moved into the crowd. The manner of entry was forceful.[38]

It also took place without warning. The aim, as the demonstrators quickly discovered, was to drive a human wedge through the crowd in order to clear a space for the Home Secretary's entrance. However, the absence of any exit route for those at the back and the sides (hemmed in as they were by the closed union doors and the side railings, respectively), meant that for them the only alternative to being crushed was to push back. This act of resistance was also fuelled no doubt by 'anger at the conduct of some of the officers'.[39] This in turn led to the police reinforcing the wedge and engaging in their task 'even more vigorously'.[40] At this point 'self protection and escape' seemed to be uppermost in demonstrators' thoughts.[41] Uppermost in police minds, judging by the way they conducted themselves, was the speedy clearance of the central steps 'by any means necessary':

> during the several minutes it took to complete the operation . . . some officers literally pushed, pulled, kicked and punched their way to the top, throwing the tightly packed demonstrators, who had no means or chance to escape, down the flight of steps or over the side railings.[42]

Indeed, so forcefully was this executed that one set of metal side railings snapped, causing about ten demonstrators to fall about six feet or so onto some bikes on the pavement below. The flavour of this clearance exercise is well caught in the following testimony of one individual, just one of 65 people in all who claimed to have witnessed or suffered similar police violence:

> C claimed to have been pushed against the doors at the top, grabbed by the back of the head, pushed down, poked in the eye, punched several times in the stomach, picked up, thrown down the steps where he landed on top of four to five students. Two to three more demonstrators landed on top of him.[43]

Not surprisingly, such police aggressiveness, together with the verbal abuse (like 'nigger', 'fucking whore', 'stupid bitch', and so on)[44] that often accompanied it, 'provoked retaliation from the demonstrators'.[45] Within ten minutes the police objective – wresting control of the space of the central steps from the students – had been secured 'as the original wedge, reinforced by other PSUs, pushed out sideways'.[46] Demonstrators were now tightly and unhappily contained behind the police lines, either 'to the left and to the right of the central steps . . . or on the pavement to the north and south of the Union building'.[47]

In this example, the paramilitary units were kept out of sight until the moment the police decided to 'take' the steps. When they appeared, their first act – the ramming of the crowd without warning or compassion – was provocative. This provocation clearly transformed the whole nature of the demonstration as the formerly good-natured crowd became incensed by the carelessly brutal police conduct. Though shields and truncheons were not in evidence, the paramilitary style clearly was. And, true to paramilitary form, the resistance of the crowd apparently confirmed (or at least could be used to justify) police expectations of trouble and their ideological notions of the demonstrators as violent subhumans ('niggers', 'whores', 'bitches') – an exercise in delegitimization which reinforces where the power lies. This resulted in the use of reinforcements and even greater 'vigour'. Both sides having had their worst fears of the other confirmed, subsequent actions from either side could only continue to have further amplifying effects.

Controlling the crowd

The period of controlling the crowd lasted for an hour: 20 minutes before the Home Secretary's arrival and a further 40 minutes thereafter. During this phase, the anger of demonstrators at their violent ejection from the steps and their subsequent tight containment behind police cordons was met by further forceful 'no-nonsense' policing. The result, in the 'pre-arrival' period, according to one witness, was 'numerous scuffles taking place in an air of mounting hostility'[48] and about ten arrests. One of these arrests usefully captures the flavour of this period:

> E was behind one of the cordons established after the step clearance. The police officer in front of him jammed his elboe [sic] in E's face. E removed the elbow and said, 'I don't want your elbow in my face, thank you.' It is not clear whether these words were delivered in a sarcastic manner. Anyhow, they proved too much for the officer who 'got hold of me around the neck and forced my head down and marched me down Oxford Road.'[49]

When the Home Secretary arrived he was rushed up the steps under police escort. A small missile was thrown at him, someone tried to hit him, and 'sporadic fighting and constant shouting and swearing'[50] accompanied the resulting surge from the crowd. This in turn led to 'at least nine arrests'[51] and yet more examples of police violence. What worsened matters for demonstrators was the presence of plain-clothes officers in the crowd making or assisting arrests. The departure of the Home Secretary at around 8.20 p.m. marked the end, as far as the police were concerned, of the demonstration, leaving only the need to disperse the crowd. By this time the crowd, which had been treated with intimidatory roughness and considerable contempt from the moment of the wedge entry onwards, and kept under the tightest control, can have felt only hurt, anger and resentment at the oppressive style of policing. And it was in no mood for the insensitive clearance that followed.

Clearance

The manner of dispersal was all of a piece with the evening's policing – rough, reckless and unwilling to brook any signs of disobedience or tokens of resistance. Once the Home Secretary had left, police impatience to clear an already thinning crowd manifested itself immediately. Those emerging from the meeting onto the steps were aggressively removed from the steps, forbidden to re-enter, and hurriedly moved off down the road. Any protest, questioning or failure to comply with instructions was liable to be dealt with by arrest[52]

which was the fate of at least six people. The following testimony illustrates all the accumulated issues of this stage: a spontaneous outburst from a hurt and angry demonstrator; the shortness of the police fuse; and the readiness to resort to violence and arrest.

> I had been pushed with a large body of students through the doors on the left-hand side of the ground floor . . . I then went out to the Union doorstep from where I saw police officers patrolling the Union steps and beginning to single people out for arrest. Very distressed at what was happening, I shouted towards the officers, 'it's all over, just go, leave the building, don't ever come back'. Immediately, a policeman grabbed me round the neck and began to drag me down the steps. I was grabbed by some friends. The two sides tugged me and I fell on the ground. My friends implored officers that I had done nothing. By then three officers had grabbed me by the hair. As they tugged me down the steps they banged my head against them. Then I was tugged to my feet, held leaning forward, and punched twice in the face until my face bled from the nose. I was then thrown into a police van and was soon joined by others.[53]

Any who complained of such treatment could suffer a similar fate, as happened to Sarah Hollis, who witnessed the above and pleaded with the officers to stop. The result: 'she was then grabbed by the hair, had her head violently and painfully jerked backwards, before being thrown down the steps',[54] where she struck her head, lost consciousness, was taken to hospital and ended up 'in a neck collar for three and a half months'.[55] Nineteen people in all mentioned witnessing acts of violence during this stage.

Though by 9 p.m. the demonstration was over and the streets cleared successfully, for the 102 eyewitnesses, 'practically all of [whom] . . . claimed that the policing was aggressive or witnessed police-initiated violence',[56] for the 48 of these who 'claimed they were assaulted in some way by a police officer or officers', for the 'approximately 40 people [who] were injured',[57] four seriously enough to require hospital treatment, and for the 40 people arrested, the nature of that 'success' must have looked rather different, as must the concrete reality of paramilitary 'effectiveness' in action.

Orgreave, 18 June 1984

One hundred days into one of the bitterest strikes in living memory, several thousand miners gathered at the strategically significant coking plant at Orgreave in another mass protest at the continuing production and distribution of coke. And, as on previous similar occasions, the police were there to ensure free passage for the plant's lifeline – the convoys of lorries fetching and carrying the coal and coke. As the pickets arrived in the early morning they were directed into one of several fields near the plant and greeted by massed ranks of police, with riot shields, dog handlers and mounted police all prominent. All was quiet until after the first ritual push on police lines in response to the arrival of the first lorry. Then the mounted police made one of several charges into the crowd, to the sound of riot shields being beaten by truncheons. Later these charges by the mounted police were accompanied by short-shield officers with truncheons drawn bringing up the rear and hitting out at any pickets who got in their way. Many miners left after these early morning clashes.

Following a mid-morning lull in the proceedings, an altercation between some miners and the police lines, which included some stone-throwing, led to further mounted-led charges on the thousand or so miners still remaining. This time arrests, and the advance of the long-shield officers, accompanied the truncheonings. With each advance and subsequent regrouping of the mounted and short-shield officers, the dispersed miners would drift back towards police lines, and recommence stoning them. But successive advances of the police line had effectively cleared protestors from the plant area so that when, around noon, some remaining miners built and lit a barricade of wrecked cars, the event was effectively over.

Altogether the morning saw the arrest of almost 100 people and many injuries, undoubtedly more than the 79 (51 of them pickets) reported in one national newspaper.[58] Those arrested were all charged with riot and unlawful assembly, but were all acquitted when the prosecution abandoned its case on the 48th day of the trial, though not before the existence of the secret ACPO public order training manual detailing various aggressive 'tactical options' had been made public.[59]

Preparation

To say that the police were well prepared for any eventuality at Orgreave is to state the obvious, for Orgreave has become probably the supreme example to date of the paramilitary approach in action. The reasons for this have partly to do with the general context, that is, a highly contentious industrial dispute for which the police had been given a high-profile strategic responsibility, and in the course of which enough provocations and violence had already taken place to make 'trouble' a routine, mutual expectation (even if in reality, 'most of the picketing . . . was peaceably conducted and as peaceably policed'),[60] and hostility a mutual fact of picketing life. They also have partly to do with the particular context, namely a series of mass-protest demonstrations at Orgreave during the immediately preceding weeks which were intended to highlight British Steel's intention to use Orgreave coke and the lack of steelworkers' support. These had produced a series of violent clashes with police and, at the biggest of these on 29 May, had exposed a certain weakness in police organizational readiness.

Against this backcloth, and given a paramilitary logic at work, the presence of 'nearly 5,000 police officers with 50 mounted men and 58 dogs' at Orgreave on

18 June comes as no surprise.[61] Importantly for my purpose, as the pickets arrived early in the morning and were escorted by police to one of three fields above and below the plant, the massive paramilitary presence was very much on view, as Bernard Jackson, one of those directed to the field above the plant, describes:

> At the bottom boundary was a thick black line of police uniforms about ten deep. The front rank carried tall, transparent long shields interlocked and forming a phalanx of glistening plastic almost the entire width of the field and out across the road. In the bushes and trees on the left-hand boundary the shadowy shapes of mounted policemen could just be made out, occasional shafts of sunlight penetrating the leaves and branches reflecting from their riot helmets. Also amongst these bushes could be heard the yelps and howls of Alsatians as they moved backwards and forwards with their handlers. Police dogs also formed a barrier on the right-hand boundary at the bottom of the banking of the far side of the road.[62]

So, although the atmosphere on arrival, in keeping with the beautiful summer weather, was relaxed with 'men standing in the sun, talking and laughing',[63] the paramilitary sights and circulating stories added a darker and more foreboding edge. Jackson, for example, talked of 'an air of tension and bitterness amongst the pickets . . . on topside';[64] he also told of the warning he received not to 'go anywhere near them, [because] they're grabbing any bugger'.[65] If the obvious paramilitary presence was responsible for transforming the 'holiday mood',[66] it should not be forgotten that this was not the first of the day's provocations for miners; for Bernard Jackson and colleagues only arrived at Orgreave *after* the frustration of having failed to get into Nottinghamshire, their first choice for picketing, because 'roadblocks were everywhere'.[67] Whether the police were seriously expecting trouble that day is not clear; but their highly visible preparations for the 'worst case' scenario were undoubtedly having a negative impact on at least some of the assembling miners.

Controlling space

Perhaps the single most memorable feature of the policing of the strike was the relentless imposition of police control of space – a policy which embraced the roads around the pit areas, where the road-block policy made road travel a police-defined event, as well as the picket lines, where the different spaces allowed the 'official' (police-defined) picket and the accompanying demonstrators were as rigidly demarcated as the areas reserved strictly for working miners and delivery lorries. So, being directed to one of three holding areas was nothing new for the pickets. What perhaps was new was 'the way in which they were ushered into the area, given parking space, and almost a welcome'.[68] This certainly 'aroused suspicion among some'.[69] For Bernard Jackson, that suspicion focused on the way police control of the space constituted virtual encirclement:

It immediately struck me that we were virtually encircled and the only possible way out of the [top] holding area was across the bridge where the road went up into Orgreave. If pickets wanted to disperse, or the police decided to do it for them, they had nowhere to go. We would all be funnelled into a fairly narrow single-carriageway road which, at its narrowest on the bridge was probably no more than twenty foot wide. We had been set up.[70]

As the day wore on, the idea of being 'set up' was one many would come to share. And, whether true or not, it can only have added to the tension among the protestors.

When the first lorry arrived around 8 a.m., the ritual push against police lines 'had gone as usual', according to Jackson.[71] Describing the same push after viewing the police-made film of the day, Gareth Peirce called it 'brief' and 'good-humoured', and she timed it at '38 seconds exactly'.[72] But what on other similar occasions had been followed simply by pickets backing off (sometimes to nurse cracked heads and bruised shins),[73] had a different outcome on this occasion – a police decision to engage in some pre-emptive paramilitary crowd control, for 'shortly after the first push the long shields parted and out rode fourteen mounted police straight into the pickets'.[74]

Controlling the crowd

Since there had been no stone-throwing before the charge, I can only assume that it was 'provoked' by the ritual push on police lines. If so, it gives some indication of just how sensitive police had become to the possibility of 'trouble'. To the miners, the charge must have appeared an unprovoked attack, and a highly intimidating one, especially since it was accompanied by a 'wall of noise' created by the sound of truncheons beating riot shields. Bernard Jackson was probably not alone in thinking this sounded like 'a declaration that we were facing an army, an army which had declared war on us'.[75] When 'the mounted men returned, having left at least one man totally immobile on the field, trampled underfoot' to a 'round of applause . . . from the police ranks' and then 'within minutes' charged a second time, the miners' worst fears can only have been confirmed.[76]

If these charges were intended by police as a 'short, sharp shock' of pre-emptive deterrence, the next tactical phase had all the hallmarks of a retributive 'settling of accounts'; for this involved the short-shield snatch squads, 'dressed in strange medieval battle dress with helmets . . . visors . . . and overalls, ensuring anonymity and invulnerability',[77] running after the mounted police with truncheons drawn, intent apparently more on injuring than taking prisoners:

> It made no difference if pickets stood still, raised their hands or ran away; truncheons were used on arms and legs, trunks and shoulders, and particularly on heads and faces. Men lay around unconscious or semi-conscious with vicious wounds on their bodies, more often than not with bloody gashes on the backs of their heads.[78]

All of this took place in front of supervisors – one of whom could be clearly heard on the police film instructing short-shield officers to go for 'bodies not heads' – and the TV cameras, which managed to film 'one man being repeatedly truncheoned by a police officer'[79] for all the country to see on the news that night. Yet neither the fear of disciplinary action, nor of adverse publicity (to say nothing of potential criminal charges) was strong enough to prevent the indiscriminate violence of the cavalry-led charges – to prevent, in other words, the dominance of the occupational dimension of the work structure. This, then, constitutes the clearest possible example of how in situations where there is a weak legal structure (remember, within 48 hours the DPP had considered and rejected the case of the 'TV truncheoning' as unsuitable for criminal prosecution,[80] and *none* of the 551 formal complaints against the police led to formal disciplinary action)[81] and a weak democratic structure (fortified enormously in this instance by the sustained ideological attack in the popular press on striking miners as an undemocratic and violent 'enemy within'), the norms and values of the occupational culture can effectively override organizational attempts at supervision because of the 'independence' of the office of constable. To talk, then, as some do, of a 'lack of supervisory control' in such situations is simply to miss the point about these 'multiple protections'; it is also to overlook the fact (which becomes comprehensible only in the light of the above point) that, as one officer subsequently put it, 'all the senior officers were getting stuck in too'.[82]

One response of the miners to this barrage of attacks was simply to leave. Thus, when Sheffield police watchers arrived on the scene at 9.45 a.m., they 'saw large numbers . . . leaving the area'.[83] With the crowd now thinned and chastened, though doubtless angered by what it had seen and experienced, there followed a lull in proceedings, during which time police riot shields were removed. But crowd anger had to manifest itself somehow and, in accord with the amplifying logic of paramilitarism, some miners got into a slanging match with the police lines and some started throwing stones.[84] This led to the return of the riot shields, further stoning, and the eventual release of a snatch squad. When stoning continued, police began to reinforce 'the line with men in full riot gear' until they had 'some 1,500 or more' in readiness.[85] This build-up of resources, though the pickets may not then have been aware of it, marked the initiation of a new and final tactic in the police strategy – dispersal.

Clearance

When preparations for the dispersal were complete, 'suddenly the police lines opened and some 8–12 mounted police charged into the pickets on the road'.[86] And behind them once more came the snatch squads. But this time, 'instead of simply getting people they now felled them and dragged them back through the lines'[87] (presumably a punishment for refusing to be intimidated into departure earlier), and the police line advanced. During what turned out to be a 'three-stage movement up the field',[88] miners continued to stone the police when they could.

Wherever the miners ran, the police followed and attacked them, even over the exit bridge to Orgreave village.[89] Those miners remaining still attempted to salvage something from the savage defeat by continuing to stone the police lines during the 'tactical retreat' following each police charge.[90] During this period Bernard Jackson was himself arrested. It is a salutary, microcosmic example of paramilitarism in action – of how violence, protected from legal or supervisory sanction and justified by a demonological view of the demonstrator, produces only anger and bitterness, thereby adding to the original grievance and amplifying the possibility of future disorder. Though Jackson may not have put it this way, his words clearly recognize the problem. Peacefully enjoying a cup of tea by a wall, he unwisely refused to run to escape a police charge on the grounds that he was 'doing nowt'.[91] Next minute, in his own words:

> An arm grabbed me around the neck from behind and I was smashed in the face with a riot shield. He encircled my neck with his other arm, took his truncheon in both hands and squeezed.[92]

Jackson's attempts to remonstrate were given short shrift, as he was told, in no uncertain terms, to 'Shut your fucking mouth or I'll break your fucking neck'.[93] As he was dragged through the police cordon the physical and verbal abuse continued:

> The coppers nearest lashed out with their truncheons, 'Bastard miner', 'Fucking Yorkie miner'. Fists, boots or truncheons, it didn't matter so long as they could have a go at you.[94]

Jackson's response – how could it have been otherwise? – was one of anger, especially at the inviolability of any and every police action:

> I wasn't frightened, but by Christ was I angry, angry and bitter that these heroes could do whatever they wanted, that they could simply please themselves how they behaved.[95]

The final act of defiance by miners – when they constructed a barricade of wrecked cars some way from the plant and then set them alight – came around noon. But by this time the clearance was effectively over. The police had clearly won the battle of Orgreave, but not without stirring up the miners' anger and leaving many with particular scores to settle later. As for the police, their response, in line with the paramilitary logic of 'anticipatory response', was to move into a new and 'heavier' gear. As McCabe and Wallington put it: 'The admission of defeat by the miners at Orgreave did not end the strike. It simply opened the door for the use of heavier police tactics at colliery gates.'[96]

An officer at the subsequent riot trial 'conceded that the purpose of the horses and the short-shield officers was to terrify'.[97] He, and the police generally, seemed blithely unaware of the damagingly amplificatory consequences, both in the short and the long term, of a policy of policing by paramilitary terror.

PARAMILITARISM: SOME EVIDENCE FROM OTHER COUNTRIES

The final stage of my argument about the amplifying consequences of paramilitary policing involves demonstrating that others, looking at public order policing elsewhere in the world – namely, the USA and Australia – have reached similar conclusions. I should add that this is not intended as an exhaustive comparative survey, nor as indicating agreement in all particulars with the following examples. Moreover, it should not be assumed that the motivations and behaviour of the participants are identical. My concern is *solely* with policing responses to perceived threats to public order. With this in mind, it seems worthy of note that three separate studies undertaken at three different times on three different continents should all draw remarkably similar conclusions about policing from their evidence. It is this that I intend to highlight in the following.

The evidence from the USA

In a study written in 1972, Rodney Stark defines a police riot as 'an event . . . when roving bands of *policemen set upon nonprovocative persons and/or property in an excessively violent manner*'.[98] Using this definition (essentially an outbreak of unprovoked police violence) all the events dealt with above – Broadwater Farm, Manchester, Orgreave – qualify as police riots. Which is to say, simply, that both Stark and I are interested in explaining similar types of 'excessive' police behaviour.

Armed with this definition, Stark then offers a model for understanding how riots develop, the 'typical series of stages'[99] through which they escalate. Starting with the initial requirement for numbers of police and civilians to be present together 'in a fairly restricted area',[100] the model suggests that a conflict of interest between assembled police and civilians 'greatly increases' the potential for escalation, and even more so if the police attempt to disperse the crowd.[101] If the police decide to use force at this stage, further escalation is likely since '*the use of force by the police tends to escalate rapidly into excessive use*',[102] especially if there is police hostility towards the crowd and/or resistance from it. Once 'the excessive use of force . . . becomes relatively widespread', the model talks of a 'limited riot',[103] and of an 'extended riot'[104] when such behaviour 'extends' beyond the particular dispersal action in progress.

With this model in mind, Stark then outlines one example of each kind of riot, and then spends the rest of the book analysing the process in more detail. He spends two chapters detailing some important background factors, what he calls the 'enduring characteristics of the police'.[105] The first of these (Chapter 2), using evidence from research studies, official commissions and community surveys, makes the by now familiar case that police violence is both routine and, to the police themselves, legitimate ('it is not a dark sin of which police are ashamed or about which they feel guilty').[106] Chapter 3, again based on an assessment of the available evidence, makes out an equally familiar case that there is much mutual prejudice, hostility and fear between the police, seen as an embattled 'minority subculture', and other minorities – like 'blacks, students, radicals, hippies and other social dissenters'[107] – with radically different outlooks and lifestyles. And the situation is worse when the police 'are . . . asked to perform tasks which are beyond their means',[108] since then they blame their 'enemies' for their plight and react accordingly. Thus it is that even before a flameproof overall is donned or a riot shield picked up, these 'enduring characteristics' (violence as routine, protester as 'enemy') make public order policing perennially problematic. However, it is the next chapter, Chapter 4, on 'Tactical Errors' that has particular relevance for our question, namely, how the specifically *paramilitary* approach worsens the situation by increasing the likelihood of violence.

In concentrating 'on those aspects of police tactics which make them prone to riot when faced with confrontations',[109] Stark first advances the argument that the police are incapable of executing 'basic riot control tactics',[110] which, he says, derive essentially from military doctrines. The reason why 'the American police cannot perform at the minimum levels of teamwork, impersonality, and discipline which these military doctrines take for granted'[111] is that policework and police training are geared towards cultivating *individuality* (given the discretionary nature of much policework) and a *personal* approach (which *particular* persons are in the wrong place at the wrong time), attributes which are almost the exact opposite of those demanded of soldiers. It is these attributes of policework which lead to the breaking of ranks and thus to the destruction of the whole *raison d'être* of the (para)military approach:

> The breaking of tactical formations – for whatever reason – violates the tactical assumptions on which riot control doctrines are based, virtually ensures a fragmentation of command, and severely weakens the police control of the crowd, thus increasing both the danger to the policemen and their anger.[112]

He then goes on to demonstrate this thesis by comparing the use of US army paratroopers on one side of town, and a combination of the Detroit police and the National Guard on the other, during the Detroit riot of 1967. The difference was dramatic:

> The Guard proved as untrained and unreliable as the police and between the two forces thousands of rounds of ammunition were expended and perhaps 30 persons were killed, while disorder continued. In paratrooper territory only 201 rounds of ammunition were fired, mostly in the first several hours before stricter fire discipline was imposed, and only one person was killed. Within a few hours . . . quiet and order were restored in the section of the city under paratroop jurisdiction.[113]

And the source of the difference? Basically, 'discipline. The paratroopers had it, the police and the guardsmen did not.'[114] Does having special 'tactical [that is,

101

paramilitary] squads'[115] make any difference? Not in Stark's experience: 'Some of the most riotous police behaviour I have witnessed . . . was the work of specially trained tactical squads.'[116]

Now some will no doubt think that all this emphasis on the importance of discipline serves only to *vindicate* Waddington's initial argument that the problem with the paramilitary approach is not the attempt to weld military discipline to the policework task but the failure (so far) to do so successfully. But this would be to miss the point, in two senses. In the first place, what Stark is pointing up is that the *reality* of policework – its individualizing, person-centred approach to situations – makes military *discipline* impossible to impose (without 'massive reforms in our police institutions').[117] This is a similar point to my argument about the 'independence' of the police office, and the discretionary freedom this grants officers, especially in public order situations where legal and democratic structures are weak (which does not mean Stark would necessarily agree with it). It is this 'independence' that ultimately impedes any attempt to impose a rigid, collective, military-style discipline, and explains why all police riots occur only *after* tactical formations have been broken – for at these moments (the release of snatch squads, 'dispersal') independent discretion as befits the police office, and not military discipline, is *necessarily* to the fore. But, secondly, it also misses the point that the direct, uncompromising and standardized nature of the *military* approach *per se*, which is the precise opposite of the discretionary, negotiating police approach, not only signifies conflict and loss of civility but, *however disciplined it may be, is inherently provocative*. This is why, of course, civilian police were introduced to replace the military originally, and why subsequently, when civil disorder has threatened, the military have been introduced only as a measure of last resort.

Thus, in relation to Stark's example, the disciplined military approach may have proved more effective than the undisciplined, discretionary, paramilitary police approach, but *both* were a provocation, I would argue (despite the fact that order was, as it always is eventually, restored). Combining policework (with its individualistic, flexible and discretionary basis) and the military approach (with its collective, inflexible and standardized basis) in a single institution, merely gives the worst of all possible worlds – provocation *minus* collective discipline.

Finally, lest there be any misunderstanding, I should add that the concept of collective military discipline does not imply that soldiers, individually or collectively, do not break ranks, act in undisciplined or illegal ways, or engage in atrocities of various kinds. My Lai, mass rape and pillage, Bloody Sunday – no history of war has been written without such acts. Nor do I mean to imply that there are not other problems associated with 'the military', given the (necessary?) hardening of recruits to conceptualize the 'enemy', deal in violence, and so on. But, since it is *not* my contention that the answer to the present problems of paramilitary policing is somehow to militarize them *properly* (an implication that some may draw from Stark), I do not feel that I need to address here (even supposing I had the necessary expertise to do so) the quite specific problems of military discipline, training, and so on.

Stark's second form of escalatory tactical error concerns the provocative nature of a show of force. He berates the police failure to understand the way

> that the sheer number of police present, and the nature and amount of weaponry they display [can] stimulate hostility towards the police . . . shape police officers' expectations of danger and define intended levels of force to be used.[118]

The parallels with my 'preparation as provocation' comments seem too obvious to labour.

The cause of the tendency towards massive deployments and general 'over-preparedness' is, Stark argues, a misguided 'obsession among the police with their own safety',[119] which, in turn, promotes the equally misguided 'search for technical panaceas'.[120] The search for technical solutions is fallacious because unjustified by the level of disorder, because weapons tend to be misused, are provocative and create a false sense of danger among police, and because, most importantly, technical solutions do not work. For, just as 'there was a strong negative correlation between the amount of force applied and the cessation of rioting in Detroit', as we saw above, so 'similar patterns were found by investigators of other civil disturbances'.[121] What my own examples (and others I have no space to cover) demonstrate is something like the other side of this thesis: that there is a strong positive correlation between the amount of (paramilitary) force applied and the degree of violence and disorder ensuing.

The technical (paramilitary) route is not the only policy. To set against this, Stark recalls an alternative:

> Consider the behaviour of 200 US marshals at the University of Mississippi in September 1962, facing a violent student and Klan mob of 2,000 who were trying to prevent the admission of James Meredith to the University. The marshals stood firm under barrages of bricks and spasmodic sniper fire for seven hours, and 29 of them suffered injuries. They never broke. They never fired. They preserved life, property and civil rights. Recalling this episode, consider how little we have now come to expect of the police and how greatly we have come to share their obsession with their own safety.[122]

For those readers thinking, 'but that was a quarter of a century ago', just recall for a moment Chief Superintendent Couch's policing of the angry demo outside Tottenham police station on the afternoon of the day the Broadwater Farm estate erupted. What both exhibit are those *perenially relevant* attributes of good policing – patience, calmness, resolution and courage. They were both, incidentally, examples of highly *disciplined* policework. And they were both, also, examples of *effective* policework.

The evidence from Australia

The annual motorcycle races at Bathurst are probably the most important event in the Australian motorcycle enthusiast's calendar. Each Easter large crowds gather for the occasion, and many stay for the weekend camped on the mountainside above the race track. Over the years, violent clashes between some of the younger enthusiasts and the police have gradually become an established feature of the event as well. *Dynamics of Collective Conflict* is a series of working papers by the research team of Chris Cuneen and his colleagues set up to look into these conflicts. Based on a mixture of sociological observation and historical reconstruction, collectively these offer some fascinating reflections upon the changing relationship between the motorcyclist subculture, policing, the criminal law and the media since the races first started in 1931. Of particular relevance for my purpose are two aspects: the relationship between the gradual institutionalization of a tougher policing regime over the years and escalating levels of violence; and the contribution of the paramilitary approach in particular to this escalation.

Before the 1960s, though motorcyclists complained of police harassment, policing tended to be 'low-key', and any 'misbehaviour' was neither particularly associated with motorcyclists nor particularly 'anti-police'.[123] All this began to change during the 1960s, as conflicts between young spectators and the police over the appropriate use of certain public spaces led to the institutionalization of anti-police sentiment and activities; the introduction of intimidatory 'saturation style [police] patrols';[124] increased media talk of 'hooligans' and the 'youth problem' especially in the wake of the British 'moral panic' about the 'mods and rockers' and the North American one about Hell's Angels; the first mention of 'riots'; and, following a mid-1960s crisis of policing and law and order in New South Wales (NSW), an increasing commitment of resources to the problem.

Thus it was that police numbers on duty at Bathurst rose from 40 before 1966 to 176 in 1966, 300 in the late 1970s and 400 in the mid-1980s, by which time it had become 'the largest single policing operation in NSW'.[125] Moreover, 'the type of police squads used . . . broadened . . . [to] include riot police, the Drug Squad and members of the Bureau of Crime Intelligence who infiltrate the crowd'.[126] Of particular significance in this broadening was the introduction of '21 division . . . a police mobile unit established to deal with . . . public disturbances',[127] since arrests in the unit's debut year (1966) trebled, an outcome for which it was mostly responsible. This pattern has continued ever since: 'for the period 1961–1984 . . . 21 division officers arrested 85% of persons who appeared before the court for offences related to the Easter weekend'.[128]

One effect of the heavier policing of the town was that

> people stopped coming into it on Saturday night, preferring to stay at the main campsite on Mt Panorama where they could engage in activities in what was technically a public place but away from police observation.[129]

But the police followed, with the result that arrests increasingly took place on the mountainside rather than in the town centre. For example: 'In 1967 over 50% of arrests were made on the Mount, whereas in previous years the figure was less than 3%.'[130] Moreover, by the end of the '60s . . . a field control unit (caravan) established a 24 hour police presence on the mountain over the Easter weekend . . . manned by a sergeant and two general duties constables.[131]

This then became a focus for discontent as 'heavier patrols of the camping area . . . triggered off growing resentment and increased anti-police activity'.[132] In 1976, for example, the Easter clash involved a siege of the police caravan by, according to a local paper, 'more than 200 screaming club weilding [sic] bikies'.[133]

Following this incident, police pushed for and got an 'upgrading of facilities on Mount Panorama',[134] namely, a permanent police compound – 'a police station . . . surrounded by a three metre high cyclone fence ribboned with barbed wire, in the middle of the campground'.[135] This then became the *permanent* focus of anti-police feelings. It 'was built in 1979', since when 'it has become the focal point of the four riots that have occurred'.[136] The siting of the police compound within 'space' felt by bikers to be 'theirs' helps explain, according to Cuneen, this focusing of bikers' resentment:

> The site chosen was a flat grassy area which had traditionally been used for games. It was a classic case of the overt colonisation of space by police in an area that had been seen to be outside their control. It had been regarded as the subculture's territory.[137]

Though my own notion of how police efforts at 'controlling space' at demonstrations provokes resentment is a far more restricted one, partly because it refers to a far more temporary form of 'colonization', the similarities seem worth noting nevertheless.

The tougher police approach continued through the 1980s, prompting regular riots, and, in their wake, the formulation of yet more coercive strategies:

> Following the 1981 riot, the NSW Police Department announced the formation of a Tactical Response Group [TRG] to control public disorder. In the aftermath of the 1983 riot, the Department pressured for stronger legislation. The Government response was that adequate penalties existed under common law. In 1985 some 95 individuals were charged with riotous assembly under common law [something quite without precedent].[138]

And in 1986 saturation policing was introduced – a strategy which successfully foiled a riot, but effectively ruined the event as well – a point I return to below. Remember the origins of this 'spiralling level of conflict':[139] the dispute between police and young spectators over the appropriate use of public space arising from the police 'decision to rigidly enforce public order legislation',[140] or, in other words, to convert aspects of the collective leisure activities of working-class male youths into breaches of public order. (The first 'riot', in 1960, was a half-hour altercation between police and youths after police attempted to arrest two from a larger group throwing firecrackers.)[141] Once this happens, 'part of the "leisure" activity becomes active opposition to the police', and once this sort of 'collective behaviour has been criminalised the object of the riot becomes the police'.[142] Once the riot stage has been reached, as we see in more detail below, 'so often the immediate consequence of police involvement . . . is to exaggerate the violence'.[143]

To summarize:

> In practice the interaction between stronger policing methods and more active resistance has served qualitatively to increase the level of violence on both sides. The history of the Bathurst motorcycle riots has demonstrated the spiralling effect as the police introduce new hardware and the crowds become more vicious in their attacks. The perceived 'public order' disturbance ten years ago of smoking marijuana and shouting insults has turned into fully-fledged attacks on police with Molotov cocktails.[144]

If the role of tougher policing generally in the route from firecrackers to Molotov cocktails is undeniable, the following case studies illustrate how paramilitarism was implicated in this escalation.

Three case studies in policing styles and violence

If the foregoing is based on a general historical reconstruction over a 25-year period, this section provides a closer look at three particular years based on detailed sociological observations conducted at the bike races. And, as luck would have it, each year witnessed a different style of policing and a different outcome, that is, 'a "non-riot" situation without major intervention [1984], a "riot" situation with intervention [1985] and a "non-riot" situation with saturation intervention [1986]'.[145]

1984

Although there were over 200 officers, including the TRG, on standby, 'from mid-afternoon there were no more than half a dozen uniformed general duties police at the opened gates of the police compound'.[146] Around 5 p.m. 'bike riders were engaged . . . in public shows of riding skill'.[147] During the early evening (around 7 p.m.), 'small groups of uniformed . . . officers',[148] about two dozen in all, were outside the compound while the bike riders, now in 'bull rings' ('a ring of people gathered round the spectacle'),[149] continued the bike-riding displays and other traditional entertainments such as 'cockfighting' (shoulder-back fights)[150] and incendiary games (such as throwing lighted petrol-soaked toilet rolls among themselves). When the crowd around the compound grew to about 200, the two dozen or so police officers retreated to the compound. Some shouting of anti-police slogans, and an arrest, followed. After a while 'more than a dozen small groups of uniformed police re-emerged'[151] from the compound, talked with several often rather drunk spectators, and seemed to quieten things down. By 8.30 p.m. there were about two dozen officers outside and 20 inside the compound. Around 10 p.m. several 'burning toilet rolls were thrown into the compound and several bottles and beer cans were hurled at the fence',[152] one of which 'hit a police officer on the head'.[153] The police response was to send 'another dozen officers into the crowd'[154] and 'for the rest of the evening the small group intervention style of policing prevailed'.[155] With sporadic exceptions, the crowd response 'was positive and involved'.[156]

The groundwork for this low-key approach had been laid apparently in the afternoon by the 'superintendent . . . and other senior officers walking throughout the camping area and discussing intended cordial relations with the spectators', and assuring them there would be no 'random breath-testing . . . on the approach road to the mountain'.[157]

To summarize:

> The policing operation, unlike previous years rested on a conscious attempt at constructive communication between the police and the bikers. To facilitate this the appearance and profile of the police on the mountain deliberately concentrated on the 'normal' (eg) the use of uniformed general duties police officers, the removal of the TRG from public view on the mountain, and the minimal use of RBT [random breath-testing] patrols on the approach road to the mountain.[158]

It may be redundant to add that 'charge rates were very low'.[159]

1985

In this year 'police strength . . . was slightly larger' and

> both on Friday and early Saturday the police had established checkpoints ostensibly under the RBT programme, at which they were also checking on identification and in certain instances were carrying out random searches of luggage.[160]

Though police briefing had stressed the need for a low-key approach similar to that of 1984, lower-ranking and TRG officers anticipated violence that evening. The crowd appeared to contain more weekend 'bikers', more inebriates and to be engaged in more early evening bike-riding displays than the previous year. Around 6.30 p.m. there were about 100 spectators around the compound, and about 10–15 police officers at the compound gate. 'At about 7.30 p.m. . . . missiles and incendiary torches [were] thrown . . . into the compound.'[161] The closure of the gates and arrests followed. Then a man was arrested inside the compound for attempting to damage a police vehicle and a 'senior officer . . . mingling with the crowd was struck by a brick'.[162] The crowd was then instructed to disperse, and 'the TRG were called out' and stationed in 'a garrison defence position around the compound'.[163] There the TRG 'became the focus for attack by the crowd',[164] with everything from cans to petrol bombs. The crowd was made up of two 'rings': 'groups of several hundred individuals (many affected by intoxicants) who taunted and attacked the TRG phalanx on three fronts',[165] and about 1,000 onlookers safely 'outside the range of TRG onslaughts'.[166] The TRG response was vigorously executed 'snatch and grab' raids against targets selected 'by police observers within the compound' and TRG sergeants.[167]

The crowd response to these police attacks was 'further . . . violence'.[168] Around 9.45 p.m., 'the spotlights outside the . . . compound were cut and the police on the western side made a significant attempt to secure a large amount of ground around the compound',[169] a tactic they repeated later on the eastern side when offering protection to some 'ambulance paramedics . . . called out to treat an injured biker'.[170] Not surprisingly, charge rates were high and included the 95 'riot' charges mentioned above.

1984 and 1985 compared
In many ways the two years seem broadly very similar in terms of crowd composition and initial activity. But they could hardly be more different in terms of policing styles and final outcomes. In 1984 the police response was to keep stop checks to a minimum, numbers down, the TRG out of sight and channels of communication open, a thoughtful and restrained approach which, despite missile attacks and an officer hit by a beer can, kept violence and charge rates to a minimum. In 1985, by contrast, stop checks were in operation from early on and the police fuse, generally, was much shorter. Thus, the first missile attacks and an officer hit by a brick produced, almost immediately, instructions to disperse (recall Stark and the dangers of 'dispersal') and the entry of the TRG, which became, first, the target for crowd violence and, later, after some aggressive 'snatching' activities, the reason why the violence escalated into a riot.

1986
The 'tough' saturation approach of 1986, a response to the previous year's riot, represents a third style of policing and a third type of outcome – the simultaneous prevention of a riot and, to all intents and purposes, the event itself. The rigorous enforcement of the new coercive restrictions on alcohol, the small-group police patrols stopping, searching and breaking up all games, and the TRG publicly on standby, breaking up 'bull-rings' and aggressively patrolling the campsite into the night, led to 'a notable exodus of bikers . . . throughout Friday and Saturday'[171] and a halving of takings at the gate and at local petrol stations and hotels. These 'high-profile' tactics, which amounted almost to turning the bikers' traditional mountainside territory into one vast public compound under police control, certainly prevented a riot, but still relied on a high level of arrests (106, mostly for breaches of the new council restrictions on alcohol).

SUMMARY AND CONCLUSION

This chapter has focused on the reality of the paramilitary approach 'in action'. And, contrary to the argument that this form of policing constitutes a more effective (because more professional) form of policing, I have concretely illustrated its amplifying consequences. Arguing that the notion of professionalism animating the argument about paramilitarism's effectiveness was idealistic, I offered an analytical sequential framework for understanding the actual social dynamics of paramilitary-style public order policing. This framework, distilled from reading numerous detailed contemporary accounts of policing public disorder, consists of a four-stage sequence – 'preparation', 'controlling space', 'controlling the crowd', and 'clearance' – in which the paramilitary elements (large numbers, military organization, protective clothing and equipment, and so on) at each stage have an inherent tendency to exacerbate the very problems of violence and disorder they seek to prevent. This framework was then employed to show how, on three representative occasions – Broadwater Farm, Manchester and Orgreave – the social dynamics of these events conformed to my model. The work of Rodney Stark in the USA, and Chris Cuneen and colleagues in Australia, was then drawn upon to show the parallels between their accounts of policing public order abroad and my own British examples.

To put it at its simplest, where large numbers of police, with both might and right on their side, are allowed to respond forcefully to provocation, the result is almost certain to be resistance, which in turn leads to tougher policing, more violent resistance, and so on around the spiral of amplification. And while this outcome can be avoided by a self-defeating 'saturation' approach, only a patient, tolerant, dialogic approach seems able to avoid riots *and* allow demonstrating crowds to give vent to their anger. This is the 'overall' message from *all* our examples taken from the 'real world of paramilitary effectiveness'. But still to be elucidated, and the subject of the next chapter, are those features peculiar to the working of specialist public order squads which collectively constitute the amplifying processes of the paramilitary approach.

NOTES

1. Jefferson, 1987a, p. 51.
2. Waddington, 1987, pp. 40–41.
3. Ibid., p. 43.
4. Cf. Johnson, 1972; Cain, 1979; James, 1979; Brogden *et al.*, 1988, pp. 80–84.
5. Jefferson, 1987a, p. 52.
6. My major source of information for this account is the most comprehensive known to me, that of Gifford, 1986. Injury figures were taken from the national press. See, for example, *Daily Telegraph*, 8 October 1985.
7. Gifford, 1986, p. 74.
8. Ibid., p. 97.
9. Ibid., p. 92.
10. Ibid.
11. Ibid.
12. Ibid.
13. Ibid., p. 97.
14. Ibid., p. 98.
15. Ibid.
16. Ibid., p. 105.
17. Ibid., p. 104.
18. *Police Review*, October 1985, quoted in ibid., p. 110.
19. Gifford, 1986, p. 110.
20. Ibid., p. 111.
21. Ibid.
22. Ibid., p. 106.
23. Ibid., p. 111.

24. Ibid.
25. Ibid., p. 120.
26. Ibid.
27. Ibid.
28. Ibid.
29. Ibid., p. 121.
30. Ibid., pp. 120–21.
31. Quoted in, for example, *Daily Telegraph*, 8 October 1985, p. 1.
32. My major source of information for this account is Manchester City Council, 1985, and the vast amount of unpublished material upon which that report was based.
33. Manchester City Council, 1985, p. 61.
34. Ibid.
35. Ibid., p. 79.
36. Ibid., p. 12.
37. Ibid., p. 13.
38. Ibid.
39. Ibid.
40. Ibid., pp. 13–14.
41. Ibid., p. 14.
42. Ibid.
43. Ibid.
44. Ibid., p. 15.
45. Ibid., p. 14.
46. Ibid., p. 15.
47. Ibid.
48. Ibid.
49. Ibid., p. 16.
50. Ibid., p. 17.
51. Ibid.
52. Ibid., p. 18.
53. Ibid.
54. Ibid.
55. Ibid., p. 19.
56. Ibid.
57. Ibid.
58. *The Guardian*, 5 March 1985.
59. My major sources of information for this account are Jackson, n.d.; Peirce, 1985; McCabe and Wallington, 1988.
60. McCabe and Wallington, 1988, p. 69.
61. Ibid., p. 76.
62. Jackson, n.d., p. 33.
63. Peirce, 1985, p. 7.
64. Jackson, n.d., p. 33.
65. Ibid.
66. McCabe and Wallington, 1988, p. 76.
67. Jackson, n.d., p. 32.
68. McCabe and Wallington, 1988, p. 76.
69. Ibid.
70. Jackson, n.d., p. 33.
71. Ibid.

72. Peirce, 1985.
73. Jackson, n.d., p. 33.
74. Ibid., pp. 33–4.
75. Ibid., p. 34.
76. Ibid.
77. Peirce, 1985.
78. Jackson, n.d., p. 34.
79. Peirce, 1985.
80. McCabe and Wallington, 1988, p. 77.
81. Ibid., pp. 166–7.
82. Peirce, 1985.
83. McCabe and Wallington, 1988, p. 183.
84. Ibid., p. 184.
85. Ibid.
86. Ibid.
87. Jackson, n.d., p. 35.
88. Ibid.
89. McCabe and Wallington, 1988, pp. 184–5.
90. Ibid., p. 185.
91. Jackson, n.d., p. 35.
92. Ibid.
93. Ibid.
94. Ibid., p. 36.
95. Ibid.
96. McCabe and Wallington, 1988, p. 112.
97. Quoted in Peirce, 1985.
98. Stark, 1972, p. 17 (emphasis in original).
99. Ibid., p. 18.
100. Ibid.
101. Ibid., p. 19.
102. Ibid., p. 20 (emphasis in original).
103. Ibid.
104. Ibid., p. 21.
105. Ibid., p. 54.
106. Ibid., p. 55.
107. Ibid., p. 124.
108. Ibid., p. 86.
109. Ibid., p. 125.
110. Ibid.
111. Ibid., p. 126.
112. Ibid., p. 128.
113. Ibid.
114. Ibid., pp. 128–9.
115. Ibid., p. 129.
116. Ibid.
117. Ibid.
118. Ibid., p. 131.
119. Ibid., p. 133.
120. Ibid., p. 135.
121. Ibid., p. 137.

122. Ibid., p. 135.
123. Cuneen *et al.*, 1986, p. 23.
124. Ibid., p. 357.
125. Ibid., p. 90.
126. Ibid.
127. Ibid., p. 359.
128. Ibid.
129. Ibid., p. 90.
130. Ibid., p. 360.
131. Ibid.
132. Ibid., p. 90.
133. *Mirror*, 20 April 1976, quoted in ibid., p. 361.
134. Cuneen *et al.*, 1986, p. 361.
135. Ibid., p. 91.
136. Ibid.
137. Ibid.
138. Ibid., p. 323.
139. Ibid., p. 331.
140. Ibid.
141. Ibid., p. 356.
142. Ibid., p. 332.
143. Ibid., p. 334.
144. Ibid., p. 339.
145. Ibid., p. 362.
146. Ibid.
147. Ibid.
148. Ibid.
149. Ibid., p. 96.
150. Ibid., p. 98.
151. Ibid., p. 363.
152. Ibid.
153. Ibid.
154. Ibid.
155. Ibid., p. 364.
156. Ibid.
157. Ibid.
158. Ibid.
159. Ibid., p. 388.
160. Ibid., p. 364.
161. Ibid., p. 366.
162. Ibid.
163. Ibid.
164. Ibid.
165. Ibid.
166. Ibid.
167. Ibid.
168. Ibid., p. 367.
169. Ibid.
170. Ibid.
171. Ibid., p. 370.

CHAPTER 6

Inside the work structure: processes of amplification

INTRODUCTION

So far I hope to have established both the historical context for the emergence, and strengthening, of the paramilitary option and the macrosociological context, namely, weak legal and democratic structures 'permitting' the dominance of the occupational dimension of the work structure. Beyond that, I have tried to demonstrate what the typical consequences of that dominance are at the microsociological level of the social dynamics of particular paramilitary operations. It only remains, therefore, to identify the precise elements which, together, constitute the processes of amplification inside the work structure. Specifically, this entails outlining those processes – of selection, training and informal socialization – which transform a number of individual officers into a team of seasoned paramilitaries, and highlighting their potential for amplification.[1]

BECOMING A PARAMILITARY

Recruitment: Wanted – active, enthusiastic men

Traditionally, the job with the biggest cachet within the police has been that of detective. Though not something all probationers aspire to, few can be unaware of the elite status of the CID, itself partly a result of the centrality of the 'good' arrest – one involving the application of traditional skills of detection – to a sense of personal satisfaction and esteem. The coming of the Special Patrol Groups has not altered any of this, but it has begun to offer, if not a rival to the pre-eminence of the CID, at least an alternative avenue to highly valued work.

Interestingly, it was not always so. Before public order work acquired its present prominence and importance, the selection of SPG personnel was taken far less seriously. Indeed, for a while it became something of a 'dumping' ground for exasperated divisional commanders with deviant 'misfits' to offload – as many, of all ranks, have attested. The resulting reputation of the SPG was one of a careless 'mob-handed' approach to arrests, and an indifference about appearance, as the following quotation from an SPG supervisor amusingly reveals:

> When it started . . . the rule of the day was 'we will take prisoners'. If anybody commits an offence of any sort we will take them . . . and it developed into a sort of . . . league I think . . . and at the same time unfortunately you have this SPG cult and if you've ever seen this . . . lay-out, drawing, it's a cartoon layout of . . . styles of the various departments, you know, the Special Branch have got a trilby and dark glasses, and the pointed beards you know and the SPG was just one mass of hair, with two little eyes. Everybody drew a full set, beard and moustache or something and the hair went longer, and their appearance became dishevelled you know, smartness wasn't one of the necessities . . . the recognition of their presence was the important thing.

But that changed with the increasing importance of public order work. The route into the SPG altered from simple application without interview to application plus appearance before an increasingly high-powered selection board. And this was accompanied by a new determination that, in the words of a senior SPG officer, 'the blokes that come here will be of the highest standard I can make them'. Precisely what such a commitment entailed, like the notion of 'good policework', is not easily defined. But, as the following quotation from another senior officer makes clear, it involves a mixture of judgement and enthusiasm:

> We have a fairly exacting . . . selection procedure to get on the group . . .
> in the first place and you don't want anybody either who's too arrest-minded and you certainly don't want anybody who's idle.

What such a requirement ideally points towards is the enthusiastic young officer possessing both the appropriate temperament to handle the difficult public order situations which characterize SPG work, and sufficient experience to use discretion wisely; in short, the keen and/or ambitious officer of four or five years' standing. And that, increasingly, became the profile of SPG recruits. For applicants themselves, the attraction of an attachment rested in the 'bit of variation' such work presented from the tedious grind of pandawork (the point of both arrival and destination for most), or in the opportunity it presented to extend experience and hence enhance career prospects.

Although the senior officer quoted earlier was anxious to emphasize the balance between arrest-consciousness and idleness sought in candidates, the fact remains that 'activity', in police terms, tends to mean 'arrests'. This is so, not simply because arrests are one of the few measurable outputs of policework but, more profoundly, because, in terms of the self-satisfaction stemming from producing something, arrests are what policework 'produces', as one SPG officer astutely recognized:

If you're working in a factory and you make something, and you can see something at the end of your day . . . you know I've made that, there's some self-satisfaction in it. The only way I feel self-satisfied is when you, if you go out – I know it's prevent crime and detect it, all this, that and the other – but . . . the only self-satisfaction I get is when you go out, get somebody, for doing something.

The result is that although a good arrest record is neither the only, nor even a required, criterion in itself for entry to the SPG, the desire for officers who are 'not idle', together with the equation of 'activity' with arrests, tends, in practice, to render arrest records important – as the following group novitiate realistically suggests:

You've got to have a fairly good arrest rate to get on the SPG because they don't want people who are just going to come on here and do nothing.

In his own particular case, he was convinced he got the subdivisional nomination (for forwarding to the SPG) over

about six others . . . basically because at that time I was arresting a lot of people, and I'd had some really good arrests for crime, for all sorts. My name was on the PIC [prisoners in custody] sheet quite often. Not for petty, silly things, but for good stuff.

He may, of course, have been mistaken about this. But, it is a fact, as we saw in Chapter 4, that all the paperwork circulating through the SPG system I observed related solely to offences, as did the only record books. In other words, the only permanent 'trace' of unit activity was confined to arrest behaviour.

If the SPG is the home of the active and the enthusiastic, it is, or certainly was, also the province of *men*. The Chief Constable, in his own wily way, insisted this was not a product of policy but of the physical unsuitability of women for the work:

I say that there is no ban on women being employed in public order situations *per se* but you work out which of the women you've got, as individuals . . . are capable of handling the kind of situation which you are sending them into, if you think they are not capable, not because of sex, but because of physical aptitude or training or whatever, OK they don't go, you haven't rejected them because they are women, their sex is just one of the factors, an additional factor that you should take into account when deploying them. And if you work on that basis I don't think you can go far wrong.

That, according to the Chief Constable, was official policy. But the result was the same either way; as a senior officer more bluntly expressed it: 'We don't have them on the group.'

As we saw in Chapter 1, such institutional discrimination has now been successfully challenged in the Metropolitan Police and we saw riot-trained policewomen in action at Wapping. It can only be a matter of time before this practice spreads elsewhere, though it will no doubt be resisted given the widespread patriarchal assumptions about policing generally, never mind its 'tougher' aspects, being a 'man's' job. But, for my purposes, this point is less significant than what the earlier absence of women tells us about the masculinist assumptions informing decisions about the appropriate response to expected disorder, and hence about the SPG's ethos. A senior officer unselfconsciously illustrates this in his doubly gender-blind remarks on the appropriate role of women. Though 'there are some public order situations where they can have a calming influence, . . . if there's going to be any violence then they are better out of it'. Long after the female sex have entered the hitherto exclusively male world of the SPG, the gender-based assumptions behind the ACC's remarks will continue, no doubt, to inform the SPG's ethos.

If the ideal candidates for the SPG are enthusiastic and ambitious young men with good arrest records and anxious to prove themselves further to their superiors, the resulting 'reality' – given the practical meaning of 'activity' and the masculinist ethos informing responses to disorder – is the firmest imaginable foundation for the construction of an amplifying spiral.

Training: techniques, drills and the absent agenda

Discussion of paramilitary training has tended to focus on its highly visible aspects, namely, the various techniques used by the shield units and the mounted police to control or disperse crowds, the testing of ever more technologically sophisticated (and dangerous) equipment, and so on. And there is little doubt that there is much of dramatic interest in all this – witness the realistic reconstructions of violent scenarios with (for comic relief) police officer 'demonstrators' vehemently 'attacking' their colleagues, so beloved of the press – as well as much of legitimate concern. But what tends to get overlooked in such a focus, and which is central to my argument, is what such training *misses out*. For, apart from some sessions on legal aspects of the work (brushing up on 'Section 5', and so on) the practice of techniques and drills *is* paramilitary training – as one SPG officer disparagingly confirmed:

> say you had ten training days, I should say nine out of the ten were taken up in how to get on and off a bus.

His complaint at the time was that training in such 'embussing' and 'debussing' techniques was of little use because, in practice, they were 'never used'. But the important point for us is not the question of relevance in this sense, the 'over-learning' of techniques that may be little used, since such training, in retrospect, would probably now be regarded as highly prescient in the light of subsequent disorders. It is, rather, the complete absence of attention to the very core of SPG activities, namely, specific (often highly contentious) incidents, and to the tricky question of how they might be handled in ways which avoid trouble. It is this which constitutes the training's real lack of relevance.

Downtime

This absence is not due simply to lack of time. For the plain truth is that there is much time available which could be used, albeit on an *ad hoc*, irregular and informal basis, for training purposes. In the first place there are the seemingly endless hours on standby which presently constitute not just dead time but, as many would agree, one of the most frustrating parts of the job:

> First two or three times you know, you don't mind. But it happens quite a lot and I think that's one of the most frustrating things, is sitting in a police station, doing nothing, just sitting there and it ain't just for an hour, it's, you know, it could be six, seven, eight hours.

Secondly, there is the time between public order calls which is spent, presently, assisting local divisions with various crime problems. In practice, I found this time largely taken up with plain-clothes patrolwork in pairs. And there is little doubt that such time could be otherwise used without significant loss, a sentiment with which the officers themselves readily agreed: 'Plain clothes is like a spare-time job really for us.'

More generally, there is time available because life in the SPG (when it is not actually in the thick of things), as most agreed, is 'a lot slower' than normal divisional work:

> It's a lot slower, used to go to work, used to be out in ten minutes, the gaffer used to say: 'come on let's have you out' whereas this . . . I think is more relaxed . . . there's nowhere to go in a hurry. If you're going to find anything cracking off you're going to find it anyway, you're going to come across it, there's no point in, like, if you're going to do a van patrol . . . we normally go on at 6 o'clock. It's no use us getting changed into uniform straight away at 6 p.m., going to ―― or ―― waiting for trouble to start, because the trouble ain't at 6 o'clock the trouble is about 9, 10 o'clock. So I mean, you just do some reports . . . any enquiries . . . we do stop actually in the station, and it's more relaxed, it's just a matter of waiting you know for the order to say: 'OK lads, let's go'.

It is not lack of time, then, that is a problem, a point that applies equally to supervisors, incidentally, since they, too, share the hours of standby, and a slower pace – the latter because they lack the range of duties of subdivisional unit supervisors, as we saw in Chapter 4.

Debriefing

To consider why there is the inattention to the question of how incidents might be handled best (and how, therefore, disasters might be avoided), it is worth considering another similarly wasted opportunity – 'debriefing' sessions. Here, though all manner of other things – whether designated procedures were followed; whether there were sufficient officers with the right equipment; whether officers were in the right places at the right times – will be considered, specific incidents, once again, escape scrutiny. This failure to use debriefing and other available time to raise such questions is, of course, too systematic to be due to accidental oversight. The simple truth is that such questions are omitted from training because, as we saw in Chapters 3 and 4, they are also neglected in operational contexts. In explaining this, I argued that once an order is given to undertake an offensive measure of some sort, ensuing incidents are governed not by supervisory but by constabulary powers. This flattening of the rank structure in the face of constabulary independence means that, as we saw then, so long as the arrest is adjudged lawful and complaints and inquiries are not forthcoming, it is *ipso facto* appropriate. Given this legalistic perspective in operational contexts, there is, at present, then, nothing to discuss in training or debriefing contexts.

'Blagging'

Yet, for the officers themselves, the appropriateness of particular responses, especially in difficult or dangerous situations, clearly affects them, often profoundly. If your partner makes a silly move, or a particular pair regularly overreacts, or anyone in the Group behaves in a manner likely to jeopardize either Group reputation or safety, the repercussions – given that the unit operates as a team – will obviously affect everybody. Faced, then, with the necessity and the opportunities for such discussions, yet precluded from doing so directly, either in training or elsewhere, by the peculiar independence of an office which routinely sanctions all manner of stupidities in the name of law, the question becomes one of how to do so.

The answer, as so often with serious matters that if raised directly would cause difficulty, is humour – more specifically, in this case, blagging. Blagging is essentially a verbal game in which characteristics of officers are caricatured. Thus, 'weaknesses' of individuals or pairs are ruthlessly exposed and wittily exaggerated, in much the same way as a cartoonist works. Success is similarly measured through the 'accuracy' and wit of presentation, as well as, in this case, the ability to outwit an opponent through verbal adroitness.

Much 'downtime' is spent in this way, thus indicating blagging's importance. Moreover, there are rules to the game – partners should not blag each other and absent colleagues should not be blagged, for example – which suggest the importance of ensuring it never gets out of hand and thereby ceases to be a game, which I never saw it do. Jointly these two observations – about its importance, and its rule-boundedness – suggest its primary function, namely, the safe airing of inevitable differences. Given a bunch of officers, all with individual responsibility for the use, often in highly difficult situations, of highly discretionary powers, who are, nevertheless, also required to operate as a team, some mechanism for amicably negotiating the differences that are bound to arise and for airing grievances in a non-antagonistic way is obviously needed. 'Blagging', as the following officer also realized, is the necessary 'safety valve':

> You have to learn to tolerate people I think . . . I mean, you get a group of eight blokes that come together, you've got to have differences, I mean it's impossible for eight blokes to come from all parts . . . of the force into a van for sometimes up to 16, 17 hours a day and not to have disagreements and fallings out . . . I think that this term 'blagging' . . . or taking the mickey . . . really it's release, it's a pressure valve, it's a relief valve really because I think if you didn't have it, it would come out probably in some other way . . . whereas blagging you see you can just laugh it off, or . . . say something back to them and that's it.

If, as I concluded earlier, the recruitment process laid a firm foundation for the construction of an amplifying spiral, the process of training does nothing to counteract this. Instead of offering some official forum for discussing ways unwanted (amplifying) consequences might be avoided, it offers only a vacuum. And this can hardly be filled by 'blagging', which can provide only a mechanism for the safe resolution of grievances and, subsidiarily, an entertaining antidote to boredom. Informal socialization, to which we now turn, fills that vacuum – and completes the construction of the amplifying spiral.

Informal socialization: comradeship, teamwork and the acquisition of competence

Socialization is about the processes involved in the passage from feeling strange to feeling comfortable in new roles. In other words, it is about learning competence. Training is the formal process involved and, as we have seen, offers little guidance to core aspects of the role. This vacuum places a premium on those time-honoured informal processes of watching and copying old hands in action.

A surrogate family?

Since socialization implies a role, it is necessary, therefore, to be aware of the precise nature of the role in question, and the way this affects the socialization process. The first significant aspect of the role stems from the SPG's overriding function to provide 'the hierarchy of the police service' with 'a pool of men that they can call on at any time to deal with any situation . . . in other words to be on twenty-four-hour standby'.

The practical effect of this aspect of the role is a working life of long and

119

unpredictable hours. Being prepared to put up with this becomes, in consequence, a precondition of joining the SPG, as many found at their recruitment interview.

> When I joined the SPG they said to me 'are you willing to stop on, are you willing to cancel your rest days, have you got a phone, are you willing to be called out in the middle of the night' . . . to get on really you got to say: 'yes'.

This aspect of the job turned out to be no idle threat, and most had heartfelt stories to tell of the disruptions to domestic and social life that they, and especially their families, had to get used to on joining.

> [I] found it very hard to adjust to the short notice . . . initially, on the SPG, the short notice of change in duties, the short notice of working extended hours, long hours. I found that hard to . . . grasp, because, . . . it caused me to have a little bit of a problem at home . . . I found it very hard actually, you know, having a little baby as well, you know, it seemed I went, at one stage, about three or four months without ever seeing my wife or family.

> On the SPG it's you know my wife, oh, moaning she's done over the last, since I've been on the Group, and especially the last three or four months, the overtime, you know, I never seem to be at home. I think that was the worst, I used to come home and I'd say 'I've got court in the morning', if I was on four 'til midnight, I'd say, 'I've got court in the morning'. She'll say 'not again' . . . So you'll be at court in the morning, then back to her, and I probably wouldn't be in the house for an hour, and then I'd say 'oh, there's a job on tonight, it could be four in the morning. Then we've got a, we are on days Saturday but we've got to stop on, there's a raid on', and she'd say 'Christ, that means we can't go out again this Saturday' . . . I say 'I'm sorry, I can't do nothing about it'. You know, the worst part of it as well is on the SPG they never tell us, sometimes they do, but more often than not they don't say 'til the night before, you know, . . . 'oh, I want you to work over tomorrow night, there's a job on', and that to me, that's short notice, you know, you could have planned something to go out, and then the Friday night they'll turn round and say, 'you got to stop on'.

As a twenty-four-hour reserve, SPG activities embrace everything from combing woods for missing children to sorting mail where letter bombs are suspected. But, the major task, as most would confirm, 'obviously is public order situations'. Even though other activities, such as plain-clothes work, can conceivably consume as much working time, these are, as we saw earlier, definitely subordinate to public order. Public order work constitutes time spent together, on standby or on van or foot patrol, and, since it always involves at least the possibility of difficult and demanding disorderly confrontations, especially in their position as 'frontline troops', it is often emotionally taxing work. The standby component also makes it frustrating work, as we saw in Chapter 5.

It is this combination of features – the long hours together, the mutually disrupted social and domestic lives, the emotionally upsetting and frustrating nature of the work – which make the mutual support of 'comradeship' probably the most important feature, to the men themselves, of life in the SPG. Certainly, many volunteered it as the most satisfying part of the job.

> The most satisfying part [of the job] I suppose is that, I would say the comradeship is . . . satisfying, as I say . . . there's eight or nine men there and you spend most of your time in that two years or so in that van stuck with those eight men and I think if you don't get on with the certain blokes or, you know, comradeship ain't there, it's going to be very difficult to work two years.

It is this comradeship, together with the long hours spent away from their real families, which provides the basis for the unit becoming, in effect, a sort of surrogate family: a substitute group characterized by relative exclusivity and the investment of much time and emotional energy. The frequency with which SPG officers themselves spontaneously make the 'family' analogy suggests the idea is not entirely fanciful:

> On a unit, as I said before, we are like a large family, and I suppose you could say the same thing about the Group.

> You have to learn comradeship a little bit more, teamwork, you have to learn to tolerate people, like I say . . . you're with them probably as much as you're with your own family and . . . I think you have to learn to know their little irritations and weaknesses.

Of course, the differences between actual family life, with its male-dominated hierarchical pecking orders and associated inequalities (between husbands and wives, male children and female children, parents and children, and so on), and life on the (all male) unit, should not be forgotten. In many ways, unit life resembles (despite rank differentials) a male club more than a family. Either way, the significance for my purpose remains the same, which is that the pressures of socialization are not easily evaded. In occupations, like lighthouse keepers or university academics, where much time is spent working alone, the pressures towards conformity to an occupational ideal (even supposing there is one), can be comfortably evaded. Indeed, eccentricity, though not an inevitable feature of both jobs, is certainly common enough in both. But in the SPG, because of the features so far outlined, whatever idiosyncracies individual officers might have had on entry will find the pressures of informal socialization to the SPG ethos – to, in other words, the learning of competence – hard to resist.

Learning teamwork

It is, indeed, this aspect of the work that provides the single most essential thing to be learned by new members – teamwork: how to operate as part of a pair and, when occasion demands, as part of a single team. Achieving this aim requires first that a new recruit is paired up with an old hand from whom he can learn the ropes. This means that in forming new partnerships 'you'd never put two new men together', as one senior officer put it. Through a process of listening, watching and questioning, the newcomer will then learn the essentials of paramilitary teamwork from his partner – never act alone; always watch out for your partner; and 'back up' other SPG members without question. As the 'front-line troops in public order situations', which means, effectively, working in the prospective trouble spots, the function of teamwork is partly concerned to ensure members' safety. Though, as one SPG officer suggested, the advantages of corroborating evidence in court make for a second important function of teamwork: 'it's always best to have two police officers to give evidence against a prisoner rather than one'.

But, because it is so different from the individualistic ways of working developed in subdivisional unit beatwork, working with a partner comes as something of a shock, as many found. It thus constitutes the area where most mistakes are initially made.

> the first couple of times I [went into the crowd at football matches], I lost [my partner] sort of thing, and he comes 'what the bloody hell's going on' sort of thing, you know, 'you should hang on here with me,' or, 'we should work as a team'. Well, I'd been bogging off on me own, you have to get used to that.

> I did once go into a crowd, football match, there was a crowd there . . . [The Group] were looking at someone causing, pushing this, that and the other in the crowd, and I could see him, and it was you know, about ten deep into the crowd, and . . . you know we was going to have him out. I thought well the best chance to get him, you know, was wait 'til it had quietened down a bit and I'd got a good view of him and go in, and . . . Mr —— says . . . 'I can see him there', and he then turned away and I went in. And then he turned round and I turned round and there was nobody behind me, and then, you know, he just saw me in the crowd and came in straight away says 'oh', you know. I thought 'oh', and hears . . . 'don't ever go in'. That was a mistake.

The essential 'back-up regardless' principle overrides hitherto sacred individual judgements, which means, effectively, the subordination of individual constabulary powers, exercised using personal judgement, to the judgement of others.

> If somebody's gone into a crowd and you think, Christ almighty, I'm not going in there, but you've got to go in behind them even though you personally probably wouldn't have gone in there. You've got to do it, and there again, you're relying . . . on somebody else's judgement, . . . hopefully they are things that will come out alright . . . you've got to go by their judgement, by what they've seen.

The trust involved in such mutual support – 'complete back-up to the hilt' – goes well beyond what they have experienced on divisions. Indeed, once on the Group, it is regarded as an axis of differentiation from 'divisionals':

> It's got to be complete back-up, because . . . there's just a couple of occasions, that's all, that I've thought . . . daft, I've thought that was wrong like, shouldn't have done that. But . . . there's got to be complete trust and you knew that you was going to get it off those [SPG] lads, whereas I could go into an incident here now . . . and say to one of the [divisional] PCs, 'you saw all that, didn't you?' . . . and they'll say, 'huh, I don't want to put a statement in', you know, 'I didn't . . . I didn't see it' whereas on the SPG you go in and you say, 'you heard him say what he said', and they says, 'oh yes'. Although they was right behind you, they heard something, but they will commit themselves not to perjure themselves, but they will commit themselves to the words that he said, that you heard, whereas . . . a lot of people wouldn't want to get involved, a lot of bobbies say 'well, no, I don't want to do it', you know.

> In the SPG, if you get in trouble they will always back you as far as I know, when I, every incident I've had, you'll never be on your own, they'll always back you up . . . you can trust them in the SPG because you work together for eight hours solid every day, eight of you in the van . . . the trust is there. On division if you ask for assistance, a lot of them would turn their back and, like I said to you before, I've seen them going the opposite way. It's unbelievable, but it's bloody right.

Acquiring the 'working norm'

Let us remember that the SPG already consists of keen young men anxious to be 'actively' involved. Now, the learning of teamwork requires absolute support no matter how foolish or ill judged. In other words, the most active of an already active Group set both the pace and hence the 'norm'. Not surprisingly, then, the result is the construction and constant reinforcement of a 'working norm' or group ethos centred on alert observation and active involvement, fearlessness in the face of difficult situations, and commitment to firm and decisive action without prior pondering of possible repercussions. Such an ethos is very different from the typical mores of divisional officers on public order work. While such a norm does not necessarily mean intervention with a view to arrest on all occasions when sanctionable behaviour is observed, it does entail refusing to ignore it – by keeping an eye on it; or having a word of 'advice', for example. In this way, the individual differences that become part of the 'blagging' mentioned earlier are accommodated, as are the consequent differences in individual arrest rates. But, given the requirement of unconditional support, which obviously precludes the emergence and sustenance of completely individualistic styles, the resulting differences in approach (and arrest rates) tend to amount to relatively small variations around the norm – which the comparative arrest rates of individual unit members bear out.

The requirement to get actively involved obviously requires learning how to spot what might need sorting out, that is, potential 'trouble'. Along with teamwork, it is one of the hardest things for newcomers to the SPG to learn. Inside a football ground, for example, the new officer is faced with a whole range of behaviour, from shouting, taunting and chanting to jumping, pushing and gesticulating, all of which is subject to a variety of responses from colleagues. Even if the newcomer is generally familiar with the goings on at football matches, through his divisional experience, for example, he will, at first, be unable to 'see' what is before his very eyes:

> The first time I went to a football match as part of a Group I was just out of my depth, the way they went in and operated . . . I found it very hard to spot, because I couldn't see what they were looking for half the time. All of a sudden you'd been standing there you'd see two blokes dart into a crowd and pull somebody out, and I thought, I'm saying, 'what's he done?' and they say, 'oh, he's throwed a beer can or something', and, no matter how hard I looked for several months I just couldn't see what they'd gone into the crowd for.

Gradually, what was but a moving kaleidoscope of meaningless activity comes into focus and the chants, the gestures and the movements begin to form part of a discernible pattern. In other words, once newcomers have learned to 'see', the various activities cease to appear random and disconnected. Rather, they are seen to involve particular groups in particular locations at particular times doing particular things. The process of learning thus entails knowing *who* and *what* to look out for, *when* and *where* to look, and *how* to expunge extraneous details from the field of vision, as the SPG supervisor quoted above eventually found. Asked what makes the difference between looking and not 'seeing' anything and being able to spot something, he said:

> I don't know, it's hard to say, just experience I suppose. It's just something that's developed. I can see it now with new officers that come on to the Group while I've been on, how they stand back, and I've said, before they've said this, they just can't see what you're looking for, it's sort of . . . what I find you, you don't look at a crowd, which is what most people do, you look at a section of a crowd, and then you break down a section of a crowd once you've picked out a trouble spot, and, as far as I'm concerned, I can see no other crowd. I can't, once I've picked a section of crowd, I just can't see nothing else.

Being competent

At this point, what was previously 'strange' has become 'known' through the process of informal socialization. Or, more precisely, the erstwhile novice has internalized the common sense or 'working norm' of the Group, and the working practices that flow from it, and become competent.

But, by this point in time, the gap between the new socialized self and the pre-socialized novice is large indeed. The old self could not even 'see' offences and was uncommitted to the idea of unconditional support; the new self can both spot offences and is also prepared to follow the lead of others, regardless of how foolhardy or bull-headed he may privately judge it. The complementing of the initial enthusiasm for active involvement characteristic of SPG recruits with a learning process that heightens observational sensitivity *and* with an ethos of mutual support that makes the ultra-active members the 'norm' setters, ensures that the resulting common sense or working norm (and accompanying practice) is centred on high levels of activity (an observation borne out by the arrest figures of SPG officers compared with those of other officers on public order occasions), and thus ensures the completion of the amplifying trigger.

Though alert activity may be seen as desirable by many, including senior officers in the force, its undesirable, amplifying potential does need to be recognized. Divisional officers – unschooled in the art of unconditional team-work and unlearned in trouble-spotting (operating, in other words, with a different 'working norm') – do seem to recognize the problem. This recognition manifests itself in the attitude of divisional officers to the SPG. Though they regard SPG professional 'efficiency', technical 'know-how' and great experience with some pride, this is mixed with a certain repugnance at what is seen as the Group's insensitive and sometimes unnecessarily aggressive response to situations – a feeling which finds colloquial expression in terms such as 'the animals' or 'the heavy mob', as SPG officers themselves know only too well:

> The only conflict [between the SPG and divisional officers] I've ever come across is when . . . like say, the . . . SPG are [tape unclear] you know, some men class it as a rent-a-mob and, you know, a load of animals in a van, you know . . . I used to think the same myself two or three years ago.

For their part, SPG officers also have an ambivalent attitude to divisional officers: they recognize, having been there, of course, the different motivation and lesser training and experience in public order work of divisional officers; but, on the other hand, they can get resentful that they are sometimes left to clear up messes resulting from, as they see it, indecisive divisional action:

> A lot of them [divisional officers] are just working over and all they want to do is go to the football match, have a good afternoon, don't want to get tied up at the end of the match, you know, at six if they got a prisoner, that means they're 8.30, 9, before they are finished, they don't want that, they just want to watch the match, get home . . . when I went to the football match, like I said before, we used to go on the coach, they used to say 'For Christ sake don't get no prisoners because you get tied up. That means the coach waiting for you and the coach will bugger off without you.'

> I think divisional men [*sic*] tend to sit back at football matches and let trouble start . . . whereas we, if we see any sign of trouble, we try to get in there straight away, react quick, get the trouble-makers out and then it tends to calm the situation down a bit.

We're more on our toes than the divisional men, because they'll stand there, watch the match, with their hands in their pockets, smoking, cups of tea at the back of the crowd.

These differences, resulting from their different socialization experiences, can erupt into real antagonisms when initiated SPG officers, with their learned working norm, 'see' offences where divisional officers, in their 'innocence', literally cannot.

I did have a row with some the other week, a few comments were passed, then, they was all jumping up and down, about six of 'em started jumping up and down and the crowd surged forward. I went in, fetched one of them out, and one of 'em says, 'what's he done', and 'if you'd opened your bloody eyes' he'd have seen like he was jumping, and all the rest, and they thought, well, that was their opinion, but they thought, bloody hell, you know, it's only my personal opinion.

It is but a short step from here to equating the SPG with trouble, which, for our purposes, amounts to a recognition (at some level) of the potential amplifying consequences of the SPG type of 'common sense'.

I can honestly say I've heard divisional men [sic] say there's no trouble, until the SPG arrives. And they, they start the trouble, well, I mean, I've heard that many times you know, the SPG start the trouble, you know. What they don't realize is that when we are there, well, when they are there, you see, they are on a football match on their own, divisional men, no SPG men there, there's probably no trouble because they are watching the match, they are probably winging pennies at each other, y'know, and shouting abuse, and the divisional men are standing there, thinking, well, you know, they are outnumbered anyway, y'know, there's a risk, like, spread out, dotted in between each other, let them get on with it . . . that's why I think all this chanting goes on and the next match, and there's eight units of SPG there, and there's a line of police officers all down the line, and these yobbos then thinking, oh, well, you know, we can sing and throw because nothing happened last week, and then they start singing and the SPG move in and then they fetch one out, and a divisional man will turn round and they start pushing, you know, and this, that, and the other, and then he'll go back to division and say, 'bloody hell, last week it was a great match, there was, you know, hardly any trouble, there was a few skir-mishes and that, and throwing, but that was nothing, but this week the SPG was on, and there were 40 arrested and, you know, there was no need for it'. I think, you know, that's the conflict between divisional men on football matches. They, they, like I say, they are overtime men. Majority are, and they don't want to get involved.

Becoming hardened

The likelihood of this greater SPG involvement leading to trouble is increased by two final features of the role, features which also complete the transformation of the novice into seasoned paramilitary – the *singularity* of the Group's focus on public order work and, within such work, the *regularity* of their use in potentially violent 'trouble spots'. Despite the potential variety of SPG work, few would dispute the narrowing down of their job function, when compared with the work of divisional officers:

> the job on the SPG was black and white as far as I was concerned . . . there was no room for grey, either we went into situations, or we didn't go into situations, it was just as simple as that.

> In the football season all we concentrate on is public order, disturbances, football matches, demonstrations. That's all we've got time really for.

This narrowness of the job leads to the 'expectation of trouble' associated with public order work being constantly confirmed and hence becoming virtually a *permanent* expectation. The regular use of the SPG in the 'front line' of potential disorders – in the trouble spots – quickly produces a hardening effect, with all the negative connotations that that entails.

SUMMARY AND CONCLUSION

The recruitment of keen young men anxious to prove themselves through active involvement, and a training programme that covers everything except what really matters – the trouble-free prevention of disorder – jointly provide the preconditions for the transformation of novices into seasoned paramilitary professionals through the processes of informal socialization. The comradeship arising from spending long, frustrating and wearing hours together cements the essential teamwork, and the commitment to alert responses to potential trouble and an ability to spot it, together constitute the key aspects of the Group's 'common sense' or working norm. Once recruits are armed with this 'common sense' telling them to get in fast and early and support colleagues doing the same, and once they have become hardened to the 'trouble' which is constantly expected, then they can be said to be properly socialized into the ethos of the Group, an ethos which is a far cry from that they were used to during their time as divisional officers.

Masculinity is central to this ethos. The absence of women, the male camaraderie, the mock cruelty of 'blagging' as the preferred mode of whiling away 'standby' hours, the equation of the job with potential trouble, the premium on decisiveness, firm interventions and toughness, the sense of being the cavalry to whom beleaguered divisions turn to for help, all help make SPG work the epitome of a certain traditional notion of 'manliness'. Though the equation of masculinity with violence is too simple, feminists are right to point to the affinities between the two. In this sense, then, masculinity must be considered part of the amplifying spiral – though, as yet, little sociology of policework has been informed directly by this concept.

Moreover, as we saw in the previous chapter, this ethos is relatively unconstrained by legal and democratic structures. This means that this common-sense 'working norm' (the occupational dimension of the work structure) dominates in operational contexts because of the void resulting from a weak legal structure, a weak democratic structure, *and* a weak organizational dimension of the work structure, this last, as we have just seen, resulting from the void of a formal training programme (training being one practical manifestation of the organizational dimension) that neglects the key issue of appropriateness. Within this void, the processes of recruitment, training and informal socialization just outlined jointly construct a potentially lethal spiral of amplification. The historical and sociological conditions underpinning the emergence of paramilitarism have, of course, been dealt with in previous chapters. It therefore only remains for me to summarize the argument and draw out certain implications by way of a conclusion. These are the tasks of the next and final chapter.

NOTE

1. The material upon which this chapter is based was taken from my four months spent as an observer of two SPG units in action, which was part of a much broader observational study of a large metropolitan county force undertaken between 1977 and 1980. The quotations are taken from the semi-structured taped interviews conducted at the end of the period of observation. Altogether, 11 interviews were conducted with SPG officers: the chief inspector in charge of the Group, one inspector, two sergeants, seven PCs and one DC. In addition, group interviews were conducted with both units, as well as the chief superintendent at headquarters responsible for the Group. The Chief Constable, his Deputy and the Assistant Chief Constable (operations) were also interviewed as part of the broader project. Interview lengths varied between one-and-a-half and six hours, the average being around two hours.

CHAPTER 7

General summary and concluding remarks

There remain, finally, just two outstanding tasks: the first is to remind the reader of the overall argument by means of a general summary; the second is to draw out the various implications of my argument.

GENERAL SUMMARY

Chapter 1 traced the story of how Britain acquired, from the 1960s onwards, a paramilitary police capacity. It examined how separate 'third force', civil defence and crime-fighting debates coalesced into a single concern with public order and terrorism, and produced the basis of the peculiarly British situation: permanent force-based Special Patrol Groups supplemented by Police Support Units, available for mobilization should extra intra- or inter-force assistance be needed. In particular, it showed how a variety of industrial, political and social confrontations helped shape developments in the 1970s: for example, the establishment of the National Reporting Centre for co-ordinating mutual aid after the 1972 miners' strike; the appearance of special protective equipment, most notably the riot shield, after the Notting Hill carnival of 1976; and, in the aftermath of Southall, in 1979, the thorough reorganization of the Metropolitan Police SPG, the first of a succession of attempts to deal with the unwanted fallout from the new paramilitarism – the SPG's growing reputation for brutality and aggression. It showed also how the inner-city disturbances of the 1980s provided the stimulus to further developments: a nation-wide revamping of organization and training; the acquisition of improved protective clothing and more lethal weaponry, particularly CS gas and plastic bullets; and the importation of 'colonial'-style tactics of aggressive dispersal. As the 1990s begin, the appearance of anonymous teams of offensively-orientated be-visored and flame-proofed paramilitaries, shield in one hand and truncheon in the other, has become a normal feature of the policing of public order.

Two common but unsatisfactory approaches to the problems posed by paramilitarism were then discussed. The first, which makes centralization (or a national riot squad) the key issue, was found wanting because of its idealistic sense of British police history. Whether arguing for or against such a squad, the shared problem for each was how best to preserve the consensual tradition. The second approach, focused on professionalism, was similarly idealistic in its reliance on the 'professional' discipline of paramilitarism as the most 'effective' way of restoring the tradition of 'impartiality' and 'restraint' threatened by the confrontations of the 1970s and 1980s. Against such idealism, a more concrete approach was proposed: one premised upon a simple definition of paramilitarism – 'the application of (quasi-)military training, equipment, philosophy and organization to questions of policing (whether under centralized control or not)' – and a less abstract history and sociology of paramilitary policing.

I then suggested that such a project effectively entailed an inversion of the idealistic 'professionalism' approach. Against this 'restrained' tradition of policing disorder, I suggested that 'unjust violence' was probably more in keeping with the experiences of the 'policed' (developed in Chapter 2). Against this notion of *impartial* policing, I pointed to the *political* nature of police discretion, and to the highly discretionary nature of public order policing (developed in Chapters 3 and 4). And, against the argument about paramilitary *effectiveness*, I proposed that the paramilitary approach *amplified* levels of disorder (developed in Chapters 5 and 6).

Chapter 2 addressed the question of the 'restrained' tradition by looking critically at the conservative reading of police history underpinning it, and supplied an alternative account. The 'history-as-progress' approach of the conservatives was outlined, whereby cross-class pressure produced the commitment to minimum force which in turn led to widespread public acceptance and the famous British 'police advantage' which must be preserved at all costs. An example was then used to illustrate concretely the problems with such an approach – Geary's conservative account of the increasingly pacific nature of industrial confrontations, which can only accommodate the renewal of violence during the miners' strike of 1984–5 by seeing it as the exception that proves the rule.

Gramsci, who saw consent as contingent upon a struggle between contending forces attempting to achieve 'hegemony' (moral authority) and history as a series of 'conjunctures' each more or less stable depending on the outcome of these ongoing struggles, was then offered as providing a more fruitful historical framework. Phil Cohen's work on the history of 'policing the working class city', with its notions of the police's contradictory mission (to enforce bourgeois law and proletarian order), of the consequent police need to compromise the letter of the law to achieve acceptability in working-class neighbourhoods, and of the structural changes in the composition of the working classes always threatening to undermine existing compromises, was then used to illustrate this idea – that both consent (and conflict) are contingent, not inevitable, features of public order policing. Using this approach to think about the mid-1960s emergence of paramilitarism necessitated a concrete examination of the postwar conjuncture. This examination, drawing heavily on *Policing the Crisis* by Hall *et al.*, traced the shift from the consensual, hegemonic 1950s, through the 'transitional' decade of the 1960s to the breakdown of hegemony in the 1970s and 1980s and the related emergence of a crisis in policing – a conjunctural return to the predominance of Foucault's 'sovereignty–law–repression'. The emergence and development of paramilitary policing outlined in Chapter 1 was seen to coincide with the moment of this dual crisis. In Cohen's terms the new tougher paramilitary response represents the reversion to the strict enforcement of 'bourgeois law' with those groups ('the new lumpen' and dissidents of various persuasions) 'created' by the structural changes – economic, political and ideological – of the 1970s and 1980s. And, in keeping with Cohen's analysis, the tougher policing response has been matched by a growth of community relations policing (a normalizing practice, in Foucaultian terms), whose job is essentially to renegotiate the terms of acceptable police entry into variously alienated communities.

Finally, because of the worsening nature of the crises, the problem of 'technological drift' (the idea that once the technology is available it becomes easier to use it and become used to it), Thatcher's commitment to a tough law and order stance, and the absence of an alternative vision, the moment renders the idea of 'restrained' policing even more idealistically abstract – especially when viewed from the 'bottom up', the vantage point of those on the receiving end of paramilitarism. This constitutes, then, the concrete historical starting point for the subsequent evaluation.

Chapter 3 was concerned to expose the idealism behind the notion of impartial law enforcement, consider the actual determinants of law-enforcement decisions, look at these 'in action', and show how things are presently getting worse. Theoretically, police officers are placed 'above politics' and granted a unique independence to ensure 'impartial' law enforcement. In reality officers of all ranks end up selectively enforcing the law: chief constables because lack of knowledge, time and resources preclude full enforcement; and constables because laws which lack clarity or the need for a complainant make subjective judgements inevitable. This discretionary, partisan nature of police decision-making, makes law enforcement inevitably political.

Conservatives tend to see the use of this discretion as benign and unpolitical, a notion challenged by radical sociologists who exposed the class-based outcomes of such decision-making. Concern with the processes through which such outcomes are achieved led first to the liberal sociologists who see discretion 'guided' either by the police subculture or by the 'environmental contexts' of policework. What was needed was a combination of the strengths of the radical critique (with its attention to outcomes, that is, the social function of law enforcement) and those of the liberal critique (with its attention to processes, that is, the *means*, through which such outcomes are achieved). Consequently, a more adequate conceptualization of the legal and extra-legal determinants of discretion, and the relationship between them, was argued to be needed. Crucial to this is the question of the *degree* of discretion in particular situations.

Making law more concrete is the first step – seeing it as a structure, with various sites where it gets defined and interpreted, and composed of various powers and demands. Regarding it thus renders offences different in their legal complexity and clarity, and in their need for complainants or witnesses – and, in consequence, different in terms of their ability to act as a constraining influence on discretion. Clearly defined legal offences, for example, are more constraining than others. A further level of constraint is the use made by citizens of the powers they possess – to complain or take civil action, for example – with a greater level of constraint associated with high usage, and vice versa.

As for the extra-legal constraints, these can be the organization itself, the public or immediate colleagues. Starting with the 'public', the question of the conditions under which various publics can influence police discretion can only be answered if police–public contacts are more concretely specified in terms of types of role, status of contacter, nature of contact and the sort of issue bringing police and public together. From this perspective, potentially 'troublesome' contacts with disreputable strangers are less constraining than friendly contacts with powerful, known, elected representatives, for example. Regarded in this way, the public is better reconceptualized as a democratic structure, as it is the principal concrete way in which a democratic influence can be brought to bear on police discretion.

Though the organization and colleagues (or 'the cop culture') are usually assumed to be separate, antithetical, influences on the use of police discretion, this assumption is not based on empirical evidence. In which case it is preferable to see both as part of a work structure with a horizontal (the 'cop culture') and a vertical (the organization) dimension. This leaves open the question of the relationship between management and the rank and file and allows the constraining influence of specific management practices (supervision, policy, and so on) on particular policing tasks to be examined separately.

The final question is how these structures of law, democracy and work, the actual determinants of discretion, are related in particular instances. Concern with being able to conceptualize both the unity and diversity of policework practices suggests that the law, ultimately, is the most important one in the sense that it determines, in particular instances, which of the structures is dominant. Applying this approach to public order policing on the ground reveals, first, that the law in this area is highly discretionary and therefore very weak as a constraint. Second, the kinds of public contact involved render the democratic structure similarly weak. As for the work structure, the vertical dimension (for example, supervision) is strong when instructions do not conflict with constabulary powers but weak when they do. In other words, when officers are instructed to clear streets, for example, the independence of the office overrides supervisory powers. Thus, in the crucial operational moments of public order policing, the structure which is dominant is the occupational dimension of the work structure – a situation determined by the weakness of the legal structure. An example of a public order arrest from my field notes followed to illustrate the above points. The further weakening of the legal and democratic structures in the present – new legislation granting police greater discretion and the ideological onslaught expanding the range of 'outsider' groups – effectively strengthens the dominance of the occupational dimension of the work structure. In so far as this effectively puts the norms and values of the police subculture at the helm of operational public order decision-making on the ground, this constitutes a worsening situation.

The purpose of Chapter 4 was to show how, because of the uniqueness of the relationship between police management and the rank and file, the occupational dimension of the work structure is dominant over the organizational dimension in public order operations. This entailed distinguishing between the various instruments of managerial control, suggesting that policy and supervision are the central instruments, offering concrete definitions of policy, policy-making and the process of policy consideration, and then illustrating the operation of policy and supervision in public order contexts using various examples drawn from fieldwork notes.

The conventional idea of policy as 'a set of instructions, guidelines or principles which ought to be followed' was discarded as idealistic because the policy data examined rarely took this form. Consequently, policy was defined as 'an authoritative statement signifying a settled practice on any matter relevant to the duties of the chief constable', a definition which enabled a distinction to be made between policy and other sorts of management statement, and between policy *consideration*, which might not culminate in a new policy statement, and policy-*making*, the moment when new policy is inaugurated. These distinctions were necessary to show that, in reality, policy-making to do with public order was a relatively infrequent event, that, consequently, little policy existed in this area, and that what little did exist was 'permissive'. Several specific examples were then looked at – various attempts to standardize public order charges, a public order policy file, and the use of dogs in crowd control – to demonstrate this effective absence of a key manifestation of the organizational dimension and, hence, why the occupational dimension is able to dominate in public order operational contexts. The effect at the level of supervision was then noted. Taking examples from both direct and indirect forms of supervising SPG work, we saw, once again, the dominance of occupational 'common sense' in operational contexts – despite close supervision, more opportunities for it and the highly visible nature of the work. The contrasts between police accounts of four public order arrests and my own field notes, and between the ease of monitoring SPG activity and the failure to use this to analyse specific incidents, provided the illustrative material.

Chapter 5 was concerned to show that a concrete examination of paramilitary policing leads to the conclusion that it amplifies disorder rather than being the most effective means of coping with it. Concluding thus entailed a critique of the 'ideal' of effectiveness, establishing a typical paramilitary policing sequence and its amplifying tendencies, illustrating the sequence using examples from contemporary public disorders and comparing these with evidence from abroad.

The idealistic notion of the effectiveness of the paramilitary option rests on a tautologous definition which simply excludes undisciplined examples and which draws sustenance from a traditional conception of professionalism long surpassed by more recent sociological approaches. The amplifying consequences of paramilitary policing emerge when a typical sequence, based upon the routine actual dynamics of such situations, is outlined. Such a sequence involves four stages: 'preparation'; 'controlling space'; 'controlling the crowd'; and 'clearance'. The amplifying elements of the preparatory stage include the provocative appearance of large numbers of riot-equipped officers, their readiness for the worst-case scenario, and the frustrations of long hours on standby. 'Controlling space', which necessarily entails moving some people, will cause resentment, the more so the more paramilitarily executed. Once crowd resentment turns into an active response, police expectations of trouble become confirmed, pre-emptive police action is undertaken, crowd expectations are confirmed and the self-fulfilling prophecy is under way. 'Controlling the crowd', if necessary by force, further heightens anger and confirms expectations. The release of snatch squads dramatically amplifies matters as the contrast between the protected police and the defenceless members of the crowd adds injustice to crowd anger. Injuries increase the anger. When the 'clearance' begins, an already angry crowd will become more so if this is executed insensitively and aggressively, especially if it is done in a paramilitary style. If knowledge of injuries is spreading, this only worsens matters. Though police eventually succeed, high levels of disorder encourage both sides to be better prepared (for violence) 'next time'. This sequence was then illustrated with three examples of recent disorders. At Broadwater Farm on 6 October 1985, the police sealed off the estate following the death of a black woman after a push by a police officer during a house search, and a night of violence followed, involving petrol bombs and gunshot and culminating in a police officer being stabbed to death. In Manchester on 1 March 1985, a peaceful demonstration by students against the visit of Leon Brittan, then Home Secretary, was aggressively broken up by TAG (Manchester's SPG) officers leaving many demonstrators hurt, injured and angry. At Orgreave on 18 June 1984, one of the mass pickets at the Orgreave coking plant during the year-long miners' strike became a public testing ground for the new and very aggressive 'colonial-style' tactics.

Evidence from other countries – Rodney Stark's examination of *Police Riots* in the USA and Cuneen and his colleagues' look at the policing of the bike races at Bathurst in Australia – was then presented in a manner which highlighted the similarities between their findings about policing and my own: how tough paramilitary policing produces resistance, tougher policing, more resistance, and so on.

Chapter 6 looked at the processes – of recruitment, training and informal socialization – which transform ordinary officers into a paramilitary team, and at how such processes can be amplifying. The typical recruit to the SPG is a keen ambitious young male officer of four or five years' standing, anxious to be 'active'. In police terms 'activity' means arrests, this being one of the few measurable outputs *and* sources of job satisfaction. Since the SPG values 'activity' and the only records kept are offence-related, arrests take on special importance. Although there is no policy excluding women, the practice is to do so. Even when women are admitted, as they now are in the Metropolitan Police

SPG, masculinist assumptions are likely to prevail. All these factors contribute, then, to the construction of an 'amplifying spiral'.

Training attends to drills and the law but completely ignores how specific incidents might best be handled. This is not due to a lack of time since standby and non-public order time is available, and the pace of the job is generally slower than for divisional officers. This neglect echoes the similar neglect in operational contexts where actions adjudged lawful, whether appropriate or otherwise, are not discussed because of the existence and primacy of constabulary powers. Consequently an informal means – 'blagging', a form of extended teasing – is adopted to air differences in a safe, non-threatening way.

Since training fails to provide an official forum for discussing the handling of incidents, this has to be learned on the job, informally, from colleagues. Given the long, unpredictable hours worked, the frustrations of standby and the emotionally taxing nature of the work, comradeship becomes the most important and satisfying feature of the job and the unit becomes a place where much time is spent, thus making the pressures of socialization difficult to avoid.

Work with a partner as part of a team is the most important and difficult thing to learn. Old hands pass on the essentials of such teamwork: never acting alone; watching out for your partner; and unquestioning 'back-up'. This unquestioning mutual support effectively subordinates individual judgements to those of others in the group, and the complete trust this entails and produces marks an important difference from the attitudes of divisional officers.

Since teamwork requires unconditional support, the most 'active' of an already keen and 'active' group of men set the pace and establish the group ethos or 'working norm'. Unsurprisingly, this is centred on alert observation, active involvement, fearlessness, firmness and decisiveness – very different mores from those of the typical divisional officer. And, since all must follow the most active, differences in style and arrest rates are small.

Once the who, what, when, where and how of spotting 'trouble' have been mastered and the novice has 'become competent' by internalizing the group working norm, the difference from divisional officers is complete, a process of differentiation not unrecognized by divisional officers, who talk of the SPG as 'the animals' or 'rent-a-mob', nor by SPG officers themselves. At this point the potential for amplification is complete. The equation of the SPG with trouble is exacerbated by the singularity of its focus on public order work and the regularity with which it is used in the trouble spots. Jointly these produce a hardening effect which only makes amplification more likely. The dominance of the Group working norm, with all its potential for the amplification of violence, is, it should be remembered, effectively unconstrained either by legal and democratic structures, which are both weak, or by a similarly weak organizational dimension of the work structure – this last illustrated here by the void in the formal training programme.

With the overall argument now, hopefully, back in mind, we are ready to turn to some concluding remarks.

CONCLUDING REMARKS: TWO POSSIBLE FUTURES

In his excellent conclusion to *Visions of Social Control*, Stan Cohen argues persuasively that it is not the job of the sociologist 'to advise, consult, recommend or make decisions'.[1] What is important for intellectual workers, however, 'is to clarify the implications of your analysis. That is, to try to understand the type of differences which do make a difference.'[2] It is with that distinction in mind that I approach this concluding section. Drawing out the implications of my analysis are thus what concerns me in what follows; recommendations and similar tasks, as Cohen says, 'belong to others'.[3]

The 'worst case' scenario

I want to start by thinking through the implications of failing to reverse present trends, that is, the 'worst case' scenario. Let us recall, first, my starting point – the notion of history as a series of conjunctures, each of which can be characterized by either a high degree of consensus (hegemony) or by the reverse (breakdown of hegemony), depending upon the particular balance of forces obtaining at the time. From this perspective, it should be recalled, the present 'moment of Thatcherism' is an example of dissensus, of the breakdown of hegemony. This has meant that upholding order, whether on the social, political or industrial front, has been (as I show in Chapter 1, for example), and continues to be (I write this as the students lick their wounds after being attacked by police during their London grants demonstration in November 1988) a fiercely contested affair. At such moments the traditional response of authorities is to go for more and 'tougher' law in the interests of better order. (This 'traditional' aspect is part of the 'regressive' side of Hall's telling characterization of Thatcherism as a project of 'regressive modernisation'.)[4] Now, as I argued in Chapter 3, those laws giving more powers to the police, such as the Police and Criminal Evidence Act 1984 and the new Public Order Act 1986, effectively grant them more *discretion*. And, as I also argued in the same chapter, because of the notion of constabulary independence and the resulting absence of guidance either from inside or outside the force as to the most appropriate use of discretion, the occupational subculture is effectively 'in command'. In such a situation, granting police more discretion is dangerous enough. But it becomes infinitely more so when the particular subcultural values 'in command' are those of the battle-hardened and action-orientated SPG. When, furthermore, such Groups are given more and 'tougher' weapons and equipment, another 'traditional/regressive' response to problems of disorder, the prospects become frightening indeed.

In other words, a projection of present trends would have to emphasize a mounting concern with disorder and a characteristically regressive 'legal-technical' response to it: greater powers and discretion to those designated to deal with it – the 'hard-cop', public order specialists – and ever more technologically sophisticated weaponry and equipment. If the deviancy amplification spiral has become an unfashionable concept, it can be usefully resurrected here. For, without suggesting an inevitability to any of this (which deliberately assumes that any counter-tendencies at work will remain relatively weak), each feature of the regressive response certainly increases the *potential* for unleashing further violence.

Changes in policing public order are, of course, linked to concerns about disorder. So, to complete this 'worst case' future, I need to draw out the implications of a failure to reverse present trends conducive to social disorder. Here I must necessarily be more speculative, but enough has been said about the social effects of Thatcherism to enable one or two projections to be made.

One undeniable feature of Thatcherism has been the creation of mass unemployment among certain sections of the young in certain areas. And many would subscribe to the view that this constitutes 'social dynamite', capable of exploding whenever there is a suitable spark of ignition. Certainly the notion that the inner-city riots were essentially an angry outburst by black and white unemployed youths – the disaffected dispossessed – is a commonplace.[5] For the sake of brevity then, I intend, in what follows, to focus solely on this question of social disorder and youth.

Let me start with a brief list of some of what I take to be the important signs of this youthful disorder.

1. Disturbances. I have in mind here not just the major eruptions of 1980, 1981 and 1985, but, particularly, the small-scale 'mini-disturbance'. Though the nature and extent of these remains obscure, mostly because there has been a tendency to play them down so as to avoid the so-called 'copycat' effect as well as, no doubt, to conceal the extent of police–youth hostility and of government inaction against inner-city deprivation, the signs are that such clashes are becoming less exceptional in major urban centres. Indeed, though I have no evidence to support it, I have a hunch that the recent outbursts of 'lager-loutism' outside the major urban centres, impressively analysed by Mary Tuck,[6] are in some way related phenomena. I should add that this is not something the Mary Tuck study explores.

2. Attacks on particular police stations, police officers, police cars, etc. These are essentially just limited versions of the above, discrete in focus, possibly simply a form of reprisal action for particular incidents. Once again, the nature and extent of these almost certainly exceeds those which do become 'newsworthy', probably for the same reasons as govern the playing-down of 'mini-disturbances'.

3. The use of lethal weapons. Whatever the relationship between the use of weapons by the police and by protestors, both have gradually turned to increasingly lethal weapons. For demonstrators, the movement has been from sticks and stones to petrol bombs and, finally, on one occasion – the Broadwater Farm disturbance in 1985 – to guns.

4. Bomb attacks. Following the police killing of Clinton McCurbin during a violent struggle following his arrest in a Wolverhampton shop, a bomb was

planted near a Wolverhampton police station by a group calling itself the Black Liberation Front. Subsequently, the same group has claimed responsibility for the Christmas week posting of three incendiary devices, one of which exploded, in the West Midlands. One was addressed to the Chief Constable, one to a local superintendent, and one to a councillor.[7]

If nothing intervenes to alter present trends, we can expect these presently *ad hoc*, occasional and relatively isolated signs of disorder to become more and more organized, regular and widespread – or, in a word, endemic. But, these signs also illustrate the progressively *tougher* nature of the responses – not unsurprisingly, of course, in the light of my argument about the amplifying effects of paramilitary policing. Now, it does not need much imagination, nor much sense of history, to see how excluded and dispossessed groups move from disaffection, through spontaneous, angry disorder, to organized opposition and resistance. The examples are all around us. So, it should not be difficult to envisage this spontaneous anger coalescing into something more organized and sustained, involving perhaps some form of urban terrorism.

If this were to happen, it is worth bearing in mind the differences between the early 1970s – a previous moment when a section of the alienated young converted open disaffection into violent, underground resistance – and the present. The Angry Brigade, in despair at the apparent stranglehold of consumer capitalism on the working classes and wishing to rouse them from their slumbers via the political education of the selectively placed bomb and accompanying explanatory communiqué, were a product (though some might say the nemesis) of the optimistic, visionary 1960s. If the more hard-headed were sceptical of utopian visions, there was at least the sense of social alternatives to existing arrangements. The present moment is very different. It is not just the changed nature of the economic foundations from 1960s 'affluence' to the heightened inequalities of the 1980s that makes it so; it is, more profoundly, the new political pessimism – the lack of any sense of how things might be different. This sense has to do both with what Stuart Hall, following Gramsci, describes as the 'proliferation of the sites of power and antagonism in modern society',[8] *and* the failure of the Left to organize this proliferation of new social forces into 'a new historical project'[9] because

It doesn't see that it is in the very nature of modern capitalist civilization to proliferate the centres of power, and thus to draw more and more areas of life into social antagonism. It does not recognise that the identities which people carry in their heads – their subjectivities, their cultural life, their sexual life, their family life and their ethnic identities, are always incomplete and have become massively politicized.[10]

The New Right, of course, has produced such a project – Thatcherism – based on, as the title of Gamble's recent book puts it, 'the free economy and the strong state'.[11] This does not involve organizing the disparate sites of power into solidaristic collectivities but, rather, the reverse, that is, encouraging the further proliferation of such sites in the pursuit of an unbridled individualism;

encouraging, in other words, the complete fragmentation of social life, albeit under the tutelage of a strong state. One consequence of the success of this project, in the context of a failure of the Left either to envisage any social alternative or to empower through a thoroughgoing democratization, *and* of ever 'tougher' policing, is that the multiple sites of power will become multiple sites of resistance – each acting alone, unconnected with other sites, and without any global, guiding vision of an alternative future. In other words, the resistance, like the power itself, will be multiple, fragmented and unpredictable. The image I have of resistance in such a 'worst case' scenario, then, is one of a volatile mixture of desperation, instability and unpredictability (which is not, of course, to suggest that *all* centres of resistance will be this disorganized).

This image, or spectre, of urban chaos – paramilitarized cops engaging 'chaotic' resistance in an amplifying spiral of bitterness and violence – was once simply the stuff of the apocalyptic nightmare visions of certain artists. In facing up to the implications of my own analysis, I have been led to conclude, regrettably, that such visions may yet prove remarkably prescient.

'But that's not the way it's got to be . . .'

Constructing a 'best case' scenario entails drawing out the implications of my concrete reconstruction of each of the terms I started out with – 'restraint', 'impartiality' and 'effectiveness'.

'Restraint' and police history 'from below'

In Chapter 2 I argued for a contingent, conjunctural view of police history based on a reading of Gramsci. However, it is important to remember that Gramsci talked of organic trends (the long-term structural tendencies within a social system) as well as conjunctural moments (the particular balance of forces at particular historical moments). Applied to a history of policing, this distinction corresponds to one often drawn between the social function of policing (the 'organic' aspect and usually taken to be 'order maintenance; which effectively boils down to policing working class culture and crime, and conflict and dissent more generally')[12] and the manner of its execution at particular moments (the conjunctural question of the degree of coercion necessary to maintain order). However, for those routinely the object of police 'order maintenance' attention – the criminals, deviants, and other powerless groups that have become, in Lee's evocative phrase, 'police property'[13] – the 'organic' nature of their relationship with the police is overriding, whatever the conjuncture. In other words, the view of policing 'from below' remains relatively constant: police violence, not restraint, is always potentially their lot; it is just a little more likely in less hegemonic times. The implications of this are that there are definite limits to the changes possible through police reform alone, *especially* when the conjuncture, as presently, is much less hegemonic, and *especially* for those designated 'police property'. This is a viewpoint echoed in various ways by many. For example:

139

The worst enemies of the current police bid for relegitimation are arguably not their overt critics but their apparent benefactors – a 'law and order' government which is unconcerned about destroying the social preconditions of consensus policing and the virtues of the British police tradition.[14]

Rather than place policing at the centre of a socialist response to crime, we would emphasise the cardinal importance of social justice as the only legitimate basis of order, and the need for a range of social and environmental measures to improve the quality of life, as well as preventing some kinds of crime, in those neighbourhoods most afflicted by crime and insecurity. Public investment, and participation by residents in decisions which affect their lives, are vital ingredients in the process of local regeneration.[15]

Problems of policework, then, cannot be solved purely by changes in policework, however radical these are.

One of the Right's characteristic responses – particularly in 'iron times' like now – is to translate broader questions of social justice into the narrow issue of crime and policing. Some criminologists, the so-called 'new realists',[16] have chosen to contest the Right on this narrow ground by 'taking crime seriously' from a left-wing rather than a right-wing perspective. Whatever the other merits or demerits of the new realist project, which cannot detain me here,[17] what it singularly fails to do is shift the whole terrain of the debate away from traditional 'common-sense' understandings of crime and policing. Hegemonic projects like Thatcherism demand hegemonic responses.[18] So, without a strategy to attack various social injustices, without attention to the way such injustices are transformed through processes of ideological signification into questions of crime and law enforcement *and* into an overattentiveness to working-class criminality, use of public space, deviance, dissent, and so on,[19] and without encouraging forms of informal social control,[20] focusing solely on the policing of crime and disorder is at best redundant and, at worst, counterproductive. Hogg's sympathetically critical review of 'new realism' also endorses this point that the importance of policing should not be overemphasized.[21] In sum, the 'best case' scenario for all of us concerned with resolving the order-maintenance problem of policing, would be to make policing *less important* to the problem of social order. To pinch Stan Cohen's argument:

> This is not because crime is 'unimportant' . . . it is rather, as therapists sometimes have to tell their patients or Zen masters their disciples, that we have to take a problem less seriously in order to solve it.[22]

If making policing less important is one important implication of a concrete consideration of the British police tradition, there is one final point to bear in mind. In so far as changes specifically within policing are concerned, these have to be judged 'from below'. In other words, in so far as we do take the question of 'restraint' or 'minimum force' seriously, the touchstone has to be the perception of the routinely restrained. I take up this issue, among others, in what follows.

'Impartiality' and the politics of police discretion

My earlier reconstruction of the notion of impartiality highlighted, first, the failure to recognize the existence of police discretion and hence the intrinsically political nature of the task of policing at all levels; and second, the fact that presently such discretion is guided by the police themselves, which in crucial operational contexts means little more than the common-sense 'rules' of the occupational subculture. This recognition of the political nature of the police task currently 'steered' by the police themselves raises the issue of who, in a democratic society, should guide the use of this discretion, and what should be the criteria informing discretionary guidelines. I intend to draw out the 'best case' implications of each of these – recognizing discretion, who should direct, and by what criteria – in turn.

Recognizing police discretion

Recognizing the existence of substantial police discretion implies 'two principal needs . . . the elimination of unnecessary discretionary power and better control of necessary discretionary power'.[23] Eliminating unnecessary discretion entails 'confining discretion' by which 'is meant fixing the boundaries and keeping discretion within them'.[24] Better control of necessary discretion entails 'structuring and checking. Structuring includes plans, policy statements and rules, as well as open findings, open rules, and open precedents . . . Checking includes both administrative and judicial supervision and review.'[25] There is no space here to develop these ideas, nor, given their extensive and admirably clear elaboration by Davis in *Discretionary Justice*, is there any need. The key to the whole exercise is the far greater use of administrative rule-making:

> *The typical failure in our system that is correctable is not legislative delegation of broad discretionary power with vague standards; it is the procrastination of administrators in resorting to the rule-making power to replace vagueness with clarity.*[26]

Davis himself was in no doubt that the police were an area desperately in need of such rule-making.

> Perhaps the greatest single area of discretionary power which legislative bodies should cut back is the power of the police to nullify legislation through non-enforcement or partial enforcement.[27]

The important point I wish to stress about continuing and controlling discretion is that such activity is relevant *wherever* the law fails to offer a clear guide to action, *and* in those situations where there is no complainant.[28] In practice, on questions of public order, this means attending *both* to the chief constable's discretion to introduce various paramilitary options and to decide how they will be used, *and* to the discretion of constables executing their public order powers, which are, as we saw in Chapter 3, highly discretionary and rarely need complainants.

Who should 'guide' police discretion?

The question of who should be responsible for this exercise in cutting back and controlling police discretion is not helpfully dealt with by Davis. This is because he operates with a notion of administrators, his potential rule-makers, as rational, disinterested professionals.

> As administrators exercise discretion they solve some of the recurring problems. Then they naturally follow precedents, for they find it inefficient to rethink a question they have once resolved to their own satisfaction, in absence of special reason to do so. The precedents accordingly grow, the opinions are soon stating some standards or other guides, and the movement may go on toward principles and, for some subjects, rules.[29]

What such an approach ignores is the possibility of substantial *conflicts* emerging in this problem-solving process: the possibility of more than one 'right' answer to the problem. In Britain, the conflict over the use of discretionary powers by the police has produced a debate over who should direct the use of police discretion. I talk, of course, about the police-accountability debate. The police themselves claim either that they are bound by law (the impartiality claim) or that only they can be trusted to exercise their discretion disinterestedly (the claim to professionalism). Either way, they should remain masters of *their* own discretion. The majority of their critics agree the need, despite important differences and some confusions about the relationship between policy and practice which should not be overlooked, for some form of democratic input into some aspects of police discretionary powers. It is by now a well-rehearsed debate and needs no repetition here.[30]

What does need stressing here, though, is that a democratic input *confined* to elected representatives is unlikely adequately to represent the voices of those most affected by policing, that is, the routinely policed.[31] And, an input that does not enable these same routinely policed to have a *decisive* role in those *operational* areas, like policing public order, that really *matter*, is likely to be seen, by those most affected, as a 'cosmetic' public relations exercise. As Morgan put it, concluding a paper on police accountability, the question is 'whether the policing of those groups most dissatisfied with the police, generally those groups most marginal economically and politically, will change'.[32] Baldwin's reply in the same journal was not hopeful on this score;[33] nor, it has to be said, does the present evidence of Morgan's work on consultative committees give much cause for optimism.[34]

What should be the criteria for informing discretionary guidelines?

Here again Davis's liberalism precludes his posing this problem. His presumption about a disinterested search for the rational rule[35] overlooks Hall's important point about the multiple points of *antagonism* in modern society.[36] In such situations, the conflicts between, in public order situations, protesters and residents, between striking and working miners, and so on, need to be opened up for public debate. *Criteria* for defending particular positions need to be stated. Roger Grimshaw and I have argued elsewhere about the importance of a notion of *public justice* to such a debate.[37] I have also been gratified to see similar notions entering the accountability debate.[38] But, whatever criteria are adopted, they have to be perceived to be just by all those groups who collectively constitute 'police property'. 'Restraint', as I argued earlier, has to be 'the view from below'. It is for this reason that my own preference is for a notion of 'socialist justice' to be the primary criterion informing discretionary guidelines. Once again, this has been dealt with more fully elsewhere.[39] The essential principle involves producing guidelines that prioritize the rights of the most disadvantaged groups — as victims *and* offenders — to compensate for their overrepresentation in both categories.

'Effectiveness' and initiating a deamplifying spiral

Drawing out the implications of a concrete consideration of 'effectiveness' involves identifying the amplifying elements of paramilitarism and taking steps to put them in reverse: to initiate a deamplifying spiral. As we saw in Chapter 6, the various features that collectively constitute the difference between SPG work and unit beat policing — teamwork, unconditional support, special equipment, the focus on public order, and so on — jointly produce and sustain the distinctive common-sense rules, or 'working norm', of the group. As I have just been arguing, the discretion that allows such common-sense rules to develop needs to be confined and controlled, with any necessary discretion 'guided' by a set of criteria preferably arrived at through public debate involving a strong democratic input, and developed in accordance with some notion of public justice. These could constitute the new 'administrative rules' for the more appropriate handling of public disorder. In addition, the features that currently sustain the 'working norm' need to be systematically inverted. Now, while a strong democratic input to the construction of the new rules would require statutory change, this does not preclude the production of such rules solely after internal debate. Nor do the systematic inversions require more than imagination and commitment. Examples of the changes I have in mind include the following:

1. Getting into the habit of *analysing incidents* with a view to:
   (i) increasing the group's self-awareness of its own 'common-sense' working rules and their amplifying potential.
   (ii) encouraging the group to conceptualize a distinction between 'necessary' and 'unnecessary' arrests. In developing the latter concept, for example, particular attention could be paid to those arrests where the only injured party is a police officer, or where arrests occur as a result of an encounter with police.
   (iii) discussing the justifications for making arrests where the 'breach of the peace' is only 'imminent', and there are no complainants.
2. Getting into the habit of *monitoring activities*, such as arrests, complaints, injury rates, in order to provide further material for analysis and evaluation. One important aim of this would be to identify patterns of bias and

discrimination and, consequently, to see whether the goal of some notion of public justice was being reached.

3. Developing criteria of success based on the achievement of trouble-free public order policing – that is, low arrest, complaint and injury rates – and rewarding its successful achievement.

4. Changing the pattern of recruitment to the SPG in the interests of combating the strong masculine ethos. Most obviously, this means choosing women, rather than men, the 'steady' rather than the 'active', the older rather than the younger, and so on. This is not, of course, to suggest that simply replacing men with women would be sufficient to dismantle the 'cult of masculinity', as feminists working in this area have variously pointed out.[40]

5. Avoiding the use of carriers except as carriers. In other words, patrols should be conducted on foot as far as possible so as to increase the amount of ordinary contacts with the public.

6. Using training, standby time and downtime to focus on the new priority, that is, how to achieve the trouble-free policing of public order.

7. Creating a genuine dialogue with the communities and groups being policed. This involves contact *especially* with those on the receiving end of policing, not just 'respectable worthies', *and* being prepared to listen *and learn* from such groups about what constitutes acceptable forms of policing disorder.

8. Encouraging an open, participatory, reflexive and above all *experimental* approach to all practices. The single question being researched amounts to this: how far it is possible to change and to adapt so as to produce non-discriminatory, trouble-free and acceptable (to the policed) policing of public order.

Though the police are much concerned with their own safety, theirs is not a particularly risky job. My own favourite anecdote concerns a police researcher inquiring about police sick days in the Met. and discovering that more working days were lost from falling down ladders while decorating than from injuries in the line of duty. Nor are the police particularly known for taking risks. The 'cover your ass' mentality is part of the occupational culture's conservatism. Genuine innovators rarely last long in what are, after all, highly conservative public bureaucracies. Thus the prospects of *radical* internal reform are not good, despite Reiner's belief that encouraging internal reform is the best bet for those wishing to promote positive changes.[41] But if significant internal reform is unlikely, other sorts of relevant change – in the structure of accountability, for example, or from the riven conflictual conjuncture of Thatcherism – seem unlikely, for reasons which should now be obvious. We thus look set more on the 'worst case' than the 'best case' path. But perhaps, in the end, change will come from unexpected quarters. The sudden turnabout in the fortunes of Mrs Thatcher, the extraordinary transformations taking place in Eastern Europe in the wake of perestroika and glasnost, and the serious attention now being devoted to comprehending the complexity of these 'new times',[42] suggest a space may be opening up for a more imaginative, critical engagement with troubling issues than has been apparent in the recent past. I hope so.

NOTES

1. Cohen, 1985, p. 238.
2. Ibid.
3. Ibid.
4. Hall, 1988, p. 164.
5. Cf. Unsworth, 1982; Scarman, 1982; Lea and Young, 1982; Kettle and Hodges, 1982; Joshua and Wallace, 1983; Sivanandan, 1985; Hall, 1988, pp. 75–9.
6. Tuck, 1989.
7. *The Guardian*, 22 December 1988.
8. Hall, 1988, p. 168.
9. Ibid., p. 170.
10. Ibid., p. 171.
11. Gamble, 1988.
12. Brogden *et al.*, 1988, p. 88.
13. 'A category becomes police property when the dominant powers of society (in the economy, polity, etc.) leave the problems of social control of that category to the police' (Lee, 1981, pp. 53–4).
14. Reiner, 1985, pp. 208–9.
15. Downes and Ward, 1986, p. 61. Ironically, Downes and Ward (1986, p. 54) accuse Grimshaw and me of assuming too much 'could flow from changes in police priorities alone'. I can only assert that this was not true of our view then, that it was a misunderstanding of the argument in *Controlling the Constable* (Jefferson and Grimshaw, 1984), and can only hope that my argument here makes it quite clear that it is also not true now.
16. Key 'new realist' texts include Matthews and Young, 1986; and Kinsey *et al.*, 1986. See also the special issue of *Contemporary Crises*, vol. 11, No. 4, 1987.
17. Emerging critiques of the 'new realist' project, informed by varying degrees of sympathy, include Hogg, 1988; Brogden *et al.*, 1988, pp. 181–90; and Sim *et al.*, 1987.
18. This is not to say that Thatcherism is 'hegemonic'. This would be ludicrous in the light of what I have already said many times about Thatcherism. What it does mean, to reiterate Hall's (1988, p. 154) concise comment, is that 'Thatcherite politics are "hegemonic" in their conception and project: the aim is to struggle on several fronts at once, not on the economic-corporate one alone . . . to reconstruct the terrains of what is "taken for granted" in social and political thought – and so to form a new commonsense'.
19. See Chapter 2; also Hall *et al.*, 1978.
20. See Hogg, 1988, pp. 42–7; and Shapland and Vagg, 1988.
21. Hogg, 1988, pp. 38–42.
22. Cohen, 1985, p. 266.
23. Davis, 1971, p. 55.
24. Ibid.
25. Ibid.
26. Ibid., pp. 56–7 (emphasis in original).
27. Ibid., p. 55.
28. Jefferson and Grimshaw, 1984, pp. 155–6.
29. Davis, 1971, p. 108.
30. The following recent writings capture the range of 'voices' in the debate: GLC, 1983; Jefferson and Grimshaw, 1984; Spencer, 1985; Scraton, 1985; Reiner, 1985;

Lustgarten, 1986; Downes and Ward, 1986. An attempt to summarize the essential differences in the debate can be found in Brogden *et al.*, 1988, Chapter 7.

31. On the problem of representing various communities on matters of policing, see Jefferson *et al.*, 1988.
32. Morgan, 1987, p. 96.
33. Baldwin, 1987.
34. Cf. Morgan, 1985.
35. Davis, 1971, p. 138.
36. Hall, 1988, p. 168.
37. Jefferson and Grimshaw, 1984, pp. 157–68.
38. For a summary of these notions, see Brogden *et al.*, 1988, pp. 192–3.
39. Jefferson and Grimshaw, 1984, pp. 163–8. See also Downes and Ward, 1986, pp. 52–63.
40. Cf. Hanmer, Radford and Stanko, 1989.
41. Reiner, 1985, Chapter 7.
42. See, particularly, Hall and Jacques, 1989.

References

Baldwin, R. (1987). 'Why accountability?', *British Journal of Criminology*, vol. 27, no. 1, Winter, pp. 97–105.

Boyle, K., Hadden, T. and Hillyard, P. (1975). *Law and State: The Case of Northern Ireland*. London: NCCL.

Boyle, K., Hadden, T. and Hillyard, P. (1980). *Ten Years on in Northern Ireland: The Legal Control of Political Violence*. London: NCCL.

Brewer, J. D., Guelke, A., Hume, I., Moxon-Browne, E. and Wilford, R. (1988). *The Police, Public Order and the State*. London: Macmillan.

Brogden, M. (1982). *The Police: Autonomy and Consent*. London: Academic Press.

Brogden, M., Jefferson, T. and Walklate, S. (1988). *Introducing Policework*. London: Unwin Hyman.

Cain, M. (1979). 'The general practice lawyer and the client: towards a radical conception', *International Journal of the Sociology of Law*, vol. 7, pp. 331–54.

Camerawork (1977). 'Lewisham: What are you taking pictures for?', *Camerawork*, no. 8, November.

Chief Constable of Avon and Somerset (1980). 'The disturbances in the St Paul's area of Bristol, 2nd April 1980', unpublished report to the Home Secretary. Taken from text published in *Police*, May 1980, pp. 8–12.

Clarke, J., Hall, S., Jefferson, T. and Roberts, B. (1976). 'Subcultures, Cultures and Class' in S. Hall and T. Jefferson (eds), *Resistance through Rituals*. London: Hutchinson, pp. 9–79.

Clift, Chief Insp. M. (1981). 'Personal view: Riot control', *Police Review*, vol. 89, no. 4617, 31 July, pp. 1482–3.

Cohen, P. (1972). 'Subcultural conflict and working-class community', *Working Papers in Cultural Studies*, no. 2, Spring, pp. 5–51.

Cohen, P. (1979). 'Policing the working class city' in B. Fine, R. Kinsey, J. Lea, S. Picciotto and J. Young (eds), *Capitalism and the Rule of Law*. London: Hutchinson, pp. 118–36.

Cohen, S. (1972). *Folk Devils and Moral Panics*. London: MacGibbon and Kee.

Cohen, S. (1985). *Visions of Social Control: Crime, Punishment and Classification*. Cambridge: Polity.

Cuneen, C., Findlay, M., Lynch, R., Sutton, J. and Tupper, V. (1986). *Dynamics of*

Collective Conflict: 'Riots at the Bathurst Bike Races'. Report to the Criminology Research Council: Sydney.

Davis, K. C. (1971). *Discretionary Justice: A Preliminary Inquiry*. Chicago: University of Illinois Press.

Dickinson, M. (1984). *To Break a Union: The Messenger, the State and the NGA*. Manchester: Booklist.

Downes, D. and Ward, T. (1986). *Democratic Policing: Towards a Labour Party Policy on Police Accountability*. London: Labour Campaign for Criminal Justice.

Dromey, J. and Taylor, G. (1978). *Grunwick: the Workers' Story*. London: Lawrence and Wishart.

Gamble, A. (1988). *The Free Economy and the Strong State*. London: Macmillan.

Geary, R. (1985). *Policing Industrial Disputes: 1893 to 1985*. Cambridge: Cambridge University Press.

Gifford, Lord, (1986). *Report of the Independent Inquiry into Disturbances of October 1985 at the Broadwater Farm Estate, Tottenham*. London: The Broadwater Farm Inquiry.

Gilbert, T. (1975). *Only One Died*. London: Kay Beauchamp.

Gordon, P. (1985). '"If they come in the morning . . ."': The police, the miners and black people' in B. Fine and R. Millar (eds), *Policing the Miners' Strike*. London: Lawrence and Wishart, pp. 161–76.

Gramsci, A. (1971). *Selections from the Prison Notebooks*. London: Lawrence and Wishart.

Greater London Council (GLC) (1983). *A New Police Authority for London*. Discussion Paper no. 1. London: GLC.

Gregory, F. (1976). *Protest and Violence: the Police Response*. Conflict Studies no. 75. London: Institute for the Study of Conflict.

Grimshaw, R. and Jefferson, T. (1987). *Interpreting Policework*. London: Unwin Hyman.

Hall, S. (1988). *The Hard Road to Renewal: Thatcherism and the Crisis of the Left*. London: Verso.

Hall, S., Critcher, C., Clarke, J., Jefferson, T. and Roberts, B. (1978). *Policing the Crisis*. London: Macmillan.

Hall, S. and Jacques, M. (eds) (1989). *New Times: The Changing Face of Politics in the 1990s*. London: Lawrence and Wishart.

Hanmer, J., Radford, J. and Stanko, E. A. (eds) (1989). *Women, Policing and Male Violence*. London: Routledge.

Hillyard, P. (1985). 'Lessons from Ireland' in B. Fine and R. Millar (eds), *Policing the Miners' Strike*. London: Lawrence and Wishart, pp. 177–87.

Hillyard, P. and Percy-Smith, J. (1988). *The Coercive State*. London: Fontana.

Hogg, R. (1988). 'Taking crime seriously: Left realism and Australian criminology' in M. Findlay and R. Hogg (eds), *Understanding Crime and Criminal Justice*. Sydney: The Law Book Company, pp. 24–51.

Jackson, B. with Wardle, T. (n.d.) *The Battle for Orgreave*. Brighton: Vanson Wardle.

James, D. (1979). 'Police–black relations: The professional solution' in S. Holdaway (ed.), *The British Police*. London: Edward Arnold, pp. 66–82.

Jefferson, T. (1986). 'Policing the miners: Law, politics and accountability' in M. Brenton and C. Ungerson (eds), *The Year Book of Social Policy in Britain 1985–6*. London: Routledge, pp. 265–86.

Jefferson, T. (1987a). 'Beyond paramilitarism', *British Journal of Criminology*, vol. 27, no. 1, Winter, pp. 47–53.

Jefferson, T. (1987b). 'The police', Part 1a, Block 3 'Delivering Justice', in Open University course D310, *Crime, Justice and Society*. Milton Keynes: Open University Press, pp. 9–38.

Jefferson, T. (1988). 'Race, crime and policing: Empirical, theoretical and methodological issues', *International Journal of the Sociology of Law*, vol. 16, pp. 521–39.

Jefferson, T. and Grimshaw, R. (1984). *Controlling the Constable*. London: Muller/ Cobden Trust.

Jefferson, T., McLaughlin, E. and Robertson, L. (1988). 'Monitoring the monitors: Accountability, democracy and police watching in Britain', *Contemporary Crises*, vol. 12, no. 2, pp. 91–106.

Jessop. B., Bonnett, K., Bromley, S. and Ling, T. (1984). 'Authoritarian Populism, Two Nations and Thatcherism', *New Left Review*, no. 147, pp. 32–60.

Johnson, T. (1972). *Professions and Power*. London: Macmillan.

Joshua, H. and Wallace, T. (1983). *To Ride the Storm: The 1980 Bristol 'Riot' and the State*. London: Heinemann.

Judge, A. (1974). 'The police and the coloured communities: A police view', *New Community*, vol. 3, no. 3, pp. 199–204.

Kahn, P., Lewis, N., Livock, R. and Wiles, P. (1983). *Picketing*. London: Routledge.

Kettle, M. (1985). 'The National Reporting Centre and the 1984 miners' strike' in B. Fine and R. Millar (eds), *Policing the Miners' Strike*. London: Lawrence and Wishart, pp. 22–33.

Kettle, M. and Hodges, L. (1982). *Uprising! The Police, the People and the Riots in Britain's Cities*. London: Pan.

Kinsey, R., Lea, J. and Young, J. (1986). *Losing the Fight against Crime*. Oxford: Blackwell.

Lea, J. and Young, J. (1982). 'The riots in Britain 1981: Urban violence and political marginalisation' in D. Cowell, T. Jones and J. Young (eds), *Policing the Riots*. London: Junction Books, pp. 5–20.

Lee, J. A. (1981). 'Some structural aspects of police deviance in relations with minority groups' in C. Shearing (ed.), *Organizational Police Deviance*. Toronto: Butterworth, pp. 49–82.

London Strategic Policy Unit (1987). *Police Monitoring and Research Group Briefing Paper no. 3: Policing Wapping – An Account of the Dispute 1986/7*. London: LSPU.

Lustgarten, L. (1986). *The Governance of Police*. London: Sweet and Maxwell.

Manchester City Council (1985). *Leon Brittan's visit to Manchester University Students' Union, 1st March 1985: Report of the Independent Inquiry Panel*. Manchester: Manchester City Council.

Manning, P. K. (1971). 'The police: Mandate, strategies and appearances' in J. D. Douglas (ed.), *Crime, and Justice in American Society*. Indianapolis: Bobbs-Merrill.

Marcuse, H. (1969). *Eros and Civilization*. London: Sphere.

Matthews, R. and Young, J. (eds) (1986). *Confronting Crime*. London: Sage.

McCabe, S. and Wallington, P. with Alderson, T., Gostin, L. and Mason, C. (1988). *The Police, Public Order and Civil Liberties: Legacies of the Miners' Strike*. London: Routledge.

McIlroy, J. 1985. 'Police and pickets' in H. Beynon (ed.), *Digging Deeper*. London: Verso, pp. 101–21.

Metropolitan Police (1986). *Public Order Review: Civil Disturbances 1981–1985*. London: Metropolitan Police.

Morgan, R. 1985. 'Police accountability: Current developments and future prospects', paper presented to the Police Foundation Conference, 'Police Research: Where Now?', Harrogate, December.

Morgan, R. (1987). 'Police accountability: Developing the local infrastructure', *British Journal of Criminology*, vol. 27, no. 1, Winter, pp. 87–96.

Morris, T. (1985). 'The case for a riot squad', *New Society*, 29 November, pp. 363–4.

Morris, T. (1987). 'Police force', *New Society*, 20 March, pp. 12–14.

National Council for Civil Liberties (1984). *Civil Liberties and the Miners' Dispute: First Report of the Independent Inquiry*. London: NCCL.

National Council for Civil Liberties (1986). *No Way in Wapping*. London: NCCL.

Northam, G. (1985). 'A fair degree of force?', *The Listener*, 31 October, pp. 3–5.

Northam, G. (1988). *Shooting in the Dark: Riot Police in Britain*. London: Faber.

Palmer, S. H. (1988). *Police and Protest in England and Ireland 1780–1850*. Cambridge: Cambridge University Press.

Peirce, G. (1985). 'How they rewrote the law at Orgreave', *The Guardian*, 12 August, p. 7.

Policing London (1983). 'A guide to the Metropolitan Police (6): The Special Patrol Group', *Policing London*, no. 8, June–July, pp. 8–11.

Policing London (1986). 'Tooling-up for confrontation', *Policing London*, no. 23, September–October, pp. 21–3.

Policy Studies Institute (1983). *Police and People in London*. Vol. 1: D. J. Smith, *A Survey of Londoners*. London: PSI.

Reiner, R. (1985). *The Politics of the Police*. Brighton: Wheatsheaf.

Reiner, R. and Shapland, J. (eds) (1987). *Why Police?, Special Issue on Policing in Britain, British Journal of Criminology*, vol. 27, no. 1, Winter.

Reiss, A. J. and Bordua, D. J. (1967). 'Environment and organization: A perspective on the police' in D. J. Bordua (ed.), *The Police: Six Sociological Essays*. New York: Wiley, pp. 25–55.

Reuss-Ianni, E. and Ianni, F. A. J. (1983). 'Street cops and management cops: the two cultures of policing' in M. Punch (ed.), *Control in the Police Organization*. Cambridge, Mass.: MIT Press, pp. 251–74.

Review Panel (1986). *A Different Reality*. Birmingham: West Midlands County Council.

Rollo, J. (1980). 'The Special Patrol Group' in P. Hain (ed.) *Policing the Police*, vol. 2. London: John Calder, pp. 151–208.

Scarman, Lord (1974). *Report of Inquiry into the Red Lion Square Disorders of 15 June 1974*, Cmnd 5919. London: HMSO.

Scarman, Lord (1982). *The Scarman Report: The Brixton Disorders 10–12 April 1981*. Harmondsworth: Penguin (originally published in 1981 as Cmnd 8427 by HMSO).

Scraton, P. (1985). *The State of the Police*. London: Pluto.

Scraton, P. (1987). 'Unreasonable force: Policing, punishment and marginalization' in P. Scraton (ed.), *Law, Order and the Authoritarian State*. Milton Keynes: Open University Press, pp. 145–89.

Select Committee on Race Relations and Immigration (1972). *Report on Police/Immigrant Relations*. HC71–72. London: HMSO.

Shapland, J. and Vagg, J. (1988). *Policing by the Public*. London: Routledge.

Sheffield Policewatch (1984). *Taking Liberties: Policing during the Miners' Strike, April–October*. Sheffield: Sheffield Policewatch.

Silverman, J. (1986). *Independent Inquiry into the Handsworth Disturbances, September 1985*. Birmingham: City of Birmingham District Council.

Sim, J., Scraton, P., and Gordon, P. (1987). 'Introduction: Crime, the state and critical analysis' in P. Scraton (ed.), *Law, Order and the Authoritarian State*. Milton Keynes: Open University Press, pp. 1–70.

Sivanandan, A. (1985). 'Britain's gulags', *New Socialist*, no. 32, November, pp. 13–15.

Skolnick, J. (1975). *Justice without Trial*, 2nd edn. New York: Wiley.

Spencer. S. (1985). *Called to Account: The Case for Police Accountability in England and Wales*. London: NCCL.

Stark, R. (1972). *Police Riots*. Belmont, Calif.: Wadsworth.

State Research (1979). 'Special Patrol Groups in Britain', *State Research*, vol. 2, no. 13, August–September, pp. 130–40.

State Research (1980). 'Policing the eighties: The iron fist', *State Research*, vol. 3, no. 19, August–September, pp. 146–68.

Thornton P. (1987). *Public Order Law Including the Public Order Act 1986*. London: Financial Training.

Tuck, M. (1989). *Drinking and Disorder: A Study of Non-Metropolitan Violence*, Home Office Research Study no. 108. London: HMSO.

Unofficial Committee of Enquiry (1980a). *Southall 23rd April 1979*. London: NCCL.

Unofficial Committee of Enquiry (1980b). *The Death of Blair Peach*. London: NCCL.

Unsworth, C. (1982). 'The riots of 1981: Popular violence and the politics of law and order', *Journal of Law and Society*, vol. 9, no. 1, pp. 63–85.

Waddington, P. A. J. (1987). 'Towards paramilitarism? Dilemmas in policing civil disorder', *British Journal of Criminology*, vol. 27, no. 1, Winter, pp. 37–46.

Wilson, J. Q. (1968). *Varieties of Police Behaviour: The Management of Law and Order in Eight Communities*. Cambridge, Mass.: Harvard University Press.

Zweig, F. (1961). *The Worker in an Affluent Society*. London: Heinemann.

Index

For Product Safety Concerns and Information please contact our EU
representative GPSR@taylorandfrancis.com
Taylor & Francis Verlag GmbH, Kaufingerstraße 24, 80331 München, Germany

www.ingramcontent.com/pod-product-compliance
Lightning Source LLC
Chambersburg PA
CBHW050517280326
41932CB00014B/2351